T0339664

PHILIPPIANS

In this commentary, Michael F. Bird and Nijay K. Gupta situate Paul's letter to the Philippians within the context of his imprisonment as well as the Philippians' situation of suffering and persecution. Paul draws the Philippians' attention to the power and progress of the gospel in spite of difficult circumstances. He also warns them about the dangers of rival Christian groups who preach out of poor motives or have a truncated gospel. Bird and Gupta unpack the rich wisdom and theology of the Christ Hymn (2:6–11). Throughout the commentary, they apply a broad range of exegetical tools to interpret this letter including historical, sociological, rhetorical, and literary analysis, and they give attention to the reception of this important Pauline text throughout history. Bird and Gupta also include short reflections on the meaning of Philippians for today.

Michael F. Bird is Academic Dean and Lecturer in Theology at Ridley College, Melbourne. He is the author of commentaries on Romans and Colossians, and the author of *An Anomalous Jew: Paul among Jews, Greeks, and Romans* (2016) and *The Saving Righteousness of God* (2007).

Nijay K. Gupta is Associate Professor of New Testament at Portland Seminary, Oregon. He has written commentaries on 1–2 Thessalonians and Colossians and is the author of *Paul and the Language of Faith* (2019). Together with Bird, he is a co-founder and served as the first editors of the *Journal for the Study of Paul and His Letters*.

# NEW CAMBRIDGE BIBLE COMMENTARY

GENERAL EDITOR: Ben Witherington III

HEBREW BIBLE/OLD TESTAMENT EDITOR: Bill T. Arnold

EDITORIAL BOARD
Bill T. Arnold, *Asbury Theological Seminary*
James D. G. Dunn, *University of Durham*
Michael V. Fox, *University of Wisconsin-Madison*
Robert P. Gordon, *University of Cambridge*
Judith M. Gundry, *Yale University*
Ben Witherington III, *Asbury Theological Seminary*

The New Cambridge Bible Commentary (NCBC) aims to elucidate the Hebrew and Christian Scriptures for a wide range of intellectually curious individuals. While building on the work and reputation of the Cambridge Bible Commentary popular in the 1960s and 1970s, the NCBC takes advantage of many of the rewards provided by scholarly research over the last four decades. Volumes utilize recent gains in rhetorical criticism, social scientific study of the Scriptures, narrative criticism, and other developing disciplines to exploit the growing advances in biblical studies. Accessible jargon-free commentary, an annotated "Suggested Readings" list, and the entire *New Revised Standard Version* (NRSV) text under discussion are the hallmarks of all volumes in the series.

PUBLISHED VOLUMES IN THE SERIES
*Acts*, Craig S. Keener
*The Gospel of Luke*, Amy-Jill Levine and Ben Witherington III
*Galatians*, Craig S. Keener
*Mark*, Darrell Bock
*Psalms*, Walter Brueggemann and William H. Bellinger, Jr.
*Matthew*, Craig A. Evans
*Genesis*, Bill T. Arnold
*The Gospel of John*, Jerome H. Neyrey
*Exodus*, Carol Meyers
*1–2 Corinthians*, Craig S. Keener
*James and Jude*, William F. Brosend II
*Judges and Ruth*, Victor H. Matthews
*Revelation*, Ben Witherington III

# *Philippians*

**Michael F. Bird**
*Ridley College*

**Nijay K. Gupta**
*Portland Seminary*

# CAMBRIDGE
## UNIVERSITY PRESS

University Printing House, Cambridge CB2 8BS, United Kingdom

One Liberty Plaza, 20th Floor, New York, NY 10006, USA

477 Williamstown Road, Port Melbourne, VIC 3207, Australia

314-321, 3rd Floor, Plot 3, Splendor Forum, Jasola District Centre, New Delhi - 110025, India

103 Penang Road, #05-06/07, Visioncrest Commercial, Singapore 238467

Cambridge University Press is part of the University of Cambridge.

It furthers the University's mission by disseminating knowledge in the pursuit of education, learning and research at the highest international levels of excellence.

www.cambridge.org
Information on this title: www.cambridge.org/9781108462914
DOI: 10.1017/9781108645201

First published 2020

*A catalogue record for this publication is available from the British Library*

*Library of Congress Cataloging in Publication data*
NAMES: Bird, Michael F., author. | Gupta, Nijay K., author.
TITLE: Philippians / Michael F. Bird, Ridley Melbourne College of Ministry, Australia, Nijay K. Gupta, Portland Seminary.
DESCRIPTION: Cambridge, United Kingdom ; New York, NY, USA : Cambridge University Press, 2020. | Series: New Cambridge Bible commentary | Includes bibliographical references and index.
IDENTIFIERS: LCCN 2019048569 (print) | LCCN 2019048570 (ebook) | ISBN 9781108473880 (hardback) | ISBN 9781108462914 (paperback) | ISBN 9781108645201 (epub)
SUBJECTS: LCSH: Bible. Philippians–Commentaries.
CLASSIFICATION: LCC BS2705.53 .B57 2020 (print) | LCC BS2705.53 (ebook) | DDC 227/.6077–dc23
LC record available at https://lccn.loc.gov/2019048569
LC ebook record available at https://lccn.loc.gov/2019048570

ISBN 978-1-108-47388-0 Hardback
ISBN 978-1-108-46291-4 Paperback

# Contents

# Acknowledgment

We extends our thanks to Ben Witherington for inviting us to coauthor this commentary on Philippians. It has been a labor of love to study and reflect on Philippians as well as to work together as cowriters. We would like to extend a special thanks to Frank du Preez for use of his transcription of a lecture series on Philippians by N.T. Wright (Regent College, 1990).

# Abbreviations

| | |
|---|---|
| 4QMMT | 4Q Miqat Maaśe ha-Torah |
| AB | Anchor Bible Commentaries |
| ABD | David Noel Freedman, ed. *The Anchor Bible Dictionary*. New Haven, CT: Yale University Press, 2008 |
| *ABR* | *Australian Biblical Review* |
| ABRL | Anchor Bible Reference Library |
| ACCS | Ancient Christian Commentary on Scripture |
| ACD | Ancient Christian Doctrine |
| ACTMS | Australian College of Theology Monograph Series |
| ANF | The Ante-Nicene Fathers |
| *Ant.* | *Jewish Antiquities* (Josephus) |
| ANTC | Abingdon New Testament Commentaries |
| AYBC | Anchor Yale Bible Commentary |
| BAFCS | The Books of Acts in Its First Century Setting |
| *BBR* | *Bulletin for Biblical Research* |
| BDAG | W. Bauer, F. W. Danker, W. F. Arnt, and F. W. Gingrich. *A Greek–English Lexicon of the New Testament and Other Early Christian Literature*. 3rd ed. Chicago: University of Chicago Press, 2000 |
| BECNT | Baker Exegetical Commentary on the New Testament |
| BGU | Berliner griechische Urkunden |
| *Bib.* | *Biblica* |
| *BibInt* | *Biblical Interpretation* |
| BNTC | Black's New Testament Commentary |
| *BSac* | *Bibliotheca Sacra* |
| BTCB | Belief Theological Commentary on the Bible |

| | |
|---|---|
| BZNW | *Beihefte zur Zeitschrift für die neutestamentliche Wissenschaft* |
| CBQ | *Catholic Biblical Quarterly* |
| CBR | *Currents in Biblical Research* |
| CEB | Common English Bible |
| CITM | Christianity in the Making |
| ConBNT | Coniectanea Biblica: New Testament Series |
| CSB | Christian Standard Bible |
| CTM | *Currents in Theology and Mission* |
| EBC | Expositor's Bible Commentary |
| ECS | Epworth Commentary Series |
| EDNT | *Exegetical Dictionary of the New Testament* |
| EEC | Evangelical Exegetical Commentary |
| EGGNT | Exegetical Guide to the Greek New Testament |
| EQ | *The Evangelical Quarterly* |
| ESV | English Standard Version |
| ExpTimes | *Expository Times* |
| HBT | *Horizons in Biblical Theology* |
| HNT | Handbuch zum Neuen Testament |
| HTR | *The Harvard Theological Review* |
| ICC | International Critical Commentary |
| IVPNT | InterVarsity Press New Testament (Commentary Series) |
| JBL | *Journal of Biblical Literature* |
| JETS | *The Journal of the Evangelical Theological Society* |
| JSNT | *Journal for the Study of the New Testament* |
| JSNTSup | *Journal for the Study of the New Testament Supplement Series* |
| JSOT | *Journal for the Study of the Old Testament* |
| JSPL | *Journal for the Study of Paul's Letters* |
| JTC | *Journal for Theology and Church* |
| JTI | *Journal of Theological Interpretation* |
| JTS | *Journal of Theological Studies* |
| Jub. | Jubilees (Old Testament Pseudepigrapha) |
| KD | *Kerygma und Dogma* |
| KJV | King James Version |
| LANE | Adolf Deissmann, *Light from the Ancient Near East: The New Testament Illustrated by Recently Discovered Texts of the Graeco-Roman World*, trans. L. R. M. Strachan. 1927; reprint, Peabody, MA: Hendrickson, 1995 |
| LCL | Loeb Classical Library |

| LN | Johannes P. Louw and Eugene A. Nida, *Greek–English Lexicon of the New Testament Based on Semantic Domains*. New York: United Bible Societies, 1996 |
| LNTS | Library of New Testament Studies |
| LSJ | Henry George Liddell, Robert Scott, Henry Stuart Jones, and Roderick McKenzie. *A Greek–English Lexicon*. Rev. and augm. Oxford; New York: Clarendon Press; Oxford University Press, 1996 |
| LXX | Septuagint (Greek Old Testament) |
| NASB | New American Standard Bible |
| NBBC | New Beacon Bible Commentary |
| NDIEC | New Documents Illustrating Early Christianity. 10 vols. |
| NeoT | *Neotestamentica* |
| NET | New English Translation |
| NIB | *New Interpreter's Bible* |
| NIBC | New Interpreter's Bible Commentary |
| NICNT | New International Commentary on the New Testament |
| NIDB | *New Interpreter's Dictionary of the Bible* |
| NIGTC | New International Greek Text Commentary |
| NIV | New International Version |
| NIVAC | NIV Application Commentary |
| NJB | New Jerusalem Bible |
| NLT | New Living Translation |
| NovT | *Novum Testamentum* |
| NovTSup | Novum Testamentum Supplement Series |
| NRSV | New Revised Standard Version |
| NSBT | New Studies in Biblical Theology |
| NTD | Das Neue Testament Deutsch |
| NTL | New Testament Library |
| NTS | *New Testament Studies* |
| NTSR | New Testament for Spiritual Reading |
| NTT | New Testament Theology |
| OTP | Old Testament Pseudepigrapha |
| OUP | Oxford University Press |
| PAST | Pauline Studies |
| PCNT | Paideia Commentary on the New Testament |
| PFG | N. T. Wright. *Paul and the Faithfulness of God*. Minneapolis: Fortress, 2013 |

PNTC      Pillar New Testament Commentary
PRS       Perspectives in Religious Studies
REBC      Revised Expositor's Bible Commentary
*ResQ*      *Restoration Quarterly*
*RevExp*    *Review & Expositor*
RSV       Revised Standard Version
SGBC      The Story of God Bible Commentary
SHBC      Smyth and Helwys Bible Commentary
SNTS      Society for New Testament Studies
SNTSMS    Society for New Testament Studies Monograph Series
SP        Sacra Pagina
TANZ      Texte und Arbeiten zum Neutestamentlichen Zeitalter
*TBT*       *The Bible Today*
ThHK      Theologischer Handkommentar zum Neuen Testament
THNT      Two Horizons New Testament Commentary
*TLNT*      Ceslas Spicq and James D. Ernest. *Theological Lexicon of the
          New Testament.* Peabody, MA: Hendrickson Publishers, 1994
TNTC      Tyndale New Testament Commentary
*TrinJ*     *Trinity Journal*
*TynBul*    *Tyndale Bulletin*
*VOICE*     *The Voice Translation.* Nashville, TN: Thomas Nelson, 2011
WBC       Word Biblical Commentary
WUNT      *Wissenschaftliche Untersuchungen zum Neuen Testament*
ZNW       *Zeitschrift für die Neutestamentliche Wissenschaft*
ZThK      *Zeitschrift fur Theologie und Kirche*

# Introduction

Codex Bezae offers an interesting variant reading of Matt 20:28: "But seek to increase from that which is small, and to become less from that which is greater."[1] This Jesus-saying (perhaps an *agraphon*) seemed to a scribe to fit within the context of Jesus' teaching about glory, honor, and "greatness." Jesus' message would have been discouraging to many readers entrenched in the agonistic Greco-Roman culture. Because honor was treated as a limited good (there was only so much of it to go around), daily one vied for honor and competed to "best" the other.[2] While modern Westerners sometimes scoff at the secret request of the mother of James and John that her sons be given prime seats at the eschatological banquet (Matt 20:20–21), it would not have been a surprise to the other disciples. They were probably upset on account of *jealousy*, not propriety! The second part of the Codex Bezae Jesus-saying – "to become less" – was utter foolishness in such a competitive world. Jesus was not actually encouraging the disciples to be underachievers; rather, he was undermining a *status quo* that locked people into shame and poverty.

---

[1]  The variant reading goes on with a teaching similar to what we find in Luke 14:8–10; see B. Metzger, *A Textual Commentary on the Greek New Testament* (Stuttgart: United Bible Society, 2012), 42.

[2]  J. E. Lendon refers to honor as the "filter through which the whole world was viewed, a deep structure of the Graeco-Roman mind, perhaps the ruling metaphor of ancient society"; *Empire of Honour: The Art of Government in the Roman World* (Oxford: Oxford University Press, 1997), 73. That this value would naturally lead to competition and rivalry is made clear by this statement by Cicero: "Nature ... has made us ... enthusiastic seekers after honour, and once we have caught, as it were, some glimpse of its radiance, there is nothing we are not prepared to bear and go through in order to secure it" (*Tusc.* 2.40.58 King, LCL), as cited in Craig Hill, *Servant of All: Status, Ambition, and the Way of Jesus* (Grand Rapids, MI: Eerdmans, 2016), 81.

What does this have to do with Philippians? Everything indeed! Philippi was a Roman colony in Paul's time, and the "values of Rome" were especially prominent and on display in such an environment. Rome supported and reinforced social stratification and operated on a system of tracks of "upward mobility." Bettering oneself is always a good thing, but, again, the system as it was often involved *my* betterment at the cost of *someone else's* degradation. The text of Phil 2:5–11, popularly dubbed the "Christ Hymn," is perhaps the most discussed and debated text in all of Paul's letters. While scholars will continue to disagree on its origins, exact literary style, and the meaning and implications of specific details, what is *not* in doubt is how countercultural Paul's portrayal of Jesus would have been to "Romanized" people. The Roman way promoted headstrong ascension. Contrastingly, the main figure of the Christ Hymn dared to *willfully* lower himself. He was not the first person in antiquity to model humility, but Paul boldly narrates the breathtaking *plunge* of Jesus, from an exceptionally high status and glory to the degradation of a common slave. He modeled the movement from "greater to lesser." Who would do such a thing and why? And who would follow and emulate such a person? These are the kinds of questions that drive Philippians and give it pride of place as one of the most theologically rich texts of the New Testament.

PHILIPPI: THE CITY AND ITS INHABITANTS

## Philippi before Roman Occupation

Ancient Philippi was located in eastern Macedonia between the mountain range of Orvilos and Mount Pangaion, with Mount Symyolon to the east. Before it was called Philippi, it was the Thasian colony of Krenides, founded in 360 BCE.[3] Only a handful of years later (356 BCE), Philip of Macedon (359–336 BC) was called up to protect the inhabitants of Krenides. He took control of the city, fortified it, and changed its name to "Philippi." He also established a royal mint there.[4] Philippi would

---

[3]   Before 360 BCE, the population consisted of tribal peoples, mostly Pieri and Edoni; see P. Oakes, *Philippians: From People to Letter* (SNTSMS; Cambridge: Cambridge University Press, 2007), 10.

[4]   C. Koukouli-Chrysantaki and C. Bakirtzis, *Philippi* (Athens: Ministry of Culture, 1995), 7–8.

have been attractive to Philip for many reasons, including its gold and silver mines and plentiful water springs ("Krenides" means "with many springs").[5]

The Romans, under general Lucius Aemilius Paulus, conquered Macedonia in 167 BCE, and captured Philippi in 148 BCE. Soon after they began construction on the Via Egnatia, the route that connected the Adriatic ports of Dyrrachium and Apollonia.[6] In 42 BCE, the battle between Brutus and Cassius against Octavian and Antony was waged just outside the western wall of Philippi. After Octavian won, he settled veterans in Philippi. From that time on the city became especially prosperous. After the battle of Actium (31 BCE), more Roman veterans were given land in Philippi.[7]

In 30 BCE, when Philippi became a Roman colony, it was renamed Colonia Iulia Philippensis; soon after it was renamed Colonia Iulia Augusta Philippensis, and new buildings were erected, fresh coins struck.[8] There were, of course, many unique advantages to being a Roman colony, including tax and tribute exemption, and greater autonomy for the local government.[9]

## Roman Philippi

Despite having the status of a Roman colony (*Ius Italicum*),[10] Philippi was a relatively small city with around 10,000 inhabitants, a fraction of the

---

[5]   See C. Koukouli-Chrysantaki, "Colonia Iulia Augusta Philippensis," in *Philippi at the Time of Paul and after His Death* (eds. C. Bakirtzis and H. Koester; Harrisburg: Trinity Press International, 1998), 5–35, here 5.

[6]   The road was built by Gnaeus Egnatius, a Roman proconsul; see A.-F. Christidis, ed., *A History of Ancient Greek from the Beginnings to Late Antiquity* (English translation; Cambridge: Cambridge University Press, 2007), 901. E. Verhoef notes that the journey from Rome to Byzantium on the Via Egnatia would take about twenty-four days; *Philippi: How Christianity Began in Europe: The Epistle to the Philippians and the Excavations at Philippi* (London: Bloomsbury, 2013), 4.

[7]   It is estimated that as many as 500 Roman veterans were settled in Philippi after Actium (Dio Cassius, *Roman History* 51.4.6).

[8]   Koukouli-Chrysantaki, "Colonia Iulia Augusta Philippensis," 14.

[9]   See J. E. Stambaugh and D. L. Balch, *The New Testament in Its Social Environment* (Philadelphia: Westminster Press, 1986), 20.

[10]  This designation meant that the parcel of land was declared legally to be "Italian soil." As A. W. Lintott poignantly writes, "such communities in the provinces had the prestigious status of roman islands in a more or less foreign sea," in *Imperium Romanum: Politics and Administration* (London: Routledge, 1993), 130.

much larger Thessalonica (ten times its size).[11] It covered a geographic space of about 2,000 square kilometers. Despite its relatively small population, Eduard Verhoef notes how Philippian residents clearly traveled and established a reputation for themselves based on the naming of Philippian men in inscriptions found elsewhere.[12]

## Economy, Inhabitants, and Social Environment

In the era of Roman rule, Philippi continued to sustain its economy on agriculture.[13] Romans comprised the ruling class. There is evidence of guilds or associations in Philippi, although these often were comprised of freedmen and slaves (and foreigners); rarely did aristocrats participate.[14] In an important study called *Philippians: From People to Letter*, Peter Oakes offers an educated guess at the social stratification of the population. He surmises the following:

1 percent Roman elite
15 percent community peasant colonists
43 percent service groups
25 percent poor
16 percent slaves[15]

The ethnic composition of Roman Philippi was comprised largely of Greeks, Macedonians, and Romans;[16] it would also have included a smaller

---

[11]  See Verhoef, *Philippi*, 6.

[12]  For example, their presence is indicated in athletic competitions and games in Delphi; and some Philippians made monetary donations to temples in Argos and Delphi; see Verhoef, *Philippi*, 3.

[13]  See Koukouli-Chrysantaki, "Colonia Iulia Augusta Philippensis," 22; Verhoef notes that some would have worked in Philippian stone quarries; *Philippi*, 13.

[14]  See in general, R. Ascough, *Paul's Macedonian Associations: The Social Context of Philippians and 1 Thessalonians* (WUNT 2.161; Tübingen: Mohr Siebeck, 2003); cf. R. Ascough, R. Harland, and J. Kloppenborg, *Associations in the Greco-Roman World: A Sourcebook* (Waco, TX: Baylor University Press, 2013); J. Hellerman, *Reconstructing Honor in Roman Philippi: Carmen Christi as Cursus Pudorum* (SNTSMS; Cambridge: Cambridge University Press, 2008). Verhoef estimates the slave population in Philippi was about 20 percent; *Philippi*, 19.

[15]  Oakes, Philippians, 60.

[16]  Oakes observes that Romans would have not been in the majority of the population; see "Re-mapping the Universe: Paul and the Emperor in 1 Thessalonians and Philippians," *JSNT* 27.3 (2016): 301–322, at 309. E. Verhoef explains that Roman veterans were in active service for more than twenty years. When they were discharged, they were granted land

population of Thracians, and foreigners from Egypt, Asia Minor, Israel, and elsewhere.[17] The question of Jewish presence in Philippi is somewhat complex. Luke narrates that when Paul came to Philippi, he sought out a "place of prayer" outside of the city gate. There he engaged with some women including Lydia, "a gentile God-worshipper" from Thyatira (Acts 16:12–14). While Luke's account here offers little detail, it would seem that his story implies the absence of a major Jewish community in Philippi, and that what Paul found there was a group of women, mostly Gentiles sympathetic to Israel's God.[18]

As for other evidence, a relevant grave stele was discovered in the west cemetery of Philippi.[19] The stele reads: "Nikostratos Aurelius Oxcholios himself furnished this flat tomb/grave [and] if someone lays down [on it] a dead body of others, he will give [a fine] to the synagogue." The name of this Jewish male includes a Greek cognomen, Roman nomen gentis, and a second Greek cognomen.[20] Koukouli-Chrysantaki surmises from this stele

---

for income. The amount of land given varied from one situation and location to the next, but a common soldier might receive thirty acres; veterans of higher status much more. Landowners could lease the property to tenant farmers or purchase slaves to work; see Verhoef, *Philippi*, 10. Despite the periodic resettlement of veterans in Philippi, Romans would have been a relatively small population in the city compared to Greeks and Thracians; see C. Koukouli-Chrysantaki, "Philippi," in *Brill's Companion to Ancient Macedonia: Studies in Archaeology and the History of Macedonia* (Leiden: Brill, 2011), 437–452, here 447. Hellerman convincingly argues, though, that even in spite of the small population of Romans, the city took on a strong Roman culture; thus, "the Romans remained an ideological majority, particularly where issues of honor, status, and social virtues were concerned, since the dispossession of local landholders by Roman veterans ultimately determined not only the social hierarchy, but also the social values, of the reconstituted settlement"; *Reconstructing Honor*, 71.

[17] See Verhoef, *Philippi*, 2.

[18] See M. C. Parsons, *Acts* (Paideia; Grand Rapids, MI: Baker), 229.

[19] See Philippi Museum inv. no. *λ1529; cf. Koukouli-Chrysantaki, "Colonia Iulia Augusta Philippensis," 28; P. Pilhofer, *Philippi: Band II: Katalog der Inschriften von Philippi* (WUNT 2.119; Tübingen: Mohr Siebeck, 2000), 465–467.

[20] As Koukouli-Chrysantaki notes, "It was very common for Jews in the Roman Empire to use the Greek language and to have Greek names" ("Colonia Iulia Augusta Philippensis," 29). Indeed, Koukouli-Chrysantaki's statement seems to align with the evidence from Rome; see further, H. Leon, *The Jews of Ancient Rome* (updated ed.; Peabody, MA: Hendrickson, 1995). Koukouli-Chrysantaki also rightly observes that just because a Jew might take a Greek or Roman name does *not* mean he or she was culturally Hellenized, or less "Jewish" in any way in terms of commitments or practice ("Colonia Iulia Augusta Philippensis," 29–30); see J. M. G. Barclay, *Jews in the Mediterranean Diaspora: From Alexander to Trajan – 323BCE to 117CE* (London: T & T Clark, 2015).

inscription that Nikostratos was a Roman citizen who probably obtained his citizenship status through Caracalla's edict of 212 CE. Along with most scholars, Koukouli-Chrysantaki dates the stele to the late third or early fourth century CE.[21] Despite the fact that this stele dates to at least two centuries after Paul's ministry in Philippi, nevertheless "it still serves as an important archaeological commentary on the Acts of the Apostles, offering the first epigraphical evidence of the existence of an organized Jewish community in the city of Philippi in the late third century CE."[22] As further evidence along these lines, Koukouli-Chrysantaki adds the discovery of another grave inscription from the same time period that mentions a Jewish male called "Simon the Smyrnion."[23] All in all, it is likely that Roman Philippi of the first century was not *devoid* of Jewish presence, but certainly Jews did not comprise a significant population group.

## Religion in Philippi

Like many of the major cities of the Greco-Roman world, Philippi was home to the worship of many gods from numerous peoples and cultures. Of course the major Greek and Roman gods were honored in Philippi, including Zeus, Athena, Apollo Comaeus, Artemis, and Dionysus.[24] There was also a Cybele cult, local worship of the Roman god of forests (Silvanus), and a cult dedicated to the Hero-Horseman. Material evidence also establishes that Philippi was home to a small sanctuary for the Egyptian gods Isis, Serapis, Horus, and probably Telesphorus.[25]

In recent years, scholars have taken a special interest in the imperial cult in the Roman world. Joseph Hellerman notes how the "Augustan character of the colony" would have guaranteed a central place of the imperial cult in the life of the city.[26] According to Hellerman, a ruler cult in Philippi is attested several centuries before Paul set foot there (in honor of Philip II, at

---

[21]   See Koukouli-Chrysantaki, "Colonia Iulia Augusta Philippensis," 30–34.
[22]   Koukouli-Chrysantaki, "Colonia Iulia Augusta Philippensis," 34.
[23]   Koukouli-Chrysantaki, "Colonia Iulia Augusta Philippensis," 35.
[24]   See Koukouli-Chrysantaki and Bakirtzis, Philippi, 28.
[25]   Koukouli-Chrysantaki and Bakirtzis, *Philippi*, 28.
[26]   Hellerman, *Reconstructing Honor*, 81; cf. L. Bormann, *Philippi: Stadt und Christengemeinde zur Zeit des Paulus* (Leiden: Brill, 1995); see especially chapter 3: "Die Caesarenreligion und der Kaiserkult in Philippi."

first, and later for Alexander the Great). Verhoef aptly sums up the evidence for the Roman period.

In the first century CE monuments were erected in Philippi in honour of the Caesarean family, and in the second century temples were even built in their honour. Priests were appointed, holidays were instituted and sacrifices to the Emperor were made. Next to the priests the so-called *seviri Augustales*, the six men working in honour of Augustus, played a role in the cult of the Emperor.[27]

## THE USE OF ACTS IN THE STUDY OF PHILIPPIANS

Of what use is Acts when it comes to understanding the Philippian church and Paul's relationship and experiences in Philippi? Scholars disagree on the historical value of Acts. Some argue that Luke's theological agenda clouds Acts' ability to serve the purposes of historical reconstruction. No doubt Luke cared about more than just relaying "facts" about particular people and events in his time. He was inspired to tell a story about Jesus and the life and times of the earliest Christians.

An important starting place for discussions about the historical value of Acts involves the matter of *genre*. Martin Hengel labels Acts an "historical monograph," even if it demonstrates certain theological biases and narrative tendencies. Any attempt to understand Paul's life and even his letters apart from Luke's accounts is futile and irresponsible and, perhaps even, impossible, Hengel posits.[28] He adds the point that just because we may label a certain passage as a "legend" or "type scene" does not obviate its historical utility, "because they tend to indicate the essential characteristics of a person or event and the general impression that they made, and because they express the earliest influence exerted by such a person or

---

[27]    Verhoef, *Philippi*, 12. Honors were offered to Claudius but he refused this homage; see B. Winter on the wider subject of rulers refusing divine honors; *Divine Honours for the Caesars: The First Christians' Responses* (Grand Rapids, MI: Eerdmans, 2015). Verhoef makes it a point to say that "There was no impediment against participation in more than one cult, though the one condition was that the veneration of the Emperor would not suffer at the hands of the other cults, because the town was dependent on the Emperor for the common good" (Verhoef, *Philippi*, 12).

[28]    M. Hengel, *Acts and the History of Earliest Christianity* (trans. J. Bowden; London: SCM, 1979), 36–38; see also B. Witherington III, *The Acts of the Apostles: A Socio-Rhetorical Commentary* (Grand Rapids, MI: Eerdmans, 1998), 2.

event."[29] Hengel also contributes the important point that Acts should be treated by modern historians of no less value than Josephus's works.[30] At the end of the day we are almost entirely reliant today on ancient writers like Luke and Josephus to piece together the world of antiquity, filling in the gaps left by our analysis of Philippians and study of material remains.

### PAUL'S MINISTRY IN PHILIPPI (ACTS 16:12–40)

Given the previous comments made about Acts, it is helpful to consider the background of Paul's letter to the Philippians with some interest in Luke's account of Paul's visit to Philippi. Acts 16 narrates Paul's missionary work in the Asia Minor cities of Derbe and Lystra (Acts 16:1–3). After Timothy joined Paul and Silas they entered the region of Phyrgia and Galatia (as the Spirit prevented their movement into Asia; 16:6). The Spirit also occluded their entry into Bithynia. Instead, they moved into Troas. There Paul received the famous vision of the "man of Macedonia": "Come over to Macedonia and help us" (16:9). Wasting no time, they crossed over by boat into Samothrace, then to Neapolis. They stopped for a period of time in an important city of the northwest, Philippi; Luke refers to it as "a leading city of the district of Macedonia and a Roman colony" (*prōtē meridos tēs Makedonias polis kolōnia*; Acts 16:12).

Luke makes it a point to say that Paul and his companions stayed in the city for several days. On the Sabbath they went outside the gate by the river[31] expecting to find a place of prayer (*proseuchē*; Acts 16:13). There is scholarly interest in what Luke means here in his use of *proseuchē*. It *could* refer to a synagogue building (cf. Philo, *In Flaccum*, 6.41), but it is more likely that Luke means that they went in search of a Jewish worship gathering.[32]

---

[29] Hengel, *Acts and the History*, 41; see similarly D. Binder, *Into the Temple Courts: The Place of the Synagogues in the Second Temple Period* (SBLDS; Atlanta, GA: SBL, 1999), 78–81: "we should consider the possibility that Luke's pattern may well be a generalization based on one or more actual incidents – a possibility that takes on greater weight when we factor in the supporting evidence we have seen from Paul's own writings" (p. 81).

[30] Hengel, *Acts and the History*, 39.

[31] J. Fitzmyer observes that this may be the Gangites river, 2.4 kilometers from Philippi; or perhaps the Crenides creek; see J. Fitzmyer, *The Acts of the Apostles* (AB; New Haven, CT: Yale University Press, 2010), 585.

[32] See C. S. Keener, *Acts: An Exegetical Commentary* (Grand Rapids, MI: Baker, 2014), vol. 3, on 16:13; cf. M. Hengel, "Proseuche und Synagoge: Jüdische Gemeinde,

Paul found a group of women (Acts 16:13) and preached to them. Luke singles out the responsiveness of Lydia whom he calls a "worshiper of God" (*sebomenē ton theon*). This was one of Luke's ways of indicating non-Jews who were sympathetic to Judaism (but who did not fully observe Torah). Such Gentiles were attracted to Jewish-style "ethical monotheism" and took interest in synagogue worship.[33] Luke adds the personal detail that Lydia was from Thyatira, and that she was, to use Luke Timothy Johnson's language, a "purple-goods merchant" (Acts 16:14). Thyatira (modern-day Akhisar) stood at the crossroads between Pergamum and Sardis. Unsurprisingly, Thyatira was known for its textile industry, and in particular for purple dying.[34] Verhoef explains that purple cloth was not purely ornamental in the ancient world; it was mainly reserved for particular (high-status) Roman military adornments in Paul's time.[35] Luke records that Lydia and her household were baptized and she prevailed upon the

Gotteshaus und Gottesdienst in der Diaspora und in Palästina," in *Tradition und Glaube: Das frühe Christentum in seiner Umwelt: Festgabe für Karl Georg Kühn* (eds. G. Jeremias et al.; Göttingen: Vandenhoek & Ruprecht, 1971), 157–184. As C. K. Barrett observes, had Luke meant that Paul went in search of a "synagogue," one would have expected him to use the word "*synagogē*"; see *Acts* (ICC; Edinburgh: T & T Clark, 1998), 2.781.

[33]  See Fitzmyer, *Acts of the Apostles*, 449–450. For more information see A. Levinskaya, "The Inscription from Aphrodisias and the Problem of God-Fearers," *TynBul* 41 (1990): 312–318; also A. Levinskaya, *The Book of Acts in Its Diaspora Setting* (BAFCS 5; Grand Rapids, MI: Eerdmans, 1996), 51–126; M. F. Bird, *Crossing over Sea and Land: Jewish Missionary Activity in the Second Temple Period* (Peabody, MA: Hendrickson, 2009), 44–52. Richard Ascough has a richly nuanced discussion of Lydia as a Gentile "worshiper of God." He rightly notes that there was no technical class of god-fearers, thus we ought to be careful about what we assume about their beliefs and practices; see *Lydia: Paul's Cosmopolitan Hostess* (Collegeville, MN: Liturgical Press, 2009), 86, and generally pp. 86–90.

[34]  See T. B. Slater, "Thyatira," NIDB, vol. 5, 591. Thyatira is also mentioned in Rev 1:11 as one of the seven churches of Asia Minor to whom John writes.

[35]  See Verhoef, *Philippi*, 19. D. Matson remarks how purple fabric was "an item of luxury in both Luke's social and symbolic worlds" indicating that Lydia was probably a "person of some means"; see *Household Conversion Narratives in Acts* (Sheffield: Sheffield Academic Press, 1996), 143; he also aptly observes how Luke's story of the rich man and Lazarus describes the former as "dressed in purple and fine linen" (Luke 16:19). M. Parsons argues that she is clearly a *dealer* of purple fine-cloth, but probably not the status of a *wearer*; he quotes Plutarch: "often we take pleasure in a thing, but we despise the one who made it. Thus we value aromatic salves and purple clothing, but the dyers and salvemakers remain for us common and low craftspersons" (*Per.* 1.3–4). Nevertheless, as Parsons points out, she proved successful enough to have her own "household"; thus, he labels her as one of relatively low status, but high income (*Acts*, 230).

apostles to stay in her home (16:15). Lydia's exact economic situation is unclear, as is the composition of her household. Obviously in the Roman world one's "household" included far more than the kinship-only "nuclear" family – it could include slaves, and household workers as well. Keener surmises that Lydia appears to be independent, and thus her household probably consisted of servants and slaves.[36]

Beginning in Acts 16:16 Luke transitions to another episode that happens while Paul and his companions were in Philippi. Again they were going to a *proseuchē* and they came upon a slave girl who had a "spirit of clairvoyance." Literally, it says that she had a "pythonic spirit." According to Greek legend, a large she-snake or dragon lived in the caves of Mount Parnassus, serving as protector of the oracle of Delphi. When Apollo came to Delphi, he slew the python, and took control of the oracle. The priestess of Apollo, "his mystic bride, Pythia, became the 'mouthpiece for the god'."[37] In an ecstatic state, she gave prophecies that were interpreted by priests (who were, assumingly, in a state of spirit possession). By Paul's time, to say someone had a "pythonic spirit" meant that they were a soothsayer or had a spirit of divination.[38] Why would her services be needed? As Esther Eidinow explains, ancient people were deeply interested in divine guidance, not only for *personal* gain, but also civic decision-making. Thucydides "mentions them almost cursorily as if they were a fact of daily life, and other evidence, both literary and epigraphic, demonstrates that it was indeed usual practice to involve oracular evidence and its interpreters in political decisions, both before and after this date."[39] As Fitzmyer surmises,

---

[36]   He does consider the possibility that she indeed has a husband but in this case they do not share the same religious interests; see C. S. Keener, *The IVP Bible Background Commentary: New Testament* (Downers Grove, IL: InterVarsity Press, 2014), 370.

[37]   See M. Dixon-Kennedy, *Encyclopedia of Greco-Roman Mythology* (Santa Barbara, CA: ABC-Clio, 1998), 266.

[38]   See Fitzmyer, *Acts of the Apostles*, 586. Might she have been one of the *engastrimuthoi*, the so-called belly-talkers who prophesied through "voices" emanating from their stomachs? These were also called "pythons" due to their association with the Delphic Pythia. Luke does not say this, but it is a tantalizing possibility; see S. Iles Johnston, *Religions of the Ancient World* (Cambridge, MA: Harvard University Press, 2004), 384–385; cf. J. P. Laycock, *Spirit Possession around the World* (Santa Barbara, CA: ABC-Clio, 2015), 17; M. Dillon, *Girls and Women in Classical Greek Religion* (London: Routledge, 2008), 180.

[39]   E. Eidinow, *Oracles, Curses, and Risk among the Ancient Greeks* (Oxford: Oxford University Press, 2012).

though, the masters of the slave-diviner in Philippi apparently used her to attract the wealth of gullible locals wanting a prophetic message.[40]

This slave took an interest in Paul's group and announced "These men are slaves of the Most High God, who proclaim to you a way of salvation" (16:17). This went on for many days. The apostles became perturbed by this, so much so that Paul called out to the spirit possessing her, "I order you in the name of Jesus Christ to come out of her" (16:18) – and it did immediately. Luke wanted to make clear that the power at Paul's disposal (in the name of Jesus Christ) trumps that of the weighty and successful Pythian spirit, a spirit that even recognizes "the Most High God."[41]

This exorcism by Paul led to strong animosity against him by the slave girl's owners. They dragged Paul and Silas before local authorities (16:19). Even though they were primarily upset about financial loss, they brought civil charges against them: "These men are disturbing our city; they are Jews and are advocating customs that are not lawful for us as Romans to adopt or observe" (16:20–21).[42] They used the naming of their ethnicity ("Jews") to discredit them.[43] As Tacitus wrote about Jews, "of all others (they have) a hostile hatred" (*Hist.* 5.5).[44]

They were accused of introducing foreign customs. C. K. Barrett posits that they were charged with proselytizing for Judaism, an illegal activity as Romans could not adopt Judaism.[45] Whatever the exact concerns, the surrounding crowd was stirred up into a mob. As a punishment, the praetors (*stratēgoi*) set up a public beating to shame them, and perhaps too to induce confession of guilt (16:22).[46] Then they were thrown in prison (16:23).

Luke recounts how Paul and Silas were not downcast in view of this series of unfortunate events, but rather joyfully sang hymns (a favorite activity for Luke to highlight; see Acts 1:14; 2:42, 47; 4:23–31; 6:4; 7:60;

---

[40]  Fitzmyer, *Acts of the Apostles*, 586.
[41]  Parsons, *Acts*, 231.
[42]  As Barrett explains, the *stratēgoi* were the praetors of the city, their status between aedile and consul. Praetors judged court cases and took charge of the public treasury; see Barrett, *Acts*, 789.
[43]  L. T. Johnson notes the xenophobia that would have plagued Roman colonies; *The Acts of the Apostles* (SP; Collegeville, MN: Liturgical Press, 1992), 295.
[44]  See Fitzmyer, *Acts*, 587; cf. Juvenal, *Satires* 14.96–106.
[45]  Barrett, *Acts*, 2.789.
[46]  See Witherington, *The Acts of the Apostles*, 496.

9:11; 10:2, 9; 12:12; 13:2–3).[47] Other prisoners were attentive to their songs (16:25b). Their sonorous prayers were interrupted by a fierce earthquake, so violent that it tore open the prison doors and released them from their shackles (16:26). This miraculous prison-break episode trumps that of Peter in Acts 12:6–11. The jailer assumed that they had escaped – and that he would be punished–so he prepared to take his own life (Acts 16:27). But Paul stopped him (16:28). In both thanksgiving and awe, the jailer facilitated their exit and asked, "Sirs, what must I do to be saved?" (16:29). They called for his trust in the Lord Jesus, preached the gospel to him, and baptized his whole household.

Somewhat ironically, the next day the magistrates sent word for the apostles' release; instead of going away quietly, Paul and Silas divulged that they were mistreated *as Roman citizens* – news that alarmed the authorities and inspired their apology. Before leaving Philippi, though, Paul and Silas paid a visit to Lydia and brought encouragement to the believers. From there, Luke narrates Paul and Silas' movement through Amphipolis and Apollonia to Thessalonica (chapter 17). This is essentially the sum of what we learn about Paul's relationship with the Philippians (aside from the brief mention of a visit in 20:6).

Again, Lucan scholars vary on how much of this account ought to be taken as historically accurate and reliable. Most interpreters of Philippians, though, value Luke's account, even while acknowledging his theological and literary penchants. The following are relevant historical features in Acts that seem to have a bearing on the interpretation of Philippians.

Paul had a strategic apostolic interest in urban centers.[48]

Paul's gospel would have been attractive to gentile sympathizers of Judaism, such as Lydia (Acts 16:4).

Philippi in the middle of the first century did not have a large Jewish population. Macedonian cities like Philippi would have been no stranger to interests in divination (even for questions of state-welfare), and disruption of this would have been taken with utmost concern.

---

[47]   Johnson points out the parallel between the apostolic joy and the words of Epictetus, "Then we shall be emulating Socrates, when we are able to write paeans in prison" (*Discourses* 2.6.26–27); also T. Joseph 8.5, "[he] sang praise in the house of darkness"; see Johnson, *Acts,* 300.

[48]   See W. Meeks, *The First Urban Christians* (New Haven, CT: Yale University Press, 1983); P. R. Trebilco, "Early Christian Communities in the Greco-Roman City: Perspectives on Urban Ministry from the New Testament," *Ex Auditu* 29 (2013): 25–48.

A highly "Romanized" city like Philippi would have been particularly concerned with anti-Roman activity and anyone guilty of disturbing the peace (Acts 16:20–21).

Roman citizens had special privileges that ought not to be infringed (Acts 16:37–38).

Now we turn to Philippians itself and offer a brief consideration of the situation behind Paul's letter.

PAUL AND THE PHILIPPIANS: EVIDENCE FROM
LETTER TO THE PHILIPPIANS

When we try and get a sense for the circumstances behind Paul's letter to the Philippians, we can pick up on various bits and pieces just by reading the letter itself. Here are some incidental clues that can be gleaned.

## Basic Information

*Timothy as Paul's Coworker.* In the epistolary prescript, we learn that Paul co-wrote/-sent the letter with Timothy. Timothy is mentioned in the prescripts of Colossians (1:1), 2 Corinthians (1:1), and Philemon (1) as well. In 1 Corinthians he is called Paul's "beloved and faithful child in the Lord" (1 Cor 4:17), and someone that not only traveled and worked closely with Paul (Rom 16:21), but also a person he trusted as his proxy as needed (see 1 Thess 3:2–6; cf. 1 Cor 16:10).

Paul mentions Timothy later in Philippians as someone whom he was wishing to send to Philippi to check in on the Christian brothers and sisters there (2:19). Paul commends him by saying, "I have no one like him who will be genuinely concerned for your welfare" (2:20). He goes on to describe him as like a son, serving as Paul's trustworthy companion in the work of the gospel (2:22).

*Philippian Partnership in Ministry.* Paul gives clear indications that the Philippians had actively participated and partnered with him in his work, "from the first day until now" (1:5). This involved financial support (4:14–16), but presumably Paul was also implying that they had an active interest and investment in his ministry work.

*Pauline Imprisonment.* As is well-known of Philippians, one of the so-called prison epistles, Paul mentions his circumstances several times, namely his imprisonment (see 1:7–14, 17). He refers to being "in chains" (*en tois desmois*), and it was likely that this should be understood literally, that is, he was chained to a guard.[49] While the exact circumstances and outcome of his situation are unclear, he showed optimism and hope that he would be "delivered" (1:19) and was confident that he would have a future ministry of encouragement with them (1:24–5).

**Emissary Epaphroditus.** Apparently part of the reason that Paul sent his letter to the Philippians was to explain his sending back of Epaphroditus, their emissary. Paul mentions that he received the gifts that the Philippian church sent to him through Epaphroditus (4:18). While he found Epaphroditus' help refreshing, he was homesick and obviously experienced some life-threatening ordeal such that it seemed necessary to return to Philippi (2:25–30).

## Situational Problems and Exigencies

The fact of the matter is that Paul tended to write letters to serve certain pastoral aims and often in view of specific problems faced by his assemblies. In 1 Thessalonians, Paul wrote a letter of comfort and encouragement to a church struggling with persecution. In Galatians, Paul was dealing with interlopers who were pressuring the Gentile Galatians to become circumcised. In 1 Corinthians, Paul was compelled to address urgent concerns about disunity, worship, and spiritual gifts. What about Philippians? There are a range of scholarly opinions on this matter. Some are rather insistent that Paul was concerned with division and disunity.[50] Others believe that false teachers were preying upon the Philippians. Others still argue that there were no overt problems or opponents – rather, Paul was offering a message of joy and peace to a church concerned for the apostle in chains.[51]

## *External Problems: Paul's Opponents According to Philippians*

Since the nineteenth century, scholars have been entranced with Paul's opponents: who were they, what did they believe, and why did Paul

---

[49]   See G. D. Fee, *Paul's Letter to the Philippians* (NICNT; Grand Rapids, MI: Eerdmans, 1995), 92.

[50]   D. Peterlin, *Paul's Letter to the Philippians in the Light of Disunity in the Church* (NovTSup 79; Leiden: Brill, 1995).

[51]   See M. D. Hooker, "Philippians: Phantom Opponents and the Real Source of Conflict," in *Fair Play: Diversity and Conflict in Early Christianity* (eds. I. Dunderberg, C. Tuckett, and K. Syreeni; NovTSup 103; Leiden: Brill, 2002), 377–395.

antagonize them? This has particularly been the case in the study of Galatians, 2 Corinthians, Colossians, the Pastoral epistles, and of course in Philippians.[52] Paul mentions several adversaries across the letter and it is worthwhile to investigate who he is referring to and if the same persons are always being spoken about.[53]

## *Phil 1:15–18: Those Who Preach Christ from Bad Motives and Stir Up Trouble for Paul*

The first group mentioned are both rivals to Paul and opponents of Paul himself. They "proclaim Christ from envy and rivalry . . . [from] selfish ambition, not sincerely but intending to increase my suffering in my imprisonment" (Phil 1:15–17, NRSV). The objection raised here is not to the rivals' message, but their motives and anti-Pauline disposition. Paul does not censure them for proclaiming a false or different gospel, for announcing a different Jesus (Gal 1:7; 2 Cor 11:4), or for being proprietors of empty philosophy and human precepts (Col 2:8, 18). Paul elsewhere states that the gospel is something that he shared with other Christian leaders, including the Jerusalem church (Gal 2:7–9, 15; 1 Cor 15:8), so the enmity here might be personal and pragmatic rather than theological. It is quite possible that Paul refers to other Christian groups, perhaps in Ephesus, maybe Petrine, Jacobine, or Johannine churches, with whom Paul shares a theological affinity but of whom he nonetheless finds unwholesome and exhibiting personal antagonism toward him. This might be the

---

[52] See J. J. Gunther, *St Paul's Opponents and Their Background: A Study of Apocalyptic and Jewish Sectarian Teachings* (Leiden: Brill, 1973); Jerry L. Sumney, *Servants of Satan, False Brothers, and Other Opponents of Paul* (Sheffield: Sheffield Academic Press, 1999); Stanley E. Porter, ed., *Paul and His Opponents* (Leiden: Brill, 2009); B. J. Oropeza, *Jews, Gentiles, and the Opponents of Paul: The Pauline Letters* (Eugene, OR: Cascade, 2012).

[53] See C. R. Holladay, "Paul's Opponents in Philippians 3," *ResQ* 12 (1969): 77–90; C. Mearns, "The Identity of Paul's Opponents at Philippi," *NTS* 33 (1987): 194–204; C. Kähler, "Konflikt, Kompromiss und Bekenntnis: Paulus und seine Gegner im Philipperbrief," *KD* 40 (1994): 47–64; H. Bateman, "Were the Opponents at Philippi Necessarily Jewish?" *BSac* 155 (1998): 39–61; Sumney, *Servants of Satan*, 160–187; Hooker, "Philippians," 377–395; D. K. Williams, *Enemies of the Cross of Christ: The Terminology of the Cross and Conflict in Philippians* (JSNTSup 223; Sheffield: Sheffield Academic Press, 2002); J. L. Sumney, "Studying Paul's Opponents: Advances and Challenges," in *Paul and His Opponents* (ed. S. E. Porter; Leiden: Brill, 2009), 25–29; and N. Nikki, *Opponents and Identity in Philippians* (NovTSup 173; Leiden: Brill, 2019).

type of factions that Paul encountered in Corinth but played out on a wider scale among churches of the eastern Mediterranean with churches loyal to different personalities and parties.[54] Of course, we should not expect Paul to have mentioned every contention he had against every rival every time he mentioned some divisions internal to the church. Paul may well have a theological, christological, or evangelical complaint against such persons and he simply chooses not to rehearse such a complaint at this point in the letter. While Paul can be juxtaposed with Apollos (1 Cor 1:12; 3:4–6, 22; 4:6), go mano e mano with Cephas (Gal 2:14), and have a falling out with Barnabas (Gal 2:13; Acts 15:29), we know that Paul's most concerted adversaries were Jewish Christ-believers from Jerusalem, and it is these he probably has in mind. All the more likely when we consider that he will mention them explicitly in Phil 3:2.

### Phil 1:28–30: Pagan Critics and Persecutors of the Church

The "opponents" mentioned in 1:28 are pagan persecutors of the churches in Philippi. Oropeza detects here "general harassment involving such things as false accusations, verbal abuse, sporadic physical violence, and social alienation that may be affecting them economically" from "their unbelieving compatriots."[55] That coincides with Luke's account in Acts 16:19–24, which narrates one particularly brutal instance of persecution with Paul and Silas flogged and imprisoned for allegedly disturbing the peace and introducing unlawful customs (Acts 16:20–21). Many Romans and Romanized Greeks considered the introduction of eastern cults to be something of a perversion of Romanitas or Roman-ness, and adherence to foreign cults, including Judaism and later Christianity, was met with stern disapproval or else violent reprisal. This would suggest that Paul was not being imprisoned for simply causing a melee in the market or a raucous ruckus with local priests, but perhaps for *maiestas*, allegedly insulting Roman gods and imperial honor by urging people to "turn to God from idols" (1 Thess 1:9) and proclaiming that "there is another king named Jesus" (Acts 17:7). The same sort of opposition and persecution that Paul experienced was now happening to the Philippians

---

[54]   See Oropeza, *Jews, Gentiles, and the Opponents of Paul*, 208 who sees here opponents somewhat akin to, but perhaps a less intense version of, "the believers who attack Paul's apostolic authority in 2 Cor."

[55]   Oropeza, *Jews, Gentiles, and the Opponents of Paul*, 207–208.

(Phil 1:30). The reason why Romans persecuted Christians is not straightforward. "The interesting question is," asks S. C. Humphreys, "whether the Romans even knew why they persecuted Christians."[56] "The most probable answer is that Christians were capital O "Other." They were not a recognized cult, they were kind-of-Jewish-but-not-quite, and given to messianic enthusiasm and apocalyptic fervor. They were regarded with suspicion for holding meetings and meals in secret, where rumors of cannibalism and sexual debauchery abounded. They were also considered effeminate and servile since their ranks consisted mostly of women and slaves. In addition, by refusing to participate in civic rites and festivals they appeared disloyal to the populace and impious to the pantheon. In fact, forcing them to offer sacrifices to the emperor was routinely used as a way of weeding them out." In the second century, Pliny, the governor of Bithynia, had some questions for Emperor Trajan as to the correct process of going about identifying Christians if a person had been so accused of being one, but, once identified, Pliny took it for granted that executing them for persisting in their Christian belief was the self-evident thing to do.[57]

## *Phil 3:2–4: Jewish Christ-Believing Proselytizers*

Paul offers an impassioned and polemical warning about Jewish Christ-believers with the memorable words: "Beware of the dogs, beware of the evil workers, beware of those who mutilate the flesh! For it is we who are the circumcision, who worship in the Spirit of God and boast in Christ Jesus and have no confidence in the flesh – even though I, too, have reason for confidence in the flesh." Paul seems to have in mind not the so-called "infection of Judaism,"[58] but far more likely Jewish Christ-believing rivals known from previous clashes in Jerusalem (Acts 15:5–6), Antioch (Acts 15:1–2; Gal 2:4–5, 11–14), and Galatia (Gal 3:1; 5:1–12; 6:12–13), and is worried that they might arrive in Macedonia.[59] These Jewish Christ-believers may

[56]  S. C. Humphreys, *Anthropology and the Greeks* (Oxford: Routledge, 2004), 189.
[57]  Pliny, *Ep.* 10.96–97.
[58]  J. B. Lightfoot, *St. Paul's Epistle to the Philippians* (London: MacMillan, 1903), 143. •
[59]  M. D. Nanos (*Reading Corinthians and Philippians within Judaism: Collected Essays of Mark D. Nanos* [Eugene, OR: Cascade, 2017], 111–140) offers a novel proposal regarding the opponents in Phil 3:2. He believes it refers to Cynic philosophers, who were given the name "dogs" (*kynos*) because they were always barking or nipping at the heels of society. Nanos creatively proposes that Paul's deployment of intense and inflammatory rhetoric,

have been partly benign in believing that they were simply completing what they perceived to be deficient in Paul's message to Gentile Christ-believers by urging Gentiles to be circumcised and to obey Torah. Or perhaps they were more entrenched in their critique of Paul by supposing that Paul's gospel was defective in that it did not adequately integrate the dispensations of Abraham and Moses, where circumcision was expected of pagan converts, into Christian faith. Or else, Jewish Christ-believers were merely attempting to resolve the ambiguous social-religious status of Gentile believers, who would normally be expected to participate in the local civic cults, and becoming Jews terminated any ambiguity as they would come under the aegis of Jewish communities who enjoyed a legal exemption to abstain from such civic events.[60] Whatever their motivations, Paul engages in the acme of sectarian polemics to disparage their message of Messiah plus proselytism to Judaism.

### *Phil 3:18–19: Gentile Apostates or Jewish Christ-Believers?*

The final remarks about opponents is as equally incendiary and reproachful as anything else in the letter. Paul declares: "For many live as enemies of the cross of Christ; I have often told you of them, and now I tell you even with tears. Their end is destruction; their god is the belly; and their glory is in their shame; their minds are set on earthly things." One could understand this in a general way, Paul is simply referring to anyone – pagan or Jewish – who opposes the Christian message. Or Paul might even have in mind apostate Gentile Christians, licentious and antinomian in behavior,

---

combined with his perceived ascetic tendencies, might have led him being mistaken for a Cynic philosopher. In fact, Nanos thinks many of the Gentile Christians might be being mistaken as such, and Paul is warning them against internalizing that identity. The problem is, as some have noted (e.g., J. Reumann, *Philippians: A New Translation with Introduction and Commentary* [AYB; New Haven, CT: Yale University Press, 2008], 472) that Phil 3:2–11 has a very Jewish ambience and reflects Paul's prior polemics against Jewish proselytism.

[60] On this last option, see M. Tellbe, "The Sociological Factors behind Philippians 3:1–11 and the Conflict at Philippi," *JSNT* 55 (1994): 97–121; sympathetic is Fee, *Paul's Letter to the Philippians*, 289, M. N. A. Bockmuehl, *The Epistle to the Philippians* (BNTC; Peabody, MA: Hendrickson, 1997), 190–191; B. Witherington III, *Paul's Letter to the Philippians: A Socio-Rhetorical Commentary* (Grand Rapids, MI: Eerdmans, 2011), 196–197; B. Thurston, *Philippians and Philemon* (SP 10; Collegeville, MN: Liturgical Press, 2005), 118–119; M. Keown, *Philippians* (EEC; Bellingham, WA: Lexham Press, 2017), 2.79–80.

who have abandoned the faith, who now oppose the gospel message, and who have returned to the idolatry and immorality that characterized Romans and Greeks.[61] However, given the context of Phil 3 as a whole, the intra-Jewish sectarian language that is employed, plus the mention of the "enemies of the cross of Christ" which seems to resonate with Gal 6:12 about those who wish to avoid being "persecuted for the cross of Christ," it is more likely than not that Jewish Christ-believers are in mind. As Watson says, "There is in fact nothing here that cannot apply to missionaries of circumcision such as the Galatian agitators."[62]

## Internal Problems: Disunity among the Philippians

In terms of problems *within* the Philippian church, we can draw some implications from the letter's emphasis on unity.

Only, live your life in a manner worthy of the gospel of Christ . . . standing firm in one spirit, striving side by side with one mind for the faith of the gospel (1:27).

[M]ake my joy complete: be of the same mind, having the same love, being in full accord and of one mind. Do nothing from selfish ambition or conceit, but in humility regard others as better than yourselves. Let each of you look not to your own interests, but to the interests of others (2:2).

Let the same mind be in you (pl.) that was Christ Jesus (2:5).

I urge Euodia and Syntyche to be of the same mind in the Lord. Yes, and I ask you also, my loyal companion, help these women, for they have struggled beside me in the work of the gospel, together with Clement and the rest of my co-workers, whose names are written in the book of life (4:2–3).

---

[61]   See R. Jewett, "Conflicting Movements in the Early Church as Reflected in Philippians," *NovT* 12 (1970): 373; Bockmuehl, *The Epistle to the Philippians*, 232; Fee, *Paul's Letter to the Philippians*, 375; Oropeza, *Jews, Gentiles, and the Opponents of Paul*, 212; L. H. Cohick, *Philippians* (SGBC; Grand Rapids, MI: Zondervan, 2013), 198–199; G. W. Hansen, *The Letter to the Philippians* (PNTC; Grand Rapids, MI: Eerdmans, 2009), 264–265.

[62]   F. B. Watson, *Paul, Judaism, and the Gentiles: Beyond the New Perspective* (Grand Rapids, MI: Eerdmans, 2007), 145; similarly G. F. Hawthorne and R. P. Martin, *Philippians* (WBC 43; Nashville, TN: Thomas Nelson, 2004), 221; Thurston, *Philippians and Philemon*, 118–119; P. Holloway, *Philippians* (Hermeneia; Minneapolis: Fortress, 2017), 149; Witherington, *Paul's Letter to the Philippians*, 181, 215–216; Reumann, *Philippians*, 469–470, 518–519, 589.

The methodological questions regarding discerning the possible presence of enemies in Philippi and whether or not there were major problems in the church are complex, and there are no perfect answers, only theories that lead to the most satisfying reading and interpretation of the letter in its original setting. Still, it is worth approaching the letter with tentative or operating assumptions. We believe a reasonable approach would be to assume the following:

(1) The Philippians were experiencing rejection and condemnation from their non-Christian relatives, neighbors, and community members. It is not necessary to postulate harassment coming from an organized group with a particular theological agenda.

(2) Paul makes clear the presence of troublemakers around him, but these are mentioned as examples, not as active threats in Philippi.

(3) Due to the stresses and pressures caused by local persecution, the Philippian church was showing signs of disunity and quarrelling. Given Paul's positive and encouraging tone overall, it would seem that the issue is not *so* extreme as to assume widespread or cataclysmic infighting. Still, the explicit mention of the fall out between Euodia and Syntyche means that the problem was dire enough to merit some kind of intervention.

Overall, Paul tackles his pastoral aims in Philippians by appealing to many examples, good and bad, as a way of "triangulating," if you will, proper Christian behavior. Timothy and Epaphroditus are held up as models, for examples, of trustworthy, hard-working, cooperative, and compassionate Christian brothers who have become indispensable contributors to the work of the gospel (see 2:19–20, 29–30). The mention of evildoers in 3:2–3 is probably exemplary, these serving as negative examples of those who destroy and tear apart for the sake of vainglory, rather than those who knit together in humility.

## The Location of Paul's Imprisonment

Philippians was written during one of Paul's many imprisonments (2 Cor 6:5; 11:23), but during which imprisonment and precisely where? It has traditionally been claimed that Paul wrote Philippians during a Roman imprisonment in the early 60s, while others have suggested Caesarea in the late 50s, and others again Ephesus as the place of writing in the mid-50s CE.

While certainty is impossible, we prefer a setting in Ephesus with a date in the mid-50s for several reasons.[63]

First, an Ephesian imprisonment is a sound inference drawn from Paul's reference to the "troubles we experienced in the province of Asia," his "many adversaries" there, his enigmatic remark about "how I fought wild beasts at Ephesus," all of which could well be allusive for an imprisonment and a potentially capital trial in Ephesus (2 Cor 1:8–9; 11:23; 1 Cor 15:32; 16:9). This situation largely agrees with Luke's report of Paul's tumultuous time there during his journey for the collection (Acts 19:1–40). True, Luke does not explicitly mention an Ephesian imprisonment, but that is most likely because his narration is an episodic and epitomized summary of Paul's career.

Second, Timothy is named as the coauthor of Philippians, yet we have no evidence that Timothy accompanied Paul to Rome and he more likely remained in Ephesus where the pastoral epistles also place him.

Third, the polemical sections in the letter to the Philippians (1:15–18; 3:2–21) suggest an anxiety in Paul that has argumentative affinity and chronological proximity with his mindset, mood, rhetoric, and reaction following the Antiochene incident (Gal 2:11–21) and the Galatian crisis (Gal 5:12) of the late 40s/early 50s. In other words, Philippians should be dated soon after Paul has energetically engaged with the problem of Jewish Christ-believing proselytizers harassing his Gentile converts in the early

---

[63] See F. S. Thielman, "Ephesus and the Literary Setting of Philippians," in *New Testament Greek and Exegesis* (eds. A. M. Donaldson and T. B. Sailors; Grand Rapids, MI: Eerdmans, 2003), 205–223; Watson, *Paul, Judaism, and the Gentiles*, 13–19; E. P. Sanders, *Paul: The Apostle's Life, Letters, and Thought* (Minneapolis: Fortress, 2015), 580–591; Reumann, *Philippians*, 13–18; M. Eugene Boring, "Philippians and Philemon: Date and Provenance," *CBQ* 81 (2019): 470–94; Michael Flexsenhar, "The Provenance of Philippians and Why It Matters: Old Questions, New Approaches," *JSNT* 42 (2019): 18–45. J. White, "The Imprisonment that Could Have Happened (And the Letters Paul Could Have Written There): A Response to Ben Witherington," *JETS* 61 (2018): 549–558; a view strongly contested by Ben Witherington, "The Case of the Imprisonment that Did Not Happen: Paul at Ephesus," *JETS* 60 (2017): 525–532; idem, "Was Paul a Jailbird? A Response to the Response," *JETS* 61 (2018): 559–562. In response to Witherington, we'd contend that Roman citizenship was no get-out-jail-free card, the judicial reality and pragmatism of governors in the provinces did not always lend itself to rule by the rule of law. According to Julia Hillner (*Prison, Punishment and Penance in Late Antiquity* [Cambridge: Cambridge University Press, 2015], 143) short-term extrajudicial arrests and detainment as a means to coerce people to change habits or pay debts was common. She writes, "Nominally Roman citizens could appeal against such treatment to the emperor, but already under the Republic and early empire it was difficult to enforce this provision, and even more so in late antiquity, where Roman citizenship did not carry much privilege anymore."

to mid-50s, rather than after his more diplomatic and sanguine remarks about Christ, Torah, and the gospel that he wrote in his letter to the Romans around 57–58 CE.

Fourth, the movements described in the captivity letters (Philippians, Philemon, Colossians, and Ephesians) are far more plausible if Paul is imprisoned in Ephesus rather than in Rome.

For instance, in Philippians alone we observe: (1) Someone traveled from wherever Paul was to Philippi to inform them of Paul's imprisonment; (2) Epaphroditus traveled from Philippi to Paul's location to provide him with material and moral support; (3) then someone traveled back from Paul's imprisonment to Philippi to let the church know that Epaphroditus was seriously ill; (4) in response, the Philippians dispatched a letter to Paul expressing their concern for both Paul and Epaphroditus; (5) Paul says that he intends to send Epaphroditus and Timothy back to Philippi in the near future; and (6) Paul expects to be reunited with the Philippians himself some time soon, which means returning to Philippi (see Phil 1:26–27; 2:22–27; 4:18). It is far more likely that these quick back and forth trips are across the Aegean Sea (250 miles) rather than across the Aegean and Adriatic Seas (800 miles).

In addition, and somewhat parallel to the movements between Paul and persons in Philippi, are the journeys to and from Colossae to Paul's place of detainment. The flight of Onesimus from Colossae to seek out Paul, Onesimus' return to Colossae with Tychichus, and Paul's stated intention to visit Philemon in Colossae is again far more plausible if Paul is imprisoned somewhere closer such as Ephesus rather than in Rome (Philm 10, 22; Col 4:7–9).[64]

Furthermore, if Paul really was in Rome when he wrote Philippians, then we know from his letter to the Romans that if he was released from custody that he was intending to head westward to Spain at first opportunity (Rom 15:23–28), which makes a prior eastern sojourn back to Macedonia and central Asia Minor not just circuitous, but patently absurd.

Fifth, while many suppose that Paul's reference to "the praetorium" and the "saints of Caesar's house" implies a Roman provenance, this is far from certain (Phil 1:13; 4:22).

---

[64] Interestingly, the Marcionite prologues suggest that Paul wrote Colossians from Ephesus.

(1) The *praitōrion* simply means "general's tent" or "headquarters." Even if it refers to the people who make up the "imperial guard" (NRSV) or "palace guard" (NIV), that guard operates in a place known as the *praetorium* and Paul is merely referring to the people who work there, whether soldiers, slaves, freedman, servants, or administrators. Now, on the one hand, it is hardly beyond comprehension that Ephesus – as the "Light of Asia" and the "First and Greatest Metropolis of Asia," holding immense strategic and economic importance, and comprising the seat of imperial worship in Asia – would have an imperial residence with administrators and a skeleton garrison of praetorian soldiers and imperial slaves. In fact, that is more than a proposal, there is inscriptional evidence that *praetoriani* were stationed in Ephesus, since members of the elite imperial body-guard supervised the imperial bank in Asia.[65] On the other hand, and more likely for our mind, the reference to the *praitōrion* designates the proconsul of Asia's own residence and the staff working in his headquarters and/or military garrison.[66]

(2) The mention of the saints of *Kaisaros oikias* ("Caesar's household") does not mean members of Nero's family and inner circle who have become believers. Far more likely, it is the Christians who worked in the residence and headquarters of the procurator who was the emperor's official representative in a region to take care of his domains and interests, perhaps imperial slaves. Whereas the proconsul was a senatorial appointee, the procurator was an imperial appointee. Tacitus tells us that at the commencement of Nero's reign (ca. 54 CE) that Iunius Silanus was the proconsul of Asia, while Publius Celer and Helius were the procurators (who, it turned out, poisoned Silanus at the behest of Agrippina, Nero's mother).[67] "Caesar's household" need not be administrators or slaves in the emperor's own residence in Rome. More likely, it refers to members of

---

[65] D. E. Garland, "Philippians," in *The Expositor's Bible Commentary* (eds. T. Longman and D. E. Garland; rev. edn.; Grand Rapids, MI: Zondervan, 2006), vol. 12, 177–261, here 180.

[66] Reumann (*Philippians*, 171–172) points out that *praetōrion* could designate the military detachment associated with the headquarters of a ruler, as the case with the governor of Syracuse; even though it was a senatorial rather than imperial province, Pilate's headquarters in Jerusalem is called a *praetōrion* (Mark 15:16; Matt 27:27; John 18:28, 33; 19:9); the same for Herod Agrippa II in Caesarea-Maritima (Acts 23:25).

[67] Tacitus, *Ann.* 13.1.

the imperial apparatus in Ephesus who worked for the procurators, persons tasked with looking after Caesar's affairs.[68]

In sum, Paul declares that members of the Ephesian proconsul's retinue know that he is chains for Christ and the Christians among Caesar's household managed by the Ephesian procurators share their greetings with the Philippians.

### THE CHURCH IN PHILIPPI

What was the church in Philippi like? How large was it? Who were the believers and what was their gender, ethnicity, and social status? Unfortunately, we glean very little information directly from Paul's letter that can answer any of these questions. Based on the meager details that can be taken from Acts as well as Paul's letter itself, Verhoef explains that the Philippian church was comprised of at least these believers: Lydia, the jailer, two "bishops," two "deacons," Epaphroditus, Euodia, Syntyche, the "companion" (4:3), and Clement. Again, able only to offer guesses, Verhoef presumes that most people within this church belonged to the "working classes" and that very few would have been considered "wealthy."[69] He estimates that the church in Philippi would have had about thirty people in all by the end of the first century.

### THE PURPOSE OF PAUL'S LETTER TO THE PHILIPPIANS

When it comes to *why* Paul wrote Philippians and what he hoped to accomplish with this letter, it appears that there is not one *all-encompassing* reason, but rather several concerns or matters he wished to address. One immediate issue involved the Philippians' giving of a gift to Paul for which he wanted to express receipt and appreciation (4:10–20). He acknowledges that they alone held to a pact of "giving and receiving" with him in the early days of his ministry (4:13). His letter to the Philippians was apparently delivered by their emissary Epaphroditus, whom he sent back to them – Paul commends Epaphroditus in his letter and encourages the Philippians to give him a warm welcome. Paul also communicates to the Philippians his fondness for them and his hope to come to them if he should be released (see 1:8).

---

[68]   See esp. Sanders, *Paul*, 580–591; Flexsenhar, "The Provenance of Philippians."
[69]   Verhoef, *Philippi*, 21.

We also learn from this letter that the Philippians were facing persecution and struggling with shame and disgrace on account of their faith in Jesus Christ. Paul addresses the problem of shame and degradation (3:20–21), which he is well aware as a prisoner for the gospel (1:20). Thus, he expresses concern for the overall stability of their faith (1:28). He exhorts them not to worry, and to know the true peace of God (4:6–7). This may reflect on their attitude toward his imprisonment. The Philippians may have begun to doubt the wisdom of this gospel of Jesus Christ in light of their own apostle potentially meeting his demise (see 2:17). But Paul informs them that, not only is the gospel surviving in light of his situation, it is actually thriving (see 1:12f.).

Finally, we can address the matter of whether or not Paul had concern over moral problems in the Philippian church. We can rule out immediately any notion that this community was struggling with major or pervasive problems. The warm and joy-filled tone of the letter seems to imply that whatever challenges the Philippians were facing, they were not in dire straits. Still, given the repeated attention Paul gives to concerns for *unity* (1:9–10, 27–30; 2:1–11) and the specific calling out of the disagreement between Euodia and Syntyche (4:2), it is probable that there was some friction within this group, and Paul wanted to address it and inspire them toward more love and cooperation.

THEOLOGICAL THEMES

## Resilient Joy

On the theme of joy in Philippians, no one has said it better than Markus Bockmuehl:

St Paul's letter to Philippi sparkles with joy – the sort of life-giving, heart-refreshing joy that is tangibly transforming in its effect on the mundane realities of everyday existence. Philippians is, at the same time, an epistle of joy tested and refined . . . It shows us Paul at his most mature, having weathered the storms of his earlier ministry . . . Near the end of his hard and adventurous road, we find a man whose faith in Christ has not merely survived but aged with grace and wisdom, refined and true as gold.[70]

---

[70] Bockmuehl, *The Epistle to the Philippians*, 1.

The theme and expression of joy is not just distinct in Philippians, but also pervasive. Paul prays with joy when he remembers the Philippians (1:4; cf. 4:1, 10). He rejoices in prison knowing that Christ is proclaimed, even if some preach with dubious motives (1:18). He hopes for further progress and increase in joy for the Philippians in view of their challenges and afflictions (1:25). He also relates his joy to their unity and well-being (2:2).

As Paul considered the possibility of his own death, he told the Philippians of his fondness for and joy because of them (2:17), and he invited them to share this same joy (2:18). Paul expects that the Philippians will welcome Epaphroditus back with joy (2:29). Some of Paul's final words in this letter to the Philippians are his famous, "Rejoice in the Lord always, again I will say, Rejoice!" (4:8).

For Paul, joy is correctly understood as a state of happiness or gladness (see LN 25.123). But it is a mistake to assume that he understood it as a fleeting emotion. Paul repeats this word in command form ("rejoice!") in order to reprogram how the Philippians reflect on Paul's situation (in prison), their circumstances (of suffering), and the hope of the gospel. Paul wished for them not simply to secure for themselves a position where they might be free from cares and concerns – imagine how irrelevant this would be to slaves! Rather, he modeled for them *resilient* joy that depended on the love of God, the remembrance of the fellowship of the saints, and leaned into the hope of the world-reconciling appearance of Christ, in spite of what can seem like dire circumstances.

## Deferential Love

Another distinctive feature of Philippians is Paul's affectionate tone. In each chapter he refers to the readers as *beloved* (1:12; 2:12; 3:13; 4:8). In 4:1, he specifically explicates how he longs for them and that they are his "joy and crown." Clearly he had a fondness and affinity for this particular church, due in no small part to their gracious concern for his well-being and their commitment to support his ministry work for the sake of the gospel of Jesus Christ.

Furthermore, though, "love" is a topical concern in this letter; one of the first moments where Paul divulges his hopes for the Philippians comes in 1:9 where he expresses his prayer that "your love may overflow more and more with knowledge and full insight." While we are not privy to the exact circumstances or considerations that inspired this prayer, we may be given a clue in 2:3–4, where Paul admonishes them not to behave in ways that are motivated by rivalry and a competitive spirit. God, in his love, calls his people to care for each other with a spirit of generosity. It is possible that when Paul mentions "consolation from love" in 2:1 he is referring to divine love, the care of God that demonstrates divine concern and affection, love that inspires deferential love and unity within the household of faith.

It would be a mistake to only look for "love" in Philippians where we find the Greek words *agapē* and *phileō*. For Paul, the best explication of love is found in the story of Christ, a tale he tells in 2:6–11 – the one who once knew the highest and best status chose to accept a low station (like a king becoming a slave) and die on a cross (which Cicero called the "tree of shame"; *Rab. perd.* 4.13) for the sake of love, both Christ's obedient love toward God his Father and Christ's compassionate love for helpless sinners (cf. Gal 2:20).

## Friendship, Partnership, and Unity

Third, we come to the interrelated themes of friendship, partnership, and unity in Philippians. Oneness is essentially what Philippians is all about, and Paul was apparently drawing from a popular friendship *topos* to underscore his concern for the Philippians' unity. George Lyons and William Malas isolate five features or values that reoccur in Greco-Roman friendship discourses: unity, equality, moral excellence, frankness, and loyalty. When it comes to Philippians, Lyons and Malas note that all five are observable and offer this conclusion:

Paul's letter to the Philippians sought to strengthen the intensity of their commitment to their friendship in the face of competing values. The virtues he promoted he found modeled in the attitude of Christ: a disposition toward unity as friends and a willingness to serve and rejoice in the interests of this partnership in spite of suffering, motivated by the glory and praise of God.[71]

While it will be argued in this commentary that Philippians is not formally a "letter of friendship," Paul remains very "friendly" (4:1) in this epistle and seeks above all to renew the bond of fellowship between him and the Philippians.

---

[71]  G. Lyons and W. Malas, "Paul and His Friends within the Greco-Roman Context," *Westminster Theological Journal* 42 (2007): 50–69, at 66.

# Suggested Reading

Items with (*) are highly recommended.

## THE GENRE OF PAUL'S LETTER TO THE PHILIPPIANS

*There continues to be a robust conversation going on in scholarship about what kind of letter category fits Philippians. Not long ago, a large number of scholars were convinced it is a "letter or friendship," but there is more hesitancy today.*

P. Holloway, *Consolation in Philippians: Philosophical Sources and Rhetorical Strategy.* SNTSMS; Cambridge: Cambridge University Press, 2001.

S. Llewelyn, "Sending Letters in the Ancient World: Paul and the Philippians." *TynBul* 46.2 (1995): 337–356.

*T. D. Still, "More than Friends?: The Literary Classification of Philippians Revisited." *PRS* 39.1 (2012): 53–66.

## BACKGROUND AND SOCIAL CONTEXT

*Especially in the late twentieth century and early twenty-first century, more academic attention has been paid to understanding the social, political, and religious context of Roman Philippi. Pauline scholars are working together with archaeologists, classicists, and historians to bring the joys, trials, and tribulations of the early Philippian Church to light.*

*R. Ascough, *Paul's Macedonian Associations: The Social Context of Philippians and 1 Thessalonians.* WUNT 2; Tübingen: Mohr Siebeck, 2003.

C. Bakirtzis, ed. *Philippi at the Time of Paul and after His Death.* Harrisburg, PA: Trinity Press, 1998.

K. Berry, "The Function of Friendship Language in Philippians 4:10–20," in J. T. Fitzgerald (ed.), *Friendship, Flattery, and Frankness of Speech: Studies on Friendship in the New Testament World.* Leiden: Brill, 1996, 107–124.

H. D. Betz, *Studies in Paul's Letter to the Philippians.* WUNT; Tübingen: Mohr Siebeck, 2015.

D. Briones, *Paul's Financial Policy: A Socio-Theological Approach.* LNTS; London: T & T Clark, 2015.

R. J. Cassidy, *Paul in Chains: Roman Imprisonment and the Letters of Paul.* New York: Crossroads, 2001.

N. A. Dahl, "Euodia and Syntyche and Paul's Letter to the Philippians," in L. Michael White and O. Larry Yarbrough (eds.), *The Social World of the First Christians: Essays in Honor of Wayne A. Meeks.* Minneapolis: Fortress, 1995, 3–15.

T. C. Geoffrion, *The Rhetorical Purpose and the Political and Military Character of Philippians: A Call to Stand Firm.* Lewiston: Edwin Mellen Press, 1993.

*J. Hellerman, Reconstructing Honor in Roman Philippi: *Carmen Christi* as *Cursus Pudorum*. SNTSMS; Cambridge: Cambridge University Press, 2005.

J. Hellerman, "μορφῇ θεοῦ as a Signifier of Social Status in Philippians 2:6." *JETS* 52.4 (2009): 779–797.

"The Humiliation of Christ in the Social World of Roman Philippi Part 1." *BSac* 160.639 (2003), 321–335.

"The Humiliation of Christ in the Social World of Roman Philippi Part 2." *BSac* 160.640 (2003), 421–433.

M. D. Hooker, "Philippians: Phantom Opponents and the Real Source of Conflict," in I. Dunderberg, C. Tuckett, and K. Syreeni (eds.), *Fair Play: Diversity and Conflict in Early Christianity*. NovTSup 103; Leiden: Brill, 2002, 377–395.

M. A. Jennings. *The Price of Partnership in Paul's Letter to the Philippians*. LNTS; London: T & T Clark, 2018.

E. Krentz, "Civic Culture and the Philippians." *CTM* 35.4 (2008): 258–263.

J. Marchal, ed. *The People beside Paul: the Philippians Assembly and History from Below*. Atlanta, GA: SBL, 2015.

D. P. Moessner. "Turning Status 'Upside Down' in Phillipi: Christ Jesus' 'Emptying Himself' as Forfeiting Any Acknowledgement of His 'Equality with God' (Phil 2:6–11)." *HBT* 31.2 (2009): 123–143.

*P. S. Oakes, "God's Sovereignty over Roman Authorities: A Theme in Philippians," in P. Oakes (ed.), *Rome in the Bible and the Early Church*. Grand Rapids, MI: Baker, 2002, 126–141.

P. S. Oakes, "Jason and Penelope Hear Philippians 1:1–11," in *Understanding, Studying and Reading: New Testament Essays in Honour of John Ashton*. Sheffield: Sheffield Academic Press, 1998, 155–164.

*Philippians: From People to Letter*. SNTSMS; Cambridge: Cambridge University Press, 2000.

"Re-mapping the Universe: Paul and the Emperor in 1 Thessalonians and Philippians." *JSNT* 27.3 (2005): 301–322.

J. M. Ogereau, *Paul's Koinonia with the Philippians: A Socio-Historical Investigation of a Pauline Economic Partnership*. WUNT 2; Tübingen: Mohr Siebeck, 2014.

D. Peterlin, *Paul's Letter to the Philippians in the Light of Disunity in the Church*. NovTSup 79; Leiden: Brill, 1995.

G. Peterman, *Paul's Gift from Philippi: Conventions of Gift-Exchange and Christian Giving*. SNTSMS; Cambridge: Cambridge University Press, 1997.

*P. Pilhofer, *Philippi: Band II: Katalog der Inschriften von Philippi*. WUNT 2.119; Tübingen: Mohr Siebeck, 2000.

L. Portefaix, *Sisters Rejoice: Paul's Letter to the Philippians and Luke-Acts as Received by Firsst-Century Philippian Women*. ConBNT20; Stockholm: Almqvist & Wiksell, 1988.

P.-B. Smit, "A Numismatic Note on Phil 2:9–11." *Biblische Notizen* 149 (2011): 101–112.

*M. Tellbe, *Paul between Synagogue and State: Christians, Jews, and Civic Authorities in 1 Thessalonians, Romans, and Philippians*. Stockholm: Almqvist & Wiksell, 2001.

*E. Verhoef, *Philippi: How Christianity Began in Europe: The Epistle to the Philippians and the Excavations at Philippi*. London: Bloomsbury, 2013.

C. de Vos. *Church and Community Conflicts: The Relationships of the Thessalonian, Corinthian, and Philippian Churches with Their Wider Civic Communities*. Atlanta, GA: Scholars Press, 1999.

J. Ware, *Paul and the Mission of the Church: Philippians in Ancient Jewish Context*. NovTSup; Leiden: Brill, 2005.

D. Williams, *Enemies of the Cross of Christ: The Terminology of the Cross and Conflict in Philippians*. JSNTSup 223; Sheffield: Sheffield Academic Press, 2002.

## THE CHRIST HYMN

*For many centuries, scholars have been fascinated with this short section of Philippians (2:6–11). Not only is there ongoing debate about its Christology, but also its origins, use of the Old Testament, conceptual influences and background, and its potential critique of Roman imperial ideology.*

D. F. Asaju, "Philippians 2:5–11: An African Reading of Paul's Christological Hymn of Exaltation." *Bangalore Theological Forum* 37.1 (2005): 198–207.

S. Biggs, "Can an Enslaved God Liberate: Hermeneutical Reflections on Philippians 2:6–11." *Semeia* 47 (1989): 137–153.

M. N. A. Bockmuehl, "'The Form of God' (Phil 2:6): Variants on a Theme of Jewish Mysticism." *JTS* 48.1 (1997): 1–23.

B. Byrne, "Christ's Pre-existence in Pauline Soteriology." *Theological Studies* 58.2 (1997): 308–330.

A. Y. Collins, "Psalms, Philippians 2:6–11, and the Origins of Christology." *BibInt* 11.3 (2003): 361–372.

C. B. Cousar, "The Function of the Christ-Hymn (2.6–11) in Philippians," in C. J. Roetzel and R. L. Foster (eds.), *The Impartial God: Essays in Biblical Studies in Honor of Jouette M. Bassler*. Sheffield: Sheffield Phoenix Press, 2007), 212–220.

S. Eastman, "Philippians 2:6–11: Incarnation as Mimetic Participation." *JSPL* 1.1 (2011): 1–22.

E. E. Ellis, "Preformed Traditions and Their Implications for Pauline Christology," in D. G. Horrell and C. M. Tuckett (eds.), *Christology, Controversy, and Community: New Testament Essays in Honour of David R. Catchpole*. Leiden: Brill, 2000, 303–320.

G. D. Fee, "Philippians 2:5–11: Hymn or Exalted Pauline Prose?" *BBR* 2 (1992): 29–46.

*G. P. Fewster, "The Philippians' 'Christ Hymn': Trends in Critical Scholarship." *CBR* 13.2 (2015): 191–206.

B. Fisk, "The Odyssey of Christ: A Novel Context for Philippians 2:6–11," in C. Stephen Evans (ed.), *Exploring Kenotic Christology: The Self-Emptying of God*. Oxford: Oxford University Press, 2006, 45–73.

J. Fitzmyer, "The Aramaic Background of Philippians 2:6–11." *CBQ* 50.3 (1988): 470–483.

M. J. Gorman, "'Although/Because He Was in the Form of God': The Theological Significance of Paul's Master Story (Phil 2:6–11)." *JTI* 1.2 (2007): 147–169.

N. K. Gupta, "To Whom Was Christ a Slave (Phil 2:7)?: Double Agency and the Specters of Sin and Death in Philippians." *HBT* 32.1 (2010): 1–16.

M. Hengel, "Präexistenz bei Paulus," in H.-J. Esckstein and H. Lichtenberger (eds.), *Jesus Christus also die Mitte der Schrift: Studien zur Hermeneutik des Evangeliums*. Berlin: de Gruyter, 1997, 479–518.

M. D. Hooker, "Adam Redivivus: Philippians 2 Once More," in S. Moyise (ed.), *The Old Testament in the New: Essays in Honour of J.L. North*. Sheffield: Sheffield Academic Press, 2000, 220–234.

L. D. Hurst, "Re-enter the Pre-existent Christ in Philippians 2:5–11." *NTS* 32.3 (1986): 449–457.

L. W. Hurtado, "Jesus as Lordly Examples in Phil 2:5–11," in P. Richardson and J. C. Hurd (eds.), *From Jesus to Paul: Studies in Honor of Francis Wright Beare*. Waterloo: Wilfrid Laurier Press, 1984, 113–126.

S. J. Kraftchick, "A Necessary Detour: Paul's Metaphorical Understanding of the Philippians Hymn." *HBT* 15.1 (1993): 1–37.

G. Lüdemann, "Phil 2,6–11 und gnostiche Christushymnen aus Nag Hammadi," in B. Kollmann, W. Reinbold, and A. Steudel (eds.), *Antikes Judentum und frühes Christentum: Festschrift für Hartmut Stegemann zum 65. Geburtstag*. Berlin: de Gruyter, 1999, 488–511.

*R. P. Martin, *A Hymn of Christ: Philippians 2:5–11 in Recent Interpretation and in the Setting of Early Christian Worship*. Downers Grove, IL: InterVarsity Press, 1997.

*Carmen Christi, Philippians 2:5–11 in Recent Interpretation and in the Setting of Early Christian Worship*. Cambridge: Cambridge University Press, 1967.

ed. *Where Christology Began: Essays on Philippians 2*. Louisville, KY: Westminster John Knox Press, 1998.

W. A. Meeks, "The Man from Heaven in Paul's Letter to the Philippians," in B. Pearson (ed.), *The Future of Early Christianity: Essays in Honor of Helmut Koester*. Minneapolis, MN: Fortress, 1991, 329–336.

U. B. Müller, "Der Christushymnus Phil 2:6–11." *ZNW* 79.1–2 (1988): 17–44.

T. H. Tobin, "The World of Thought in the Philippian Hymn (Phil 2:6–11)," in J. Fotopoulos (ed.), *The New Testament and Early Christian Literature in the Greco-Roman Context: Studies in Honor of David E. Aune*. Leiden: Brill, 2006, 91–104.

C. A. Wanamaker, "Philippians 2:6–11: Son of God or Adamic Christology?" *NTS* 33.2 (1987): 179–193.
S. Winter, "'Obedient to Death': Revisiting the Rhetorical Function of Philippians 2:6–11." *ABR* 63 (2015): 1–13.
R. A. Wortham, "Christology as Community Identity in the Philippians Hymn: The Philippians Hymn as Social Drama (Philippians 2:5–11)." *PRS* 23.3 (1996): 269–287.

## THEOLOGICAL STUDIES ON PHILIPPIANS

*In previous generations, the academic energy tended to be concentrated on Christology and Soteriology in Philippians; that interest continues, but increasing attention has turned to questions about mission and evangelism, and friendship and unity.*

\*K. P. Donfried and I. H. Marshall, *The Theology of the Shorter Pauline Letters*. NTT; Cambridge: Cambridge University Press, 1993.
S. Fowl, "Know Your Context: Giving and Receiving Money in Philippians." *Interpretation* 56.1 (2002): 45–58.
"Learning to Narrate Our Lives in Christ," in C. Seitz and K. Greene-McCreight (eds.), *Theological Exegesis: Essays in Honor of Brevard S. Childs*. Grand Rapids, MI: Eerdmans, 1999, 339–354.
\*M. J. Gorman, *Becoming the Gospel: Paul, Participation, and Mission*. Grand Rapids, MI: Eerdmans, 2015.
\*M. J. Gorman, *Participating in Christ*. Grand Rapids, MI: Baker, 2019.
F. Matera, "A Theology from Prison: Philippians, Philemon, Colossians, and Ephesians," in *New Testament Theology*. Louisville: Westminster John Knox, 2007, 199–239.
G. W. E. Nickelsburg, "The Incarnation: Paul's Solution to the Universal Human Predicament," in B. Pearson (ed.), *The Future of Early Christianity: Essays in Honor of Helmut Koester*. Minneapolis: Fortress, 1991, 348–357.
P. Perkins, "Philippians: Theology for the Heavenly Politeuma," in J. M. Bassler (ed.), *Pauline Theology, Volume I: Thessalonians, Philippians, Galatians, Philemon*. Minneapolis, MN: Fortress, 1991, 89–114.
J. Reumann, "Christology in Philippians, Especially Chapter 3," in C. Breytenbach and H. Paulsen (eds.), *Anfänge der Christologie: Festschrift fü Ferdinand Hahn zum 65. Geburstag*. Göttingen: Vandenhoeck & Ruprecht, 1991, 131–140.
S. K. Stowers, "Friends and Enemies in the Politics of Heaven: Reading Theology in Philippians," in J. M. Bassler (ed.), *Pauline Theology*. Minneapolis, N: Fortress, 1991, 105–121.

## COMMENTARIES

*A quick glance at the following list will demonstrate how much has been written on this short epistle. Gordon Fee's work continues to stand the test of time as a cogent exegetical and theological study of Philippians. Reumann reads more like an encyclopedia than a traditional commentary, but it is a goldmine of word studies, quick surveys of scholarly views, and brief descriptions of interpretive options. Hellerman offers a well-researched, but concise discussion of the Greek text in a clear format. Bockmuehl's and Hooker's shorter commentaries provide sound exposition without getting bogged down in all the academic squabbles and complex details.*

K. Barth. *The Epistle to the Philippians*. Trans. J. Leitch; English ed.; Richmond: John Knox Press, 1962.
\*M. N. A. Bockmuehl. *The Epistle to the Philippians*. BNTC; Peabody, MA: Hendrickson, 1997.
F. F. Bruce. *Philippians*. NIBC; Peabody: Hendrickson, 1989.
L. H. Cohick. *Philippians*. SGBC; Grand Rapids, MI: Zondervan, 2013.
C. B. Cousar. *Philippians and Philemon: A Commentary*. NTL; Louisville, KY: Westminster John Knox Press, 2009.

M. J. Edwards (ed.). *Galatians, Ephesians, Philippians.* ACCS; Downers Grove, IL: InterVarsity Press, 1999.

*G. D. Fee. *Paul's Letter to the Philippians.* NICNT; Grand Rapids, MI: Eerdmans, 1995.

D. Flemming. *Philippians: A Commentary in the Wesleyan Tradition.* NBBC; Kansas City, MI: Beacon Hill Press, 2009.

*S. Fowl. *Philippians.* THNT; Grand Rapids, MI: Eerdmans, 2005.

D. E. Garland. "Philippians," in D. E. Garland and T. Longman III (eds.), *Ephesians, Philippians, Colossians, Philemon.* REBC; Grand Rapids, MI: Zondervan, 2006.

J. Gnilka. *The Epistle to the Philippians.* NTSR; London: Sheed & Ward, 1971.

G. W. Hansen. *The Letter to the Philippians.* PNTC; Grand Rapids, MI: Eerdmans, 2009.

M. S. Harmon. *Philippians.* Mentor; Fearn: Christian Focus, 2015.

G. F. Hawthorne and R. P Martin. *Philippians.* WBC 43; Nashville, TN: Thomas Nelson, 2004; 1st ed., 1983.

*J. Hellerman. *Philippians.* EGGNT; Nashville, TN: Broadman & Holman, 2015.

M. D. Hooker. "The Letter to the Philippians," in L. E. Keck et al. (eds.), *NIB* 11. Nashville, TN: Abingdon, 2000: 467–550.

J. L. Houlden. *Paul's Letters from Prison: Philippians, Colossians, Philemon, and Ephesians.* Harmondsworth: Penguin, 1970.

M. J. Keown. *Philippians.* EEC; Bellingham, WA: Lexham Press, 2017

J. B. Lightfoot. *St. Paul's Epistle to the Philippians.* London: Macmillian, 1903.

I. H. Marshall. *Epistle to the Philippians.* ECS; London: Epworth, 1993.

R. P. Martin. *Philippians.* TNTC; Downers Grove, IL: InterVarsity Press, 2007.

Daniel L. Migliore. *Philippians and Philemon.* BTCB; Louisville, KY: Westminster John Knox, 2014.

U. B. Müller. *Der Brief des Paulus an die Philipper.* ThHK; Leipzig: Evangelische Verlag, 1993.

C. Osiek. *Philippians, Philemon.* ANTC; Nashville, TN: Abingdon, 2000.

J. Reumann. *Philippians: A New Translation with Introduction and Commentary.* AYBC; New Haven, CT: Yale University Press, 2008.

W. Schenk. *Die Philipperbriefe des Paulus: Kommentar.* Stuttgart: Kohlhammer, 1984.

H. Schlier. *Der Philipperbrief.* Einsiedeln: Johannes Verlag, 1980.

M. Silva. *Philippians.* BECNT; Grand Rapids, MI: Baker, 2007, 2nd ed.

T. D. Still. *Philippians and Philemon.* SHBC; Macon, GA: Smyth & Helwys, 2011.

F. Thielman. *Philippians.* NIVAC; Grand Rapids, MI: Zondervan, 1995.

J. W. Thompson and B. W. Longenecker. *Philippians and Philemon: Paideia.* Grand Rapids, MI: Baker Academic, 2016.

B. Thurston. *Philippians and Philemon.* SP 10; Collegeville, MN: Liturgical Press, 2005.

N. Walter et al. *Die Briefe an die Philipper, Thessalonicher und an Philemon.* NTD 8.2; Göttingen: Vandenhoeck & Ruprecht, 1998.

B. Witherington III. *Paul's Letter to the Philippians: A Socio-Rhetorical Commentary.* Grand Rapids, MI: Eerdmans, 2011.

# Commentary

## 1:1–2: GREETINGS

1:1 Paul and Timothy, servants of Christ Jesus, to all the saints in Christ Jesus who are in Philippi, with the bishops and deacons:

² Grace to you and peace from God our Father and the Lord Jesus Christ.

Paul's letter openings are not perfunctory and prosaic formalities nor necessary yet tedious niceties, rather, they are significant because they set the tone for the letter, hint at topics covered in the letter, and provide the initial texture for Paul's message. Paul's letter to the Philippians begins by following standard Hellenistic letter-writing conventions of sender, addressee, salutation, and thanksgiving, but with distinctive glosses (in Christ, grace and peace, God our Father, Lord Jesus Christ). Paul, as is his custom, uses his Greek name *Paulos* rather than his Hebrew name *Sha'ul*. Interesting too is that Paul, along with the letters to the other Macedonian churches in Thessalonica, does not call himself an "apostle." This is most probably because, unlike the letters to the Galatians and the Corinthians, there was no need to accent his apostolic credentials in the face of any mounting dissent to his apostolic ministry or disparagement of his personality from the Macedonian assemblies. Paul nominates himself as lead author, hence the biographical "I" sections throughout, and other persons are referred to only in the third person. Even so, the letter is coauthored with or at least composed in cooperation with Timothy, much like several other Pauline letters (2 Cor 1:1; Col 1:1; Philm 1; cf. Paul, Timothy, and Silas in 1 Thess 1:1; 2 Thess 1:1). Timothy was Paul's traveling companion from the city of Lystra in the province of Galatia. Timothy was an ostensibly Hellenistic Jew (he had a Jewish mother and Greek father), who joined Paul during his second missionary journey (Acts 16:1–3), and assisted him in founding the churches of Macedonia and Achaia (Acts 17:1–18:18). Timothy was also with Paul during part of his Ephesians ministry ca. 54–56 CE (Acts 19:1–20), including his Ephesian imprisonment (see Introduction), and Paul would eventually dispatch Timothy to Macedonia to visit the churches there including Philippi (Phil 2:19; Acts 19:22). He would be remembered in church tradition as one of the first bishops of Ephesus (1 Tim 3:1–7; Eusebius, *Hist. Eccl.* 3.4). Timothy is mentioned as co-sender of the letter, not as a matter of courtesy or modesty by Paul, but most likely because Timothy too enjoyed a special relationship with the Philippians and his name adds a stronger sense of personal warmth and authority and so contributes to the letter's overall persuasive appeal.[1]

Paul describes Timothy and himself as *douloi Christou Iēsou* (cf. Rom 1:1; Gal 1:10; Titus 1:1), which means not the sanitized "servants" of Messiah Jesus (contra NIV, NRSV, ESV, NJB), but more properly "slaves" of Messiah Jesus (with CEB, CSB, NET, NLT). While slavery itself could be an ignominious and harsh condition, many slaves were managers for wealthy patrons, positions that could be financially lucrative and even socially privileged. To be a slave in the service of someone great was a position of authority and legitimacy.[2] Plus, to be the slave of a deity had a certain oriental ring to it, like being a slave of Serapis or Isis, which would convey either revulsion or attraction depending on one's disposition. The metaphorical mention of slavery underscores Paul and Timothy's sense of belonging, allegiance, and service to the Lord Jesus, who, Paul says elsewhere, purchased them with his own blood (1 Cor 1:30; 6:20; 7:23; Col 1:14; Eph 1:7, 14; Rom 3:24). However unpalatable the notion of slavery is, to ancient and modern audiences, it hints at a serious theological truth: all people are slaves to either God or to non-gods (1 Thess 1:9; Gal 4:8; Rom 6:16–22) and all people serve either the kingdom of the beloved Son or the domain of darkness (Col 1:13). As the Book of Common Prayer declares, Christians are bound to God "in whose service is perfect freedom." We might say that redemption from sin and evil means slavery to Christ,

---

[1]   J. A. D. Weima, *Paul the Ancient Letter Writer: An Introduction to Epistolary Analysis* (Grand Rapids, MI: Baker, 2016), 31.

[2]   D. B. Martin, *Slavery as Salvation: The Metaphor of Slavery in Pauline Christianity* (New Haven, CN: Yale University Press, 1990), 54–55.

which entails freedom to be the type of human beings that God always intended us to be.

Greetings are extended "to all the saints in Christ Jesus who are in Philippi," marking them, like Israel, as God's holy people. The designation *hagioi* for "saints" is common in Greco-Roman, Jewish, and Christian religious language for people "set apart," like priests, vestal virgins, or persons specially consecrated to a deity. Paul regards Gentile Christ-believers as no longer pagan or profane ("You know that when you were pagans" [1 Cor 12:2]) but dedicated to God and sanctified by God ("You were washed, you were sanctified, you were justified in the name of the Lord Jesus Christ and in the Spirit of our God" [1 Cor 6:11]). These saints in Philippi, however diverse they are in terms of ethnicity, social strata, and gender, are now united together "in Christ Jesus." The phrase "in Christ" can be used in multiple ways but here operates as a periphrasis for all believers (see Phil 1:13; 4:21)[3] and indicates "those who belong to Christ Jesus, as those whose lives are forever identified with Christ."[4] They are an assembly of believers in the city of Philippi, a Romanized Greek city, the *Colonia Iulia Augusta Philippensium*, located along the Via Egnatia in the province of Macedonia. This Roman colony in Macedonia now has within it a heavenly colony with diametrically opposed symbols, stories, benefactions, and allegiances. Paul could well say, as he does elsewhere, that this cluster of the faithful in Philippi and Macedonia more broadly are not alone, but have solidarity with those elsewhere who also "call on the name of the Lord" (1 Cor 1:2) and who's faith is part of the worldwide assembly of confessing churches (Col 1:6; Rom 1:8). The Philippian churches, by virtue of their relationship to Christ, and with respect to their connection to the Pauline network of churches, are members of a wider and interlocking body of believers and fellow-slaves of Messiah Jesus.

Paul then does something he does in no other letter, he greets the specific, but hereto unnamed, leaders of the Philippian assemblies. He moves from a general greeting to all the saints to offering specific greetings to the "bishops and deacons"[5] of the Philippian churches. This is most

---

[3]   C. R. Campbell, *Paul and Union with Christ: An Exegetical and Theological Study* (Grand Rapids, MI: Zondervan, 2012), 120–125.

[4]   Fee, *Paul's Letter to the Philippians*, 65; cf. Reumann, *Philippians*, 84; Hellerman, *Philippians*, 11–12.

[5]   Some manuscripts (e.g., B², K, 33) read *fellow-bishops*, but this is a later alteration probably designed to make Paul a bishop of the ancient church. Bishops and deacons

likely because, as John Chysostom first suggested, the bishops and deacons are the ones who organized the gift that was sent via Epaphroditus.[6] Now we should be careful not to anachronistically read the much later formalized threefold offices of bishops, elders, and deacons into the situation in Philippi (hence, the CEB opts for "supervisors and servants" to imply that they were functionaries rather than strict officers or persons ordained to clerical positions). These are more properly leadership functionaries with specific roles, not holy orders within an elaborate ecclesial hierarchy. Paul does not address them as leaders *over* the church as much as people, who, *together with* the church share in the partnership of the gospel.[7] The leaders named here probably pertain to those who have assorted pastoral, financial, didactic, and social responsibilities in their various house churches. But whether these leadership roles were temporary or permanent, whether they were formal or informal, we cannot say for certain. As to what these offices and roles of "bishop" (*episkopos*) and "deacon" (*diakonos*) actually meant, they are of course disputed.

First, *episkopos* denotes an office of oversight and guardianship exercised by an appointee in something like a temple or a voluntary association. In Christian usage the term refers "to one who served as *overseer* or *supervisor*, with special interest in guarding the apostolic tradition."[8] In Acts, Paul exhorted the Ephesian elders to "Keep watch over yourselves and over all the flock, of which the Holy Spirit has made you overseers" (Acts 20:28). Paul instructed Timothy and Titus about the qualifications for a bishop/overseer (1 Tim 3:1–7; Tit 1:7–9). While the office of bishop/overseer became exceedingly prominent in the post-apostolic era, especially in the letters of Ignatius and Clement, and in the writings of Irenaeus, the designation itself is not found in the undisputed Pauline letters outside of Phil 1:1. The reason is perhaps that *episkopos* had currency in Macedonian associations for describing the lead person in a local school, collegium, guild, or temple-cultus, which was then taken up by the Philippians

---

  are also named together (without mention of elders) in *1 Clem.* 42.4–5; *Did.* 15.1; Ignatius, *Eph.* 2.1; Hermas, *Vis.* 3.5.1. Technically, *episcopois kai diakonois* could be a hendiadys, that is, "overseers who serve," but few exegetes take that option.

6  Chrysostom, *Hom. Phil.* 1; Hooker, "Philippians,"481; Reumann, *Philippians*, 88–89; Hansen, *Philippians*, 42.

7  Hansen, *Philippians*, 42.

8  BDAG, 379 (italics original).

for their own internal usage and Paul in turn acknowledges this arrangement.[9] Alternatively, many believe that *episkopos* ("bishop") and *presbyteros* ("elder") are completely synonymous and comprise merely different words for the same office and leadership function (see, e.g., *1 Clem.* 44.4–5).[10] One intriguing possibility argued by Alistair C. Stewart is that the offices of bishop and elder are not synonyms but "perionyms," that is, they are overlapping terms. Stewart proposes that each assembly in the Pauline circle had its own bishop/overseer, not a monepiscopacy over a diocese, but the leader of a house-church or an analogous assembly.[11] However, when the various bishops (*episkopoi*) of the individual churches from a city or region met together, they formed a collective of elders (*presbyteroi*), so a church's bishop becomes their representative elder at a meeting of all local Christian leaders. This explanation resonates with (1) the scene in Acts where the Ephesians elders are summoned together and are exhorted to exercise a ministry of oversight in their respective congregations (Acts 20:17, 28); and (2) the exhortations in Titus, where Paul instructs Titus to appoint *kata polin presbyterous*, which, taken adjectively, does not mean elders in each town, but town-elders, that is, to create a federation of elders for the town drawn from the local bishops over the various Cretan assemblies (Titus 1:5–9).[12] Later, in the mid-second century, when Polycarp wrote to the Philippian churches, he explicitly mentions the elders and deacons, but not bishops/overseers, probably because by this

---

[9] Contrast Bockmuehl, *The Epistle to the Philippians*, 54 and Reumann, *Philippians*, 87–89 on the relevance of Macedonian associations for *episkopos*.

[10] Chrysostom (*Hom. Phil.* 1) reasons that each city had only one bishop (i.e., *monepiskopos*) so the plural *episkopoi* must mean the same as *presbyteroi*, a plurality of elders. See also, Lightfoot, *Philippians*, 95–99 and more recently B. L. Merkle, *The Elder and Overseer: One Office in the Early Church* (Frankfurt: Peter Lang, 2003). Alternatively, "elders" (*presbyteroi*) might refer to the whole leadership collective including overseers and deacons (Fee, *Paul's Letter to the Philippians*, 68 n. 52) or else it is an honorific term for benefactors or emeritus overseers and some inscriptional evidence supports this; see A. C. Stewart, *Original Bishops: Office and Order in the First Christian Communities* (Grand Rapids, MI: Baker, 2014), 131–132.

[11] Fee (*Paul's Letter to the Philippians*, 67 n. 46) strangely claims that "No evidence exists for a single leader as the 'head' of the local assembly in the Pauline churches" but then gives a footnote undermining his point by saying, "Although it seems very likely on sociological grounds that the head of the household, the *paterfamilias*, functioned in a similar role of leadership in the house church that met in his or her household as he or she did in the household itself."

[12] Stewart, *Original Bishops*, 11–53.

time a three-tiered system had emerged with a monepiscopacy, a presbytery, and diaconate.[13]

Second, *diakonos* is "one who serves as an intermediary" and can refer to the general role of service to others (see, e.g., Matt 20:26; 1 Cor 3:5–6; 2 Cor 6:4; 11:15, 23; Eph 3:7; 6:21) or to the specific office of deacon a person could be appointed by a church (Rom 16:1; 1 Tim 3:8–13; cf. Acts 6:1–6; *1 Clem.* 42.4–5; Ignatius, *Eph.* 2.1, *Magn.* 2.1, *Smyrn.* 8.1; Polycarp, *Phil.* 5.2–3).[14] Of course, *diakonos* was not a technical Christian term, it could be used to describe people who performed the role of waiters at religious festivals and those who distributed meats after sacrifice and cooking. John N. Collins suggests that the close association of bishop and deacon in Phil 1:1 means that deacons acted under the supervision of the bishop; they were assistants to the bishop in some religious capacity, especially at meals, which accords with later tradition where Justin says that the role of deacons is to distribute the bread and wine at celebrations of the eucharist (Justin, *1 Apol.* 65.5).[15] The office of deacon even developed some prestige. Bishop Ignatius of Antioch, on the way to his martyrdom in Rome, wrote to the Trallians about deacons as custodians of "the mysteries of Jesus Christ" and that deacons are not "servants of food and drink but are executives of the church of God" (*Trall.* 2.3 [trans. M. Bird]).

Instead of the usual "greetings" (*chairein*) found in most Hellenistic letters (see, e.g., Acts 15:23; 23:26; Jas 1:1), Paul greets the Philippians with the formula "grace and peace" which is a distinctive variation of Hellenistic letter forms. Paul turns *chairein* ("greetings") to *charis* ("grace" or "beneficence") and adds *eirēnē* ("peace"), which can be found in some Hebrew and Aramaic letters (see Ezra 4:17–22; 5:7–17).[16] Thus, Sean Adams writes: "It appears that Paul was incorporating the Hebrew greetings into his letters and combined it with the noun form of the verb *charein* to create his letter greetings."[17] Whereas "peace" means the absence of hostilities and a state of wholeness (cf. Phil 4:7, 9), "grace" in Pauline discourse refers to

---

[13] Polycarp, *Phil.* 5.2–3; 6.1, 11.1, see Stewart, *Original Bishops*, 47.

[14] BDAG, 230.

[15] J. N. Collins, *Deacons and the Church: Making Connections between Old and New* (Harrisburg, PA: Gracewing, 2002), 89–93.

[16] See 2 *Bar* 78.2 which mentions "mercy and peace."

[17] S. A. Adams, "Paul's Letter Opening and Greek Epistolography," in *Paul and the Ancient Letter Form* (eds. S. E. Porter and S. A. Adams; PAST 6; Leiden: Brill, 2010), 33–55, here 47; Weima, *Paul the Ancient Letter Writer*, 42–43.

divine blessings given without regard for the worthiness of the recipients (cf. Phil 1:29; 4:23).[18] Added to that is an explicitly Christian and binitarian benediction that makes "God our Father and the Lord Jesus Christ" the source of peace and grace that is extended to the addressees. Placing God the Father and Lord Jesus Christ in such proximity "reinforces the idea of their common purpose and agency" and intimates the high christology that will be expounded in the letter in Phil 2:6–11.[19] Paul, in his letter openings, could never refer to God the Father without the Lord Jesus, nor the Lord Jesus without God the Father, since Paul firmly believed that election, salvation, ethics, and Christian hope is bound up with what God the Father has done, is doing, and will yet do through the Lord Jesus.

Paul's letter to the Philippians seeks to buttress the relationship between himself and the Philippians by a mixture of thanksgiving, information update, ethical exhortations, and facilitating reciprocal exchanges of money, people, and services. The letter has, therefore, been characterized as a *letter of friendship*[20] or a *family letter*.[21] On the one hand, Paul does not use the term "friend" (*philos*) and he employs instead familial language of "brothers (and sisters)" (Phil 1:12, 14; 3:1, 13, 17; 4:1, 8, 21) and "beloved" (Phil 2:12; 4:1). Then again, there is no escaping the element of reciprocity in the letter (Phil 4:10–20) and the kinship described is not biological, legal, or domestic, but based on membership in a religious association and partnership with the Pauline mission. Thus, as a variation, we might better label the letter to the Philippians as a *letter of fellowship*, a justifiable description given the ample references to *koinōnia* scattered across the letter (Phil 1:5; 2:1; 3:10; 4:15), and the need to account for the relationships,

---

[18]   J. M. G. Barclay, *Paul and the Gift* (Grand Rapids, MI: Eerdmans, 2015), 354.

[19]   Bockmuehl, *The Epistle to the Philippians*, 57.

[20]   See, for example, Fee, *Paul's Letter to the Philippians*, 2–14; Hansen, *Philippians*, 6–12; L. M. White, "Morality between Two Worlds: A Paradigm of Friendship in Philippians," in *Greeks, Romans, and Christians: Essays in Honor of Abraham J. Malherbe* (eds. D. L. Balch and E. Ferguson; Minneapolis: Fortress, 1990), here 201–205; J. T. Fitzgerald, "Philippians in Light of Some Ancient Discussions on Friendship," in *Friendship, Flattery, and Frankness of Speech: Studies on Friendship in the New Testament World* (ed. J. T. Fitzgerald; NovTSup 82; Leiden: Brill, 1996), 141–160.

[21]   See, for example, Bockmuehl, *The Epistle to the Philippians*, 35; Witherington, *Paul's Letter to the Philippians*, 17–21; L. Alexander, "Hellenistic Letter-Forms and the Structure of Philippians," *JSNT* 37 (1989): 87–101; M. A. Jennings, *The Price of Partnership in the Letter of Paul to the Philippians: "Make My Joy Complete"* (LNTS 578; London: T&T Clark, 2018), 16–18.

reciprocity, rhetoric, and religious texture evident in the letter. Viewed this way, the letter celebrates the Philippians' partnership in the gospel and Paul thanks them for their practical support, that is, their financial aid, and for the services that Epaphroditus has provided to him (Phil 2:25–30; 4:10–20).

Paul, it seems, had entered into financial arrangement with the Philippians; a move that stands in stark contrast to his refusal to accept money from Corinthians, a decision that was perhaps prompted by his concern that some of the Corinthians might erroneously think that by providing for Paul they therefore "owned" him. For Paul, his arrangement with the Philippians was reciprocal: they supported him materially in his ministry, and they in turn shared in the fruits of his ministry (Phil 4:15; 2 Cor 8:1–3). That said, in this letter Paul does more than provide some receipts and a "thank you" note. He informs the Philippian believers of his rather perilous predicament, exhorts them toward unity and humility, reminds them to strive toward the prize still ahead of them, sternly warns them about enemies, mediates a dispute between two female leaders, and above all exhorts the Philippians to live out the Messiah story as a counter-imperial colony of heavenly citizens hidden right under Caesar's nose.

## 1:3–11: THANKSGIVING AND INTERCESSION

³ I thank my God every time I remember you,

⁴ constantly praying with joy in every one of my prayers for all of you,

⁵ because of your sharing in the gospel from the first day until now.

⁶ I am confident of this, that the one who began a good work among you will bring it to completion by the day of Jesus Christ.

⁷ It is right for me to think this way about all of you, because you hold me in your heart, for all of you share in God's grace with me, both in my imprisonment and in the defense and confirmation of the gospel.

⁸ For God is my witness, how I long for all of you with the compassion of Christ Jesus.

⁹ And this is my prayer, that your love may overflow more and more with knowledge and full insight

[10] to help you to determine what is best, so that in the day of Christ you may be pure and blameless,

[11] having produced the harvest of righteousness that comes through Jesus Christ for the glory and praise of God.

Most Greco-Roman letters proceed to a health wish or prayer for the recipient. For example, John the Elder wrote to Gaius, "Beloved, I pray that all may go well with you and that you may be in good health, just as it is well with your soul" (3 John 2); and in a second- or third-century CE Egyptian letter between two brothers, we read: "Irenaeus to Apollinaris, his dearest brother, many greetings. I pray continually for your health, and I myself am well."[22] Paul adapts this convention of a health wish in two ways. First, Paul deviates from thanking God for the health of the recipients and instead thanks God for the faithfulness of the recipients (Phil 1:3–8). Second, Paul also forecasts topics to be discussed later in the letter, including partnership in the gospel, the Philippians assurance of being received by God, Paul's own circumstances, and their noetic transformation and ethical conformity to the pattern of Christ Jesus (Phil 1:3–11).[23]

The thanksgiving in the letter is paraenetic, pastoral, fulsome, and unusually solemn at points. The first part of the thanksgiving in vv. 3–4 includes Paul's assurance that he frequently petitions God about everyone in the entire Philippian assembly, amidst joyful prayer, as he is moved by his regular remembrance of them. It is the epitome of Pauline spirituality: thanksgiving, prayer, filled with joy, on behalf of all.[24] The prayer report is remarkable for its claims to inclusivity ("all of you") and repetition ("everyone of my prayers" or "every time"). However, the emphasis on "all" (*pas*) – whether "all of you" or "all the time" – is not a "studied repetition" accented across the letter because the Philippians were a divided bunch constantly at each other's throats.[25] Rather, this language pertains to Paul's persistence in prayer for them and his concern for each

---

[22] BGU 27, cited in C. K. Barrett, *The New Testament Background: Selected Documents* (rev. edn.; London: SPCK, 1987), 30.

[23] S. E. Porter, *Paul the Apostle: His Life, Thought, and Letters* (Grand Rapids, MI: Eerdmans, 2016), 146.

[24] Fee, *Paul's Letter to the Philippians*, 81.

[25] Lightfoot, *Philippians*, 83 as followed by most commentators.

and every one of them. It is the language of earnest pastoral prayer and we are wise not to read too much into it.[26]

The reason for Paul's joy in his thanksgiving is spelled out in v. 5 as "your sharing in the gospel from the first day until now." This *koinōnia*, a "participation" (NET, NASB) or "partnership" (CSB, ESV, NIV, NJB), refers to "a close association involving mutual interests and sharing"[27] defined in relation to the gospel. Accordingly, when *koinōnia* is put in relation to the *euangelion*, it refers to the Philippians' material provision to promote the gospel in the Pauline mission. This is no empty commendation for being a distant supporter of a religious cause; instead, it celebrates the Philippians' participation and partnership by their tangible cooperation and financial contribution in aid of the gospel. Cohick comments: "Paul sees their unflagging enthusiasm for the gospel and his own ministry as evidence of God's grace in much the same way as he senses God's grace uplifting him while in prison."[28]

The Philippians' partnership in the gospel has lasted from "the first day until now," referring to the beginning of Paul's missionary work in Macedonia to his more recent missionary endeavors in Achaia and Asia Minor (see Phil 4:15). Paul rejoices in the Philippians reception of the gospel and their support for the gospel in Philippi. Silva rightly notes how Paul writes with "emphatic repetitions and emotional intensity" because "the apostle's joyful gratitude flows from an appreciation of his converts' consistent support of his ministry and care for his needs, from the very beginnings of their Christian experience to the most recent contribution, which in effect occasioned the present letter."[29] Importantly, this is the only Pauline thanksgiving that mentions "joy" most probably because the theme of joy is indeed characteristic of the letter and Paul's relationship with the Philippians in general (see Phil 1:4, 18, 25; 2:2, 17, 18, 28, 29; 3:1; 4:1, 4, 10). Paul rejoices both out of the encouragement he has received from the Macedonian churches (1 Thess 2:19–20; 3:9), who are themselves characterized by joy (see 1 Thess 1:6; 2 Cor 8:2; Pol. *Phil.* 1.3), but also out of an

---

[26]   See too Cousar, *Philippians and Philemon*, 28.
[27]   BDAG, 552.
[28]   Cohick, *Philippians*, 35.
[29]   Silva, *Philippians*, 45.

eschatological joy that typifies the age to come (e.g., Isa 12:1–6; 26:19; 35:1–6; 42:11; 52:8–9; 54:1; Jer 31:12–13; 33:11).

We have in Phil 1:6 something of an aside with Paul celebrating God's initial, continuing, and completing work in the lives of the Philippians. The continuation of their partnership in the gospel is not dependent solely on their own initiative or resilience, but relies upon God's purposes in the gospel coming to fruition through them.[30] Thus, Paul is "persuaded" or "convinced" (*peithō*) that God[31] who has begun a "work"[32] in the Philippians – a salvific work, the effect of the gospel, the efficacy of grace – "will bring it to completion by the day of Jesus Christ." The "Day of Jesus Christ" is the day when Christ subdues all cosmic opposition, consummates the Father's kingdom, and begins judgment (Phil 1:10; 2:16; 3:20–21; Rom 2:16; 1 Cor 1:8; 3:13; 5:5; 1 Cor 15:21–28; 2 Cor 1:14; 1 Thess 5:2–9). Paul will repeat the sentiment again in v. 10, although with a subtle hint of conditionality, hoping the Philippians practice discernment "so that in the day of Christ you may be pure and blameless." Similarly, he continues later in 2:12–13 to straddle the tension between God's faithfulness to ensure their eschatological passage and the Philippians' own responsibility to persevere when he instructs them to "work out your own salvation with fear and trembling," with the explanation "for it is God who is at work in you, enabling you both to will and to work for his good pleasure." Paul has expressed similar notions elsewhere; God in his faithfulness will keep an assembly of believers faithful until the return of the Lord Jesus who is judge and inaugurator of the new creation (see 1 Cor 1:8–9; Col 1:21–23). Even as Paul stresses the urgency of their own agency in salvation, and even urges them to a specific christocentric vision of moral formation (Phil 2:1–13), he nonetheless believes that God's grace precedes and pervades all

---

[30]  Hansen, *Philippians*, 50.

[31]  The substantive participle *ho enarxamenos* refers to God.

[32]  While some understand the "work" (*erga*) here to refer exclusively to the Philippians' financial gift for Paul and their good work in participating in the gospel (Lightfoot, *Philippians*, 84; Hawthorne and Martin, *Philippians*, 24–25; Silva, *Philippians*, 45–46; Bockmuehl, *The Epistle to the Philippians*, 62; Cousar, *Philippians*, 29–30; Hansen, *Philippians*, 50; Keown, *Philippians*, 1:138–139), we do better to locate this statement in the wider soteric-eschatological arc that Paul draws in the broader context of the letter as related to their faith (see Gnilka, *Philippians*, 46; Fee, *Paul's Letter to the Philippians*, 85; Thielman, *Philippians*, 38–39; Reumann, *Philippians*, 151–152; Hellerman, *Philippians*, 25).

that they do.[33] Paul's remarks in Phil 1:6 reveals his unwavering conviction that the Philippian community will be preserved by God and will persevere by their endurance even in spite of the persecution that they are experiencing (Phil 1:28; 2:15; 3:17–21). Salvation is entirely from God and operates in three phases: faith-initiation, faithful continuation, and final consummation. Put paraphrastically, Paul argues: "There has never been the slightest doubt in my mind that the God who started this great work in you would keep at it and bring it to a flourishing finish on the very day Christ Jesus appears" (The Message Bible).

Paul returns to his train of thought from vv. 3–5 by giving further thanks for the Philippians in v. 7 on account of his deep affection for them and their partnership in the grace. Paul's thanks, joy, and confidence in the Philippians is considered "right" or "fitting" (*dikaios*), it is entirely appropriate that he thinks in such a way about them, "because I have you in my heart,[34] and you are all partners with me in grace" (CSB). Paul here demonstrates his deep affection for the Philippians, carrying them metaphorically in his heart, while commending their partnership in a shared grace that is his ministry just as he previously commended their partnership in the gospel in v. 5. While "gospel" (*euangelion*) and "grace" (*charis*) are certainly not synonyms, they are not unrelated terms (on gospel and grace, see Acts 20:24; Gal 1:6; Eph 3:7), and Paul here conflates his evangelical ministry with the apostolic grace that it embodies (see Rom 1:5; 12:3; 15:15; 1 Cor 3:10; Gal 2:9). That solidarity with Paul is at work even while he is undergoing an "imprisonment" (NRSV) or "chains" (NIV), and Paul resultantly will be compelled to provide a "defense and confirmation of the gospel" in a forthcoming arraignment.[35] Despite that, Paul rejoices in his

---

[33]   J. R. Wagner, "Working out Salvation: Holiness and Community in Philippians," in *Holiness and Ecclesiology in the New Testament* (eds. K. E. Bower and A. Johnson; Grand Rapids, MI: Eerdmans, 2007), 257–274.

[34]   The Greek *dia to echein me en tē kardia hymas* is an articular infinitive so that the accusative pronoun *me* functions as a nominative subject of the action ("I") while *hymas* ("you") makes the Philippians the object of the action, that is, "I have you in my heart" (NIV) rather than "you hold me in your heart" (NRSV). See Chrysostom, *Hom. Phil.* 1; S. E. Porter, *Idioms of the Greek New Testament* (Sheffield: Sheffield Academic Press, 1992), 203; Fee, *Paul's Letter to the Philippians*, 90; Silva, *Philippians*, 27 n. 34; Hellerman, *Philippians*, 26–27.

[35]   The words *apologia* ("defence") and *bebaiōsis* ("confirmation") are technical legal terms used in forensic contexts, see BDAG, 117, 173; *EDNT* 1.137, 210.

love for the Philippians because they share in his ministry, his message, and metaphorically even in his manacles.

Paul reiterates his deep affection for the Philippians in 1:8 and invokes God "as my witness," as he does elsewhere (Rom 1:9; 2 Cor 1:23; Gal 1:20; 1 Thess 2:5, 10), to vouchsafe "how I long for all of you with the compassion of Christ Jesus." Beside once again repeating "all" (*pas*) to stress the inclusive scope of his affection for them, the "compassion of Christ Jesus" (*splagchnois Christou Iēsou*) defines the mode of Paul's longing for the Philippians. Paul's deeply affectionate language, says Bockmuehl, is not principally a sign of "gushing temperament, but of a gushing christ-ology!"[36] Paul's affection is an expression of his devotion to Christ Jesus. The word *splagchnon* means literally "inward parts" (see Acts 1:18), and used metaphorically it conveys the idea of being moved to the point of one's bowels – or, we might say, to be persuaded from the pit of one's stomach – with profound feelings of compassion, sympathy, pity, and mercy for someone (see Mk 1:41; Luke 1:28; Col 3:12; Philm 7, 12, 20). Lightfoot notes that such a metaphor describes how the "believer has no yearnings apart from his Lord, his pulse beats with the pulse of Christ; his heart throbs with the heart of Christ."[37] While Paul's longing for them is his own, his compassion for them derives from Christ, about which God can attest. This deep affection overflows from Paul's spirituality, which is rooted in the gospel.

Paul's prayerful petition for the Philippians in vv. 9–11, similar to other prayers in his letter openings (esp. Col 1:9–11), gives emphasis to love abounding, noetic transformation, spiritual discernment, right behavior, eschatological approval before Christ, all unto divine glory. Paul's prayer consists of three escalating purposes clauses with a further participle clause.

First, Paul desires that their "love may overflow more and more." Paul desires their love to abound and grow, presumably toward himself in their continued contribution to his needs, but also toward one another, given the need for humility and unity, as the rest of the letter will make clear. This love should not be fleeting or purely emotive, but be exercised with respect to "knowledge and full insight." The combination of knowledge (*epignosis*)

---

[36] Bockmuehl, *The Epistle to the Philippians*, 65.
[37] Lightfoot, *Philippians*, 85.

and insight (*aisthēsis*)[38] is a "stylistic reinforcement" for one's cognitive awareness and moral faculties.[39] Of course, such knowledge is more than facticity and sense of duty as it refers to a "profoundly existential, relational and responsive" form of knowing in relation to God.[40] Knowledge and love are "mutually necessary" because knowledge without love is not edifying (see 1 Cor 8:1; 13:2), while love without knowledge proves to be fleeting and fadish.[41]

Second, the result of this love and insight is that they will, to put it blandly, "help you to determine what is best" (NRSV) or "decide what is best" (NET). A better rendering is "to approve the things that are superior" (CSB), since *dokimazō* means to render judgment as approved,[42] while *diapherō* pertains to judging something to have superlative worth (see Rom 2:18 where the same expression is used).[43] Paul envisages a spirituality where love begets discernment for what is better.

Third, Paul hopes that the exercise of this love, insight, and discernment will yield them as "pure and blameless," that is, without any moral stain or innate corruption that would see them disqualified at the "Day of Christ." Such a "Day" is the day of judgment executed by the Lord Jesus Christ. The point is not absolute purity but the eschatological purposes for which believers have oriented their entire lives. Paul's letter is eschatologically infused since eschatology is intrinsic to its christological narrative and redemptive hopes for the future (see Phil 1:6; 3:7–14, 20–21). Paul entertains here, says Bockmuehl, "neither a pious platitude nor a millenarian obsession, but a way of life concretely attuned to the conviction that 'redemption is nearer to us now than when we first believed' (Rom. 13.11), and that his own ministry might hasten its consummation (Rom. 11.13ff.; cf. 2 Pet. 3.12)."[44]

---

[38]  The noun *aisthēsis* is a *hapax legomenon*, the cognate term *aisthētēria* occurs in Heb 5:14, and Silva (*Philippians*, 50) comments that, "Paul chose *aisthēsis* to specify the practical outworkings of the knowledge in view." In the LXX it is used, principally in Proverbs, with the sense of wisdom pertaining to moral judgment.

[39]  Silva, *Philippians*, 50.

[40]  Bockmuehl, *The Epistle to the Philippians*, 67.

[41]  Bockmuehl, *The Epistle to the Philippians*, 67; Thompson and Longenecker, *Philippians and Philemon*, 32.

[42]  BDAG, 255; LN 30.114; Hellerman, *Philippians*, 32–33.

[43]  BDAG, 239; LN 65.6

[44]  Bockmuehl, *The Epistle to the Philippians*, 68.

Fourth, the participle clause in v. 11 expresses the result of the exhortations in vv. 9–10, so that, if they become everything that Paul prays they would be, they would resultantly be filled (*peplērōmenoi*)[45] with the "fruit of righteousness" (see Prov 11:31; Amos 6:12; Jas 3:18).[46] This means "being filled with respect to the fruit of righteousness."[47] The "fruit of righteousness," as a genitive of apposition, is the fruit consisting of righteousness,[48] it marks out ethical conformity to a life of righteousness, which happens instrumentally "through Jesus Christ" and the effect of such lives is that God receives "glory and praise."[49]

---

### Closer Look: Paul, the Gospel, and the Philippians

The gospel (*euangelion*) is an important topic in Paul's letter to the Philippians as it announces salvation, pertains to their faith in Jesus Christ, it comprises the cause of their common partnership, it implies a certain ethic, and solicits their devotion and support. In the end, "The gospel of Christ takes first place in Paul's mission and his letter."[50] A cursory glance at Paul's statements about the gospel confirm this priority and preeminence:

I thank my God every time I remember you, constantly praying with joy in every one of my prayers for all of you, because of your **sharing in the gospel** from the first day until now. (Phil 1:3–5)

It is right for me to think this way about all of you, because you hold me in your heart, for all of you share in God's grace with me, both in my imprisonment and in the **defense and confirmation of the gospel**. (Phil 1:7)

I want you to know, beloved, that what has happened to me has actually helped **to spread the gospel**. (Phil 1:12)

I am put here for the **defense of the gospel**. (Phil 1:16)

---

[45] Probably a divine passive meaning "filled *by God*" (so Bockmuehl, *The Epistle to the Philippians*, 69).

[46] On the result participle, see D. B. Wallace, *Greek Grammar beyond the Basics* (Grand Rapids, MI: Zondervan, 1996), 637–639.

[47] Porter, *Idioms*, 66.

[48] See, for example, Silva, *Philippians*, 61; Fee, *Paul's Letter to the Philippians*, 104; Hawthorne and Martin, *Philippians*, 33–34; Hansen, *Philippians*, 63.

[49] On the curious array of textual variants for the end of v. 11 concerning "the glory and praise of God" (*eis doxan kai epainon theou*), see Metzger, *Textual Commentary*, 611.

[50] Hansen, *Philippians*, 31.

Only, live your life in a **manner worthy of the gospel of Christ**, so that, whether I come and see you or am absent and hear about you, I will know that you are standing firm in one spirit, striving side by side with one mind **for the faith of the gospel**. (Phil 1:27)

But Timothy's worth you know, how like a son with a father he has served with me **in the work of the gospel**. (Phil 2:22)

I ask you also, my loyal companion, help these women, for they have struggled beside me **in the work of the gospel**, together with Clement and the rest of my co-workers, whose names are in the book of life. (Phil 4:3)

You Philippians indeed know that in **the early days of the gospel**, when I left Macedonia, no church shared with me in the matter of giving and receiving, except you alone. (Phil 4:15)

In light of all this, Gordon Fee comments:

It does not take much reading of Paul's letters to recognize that the gospel is the singular passion of his life; that passion is the glue that in particular holds this letter together. By 'gospel,' especially in Philippians, Paul refers primarily neither to a body of teaching nor to proclamation. Above all, the gospel has to do with Christ, both his person and his work. To preach Christ is to preach the gospel, which is all about Christ; to preach the gospel is to proclaim God's good news of salvation that he has effected in Christ. As elsewhere, 'Christ' and 'the gospel' are at times nearly interchangeable. Living 'worthy of the gospel of Christ' in 1:27, therefore, means to live worthy of Christ as he has been made known and proclaimed in the gospel which has him as its focus and content.[51]

## 1:12–26: THE ADVANCE OF THE GOSPEL

[12] I want you to know, beloved, that what has happened to me has actually helped to spread the gospel,

[13] so that it has become known throughout the whole imperial guard and to everyone else that my imprisonment is for Christ;

[14] and most of the brothers and sisters, having been made confident in the Lord by my imprisonment, dare to speak the word with greater boldness and without fear.

---

[51]   Fee, *Paul's Letter to the Philippians*, 82.

[15] Some proclaim Christ from envy and rivalry, but others from goodwill.

[16] These proclaim Christ out of love, knowing that I have been put here for the defense of the gospel;

[17] the others proclaim Christ out of selfish ambition, not sincerely but intending to increase my suffering in my imprisonment.

[18] What does it matter? Just this, that Christ is proclaimed in every way, whether out of false motives or true; and in that I rejoice. Yes, and I will continue to rejoice,

[19] for I know that through your prayers and the help of the Spirit of Jesus Christ this will turn out for my deliverance.

[20] It is my eager expectation and hope that I will not be put to shame in any way, but that by my speaking with all boldness, Christ will be exalted now as always in my body, whether by life or by death.

[21] For to me, living is Christ and dying is gain.

[22] If I am to live in the flesh, that means fruitful labor for me; and I do not know which I prefer.

[23] I am hard pressed between the two: my desire is to depart and be with Christ, for that is far better;

[24] but to remain in the flesh is more necessary for you.

[25] Since I am convinced of this, I know that I will remain and continue with all of you for your progress and joy in faith,

[26] so that I may share abundantly in your boasting in Christ Jesus when I come to you again.

Paul proceeds to narrate the details surrounding his dire and deadly circumstances in his Ephesian imprisonment, how it has paradoxically led to a promotion of the gospel, as well as his hope to be released and to find respite by being reunited with the Philippians. Paul describes how his imprisonment has served to advance rather than hinder the gospel (vv. 12 -14), how the gospel spreads even through the proclamation of his self-interested rivals (vv. 15 -18b), he rejoices at the hope of being released from imprisonment (vv. 18c -20), he engages in a soliloquy at the prospect of death and departing to be with Christ or remaining alive and refreshing the Philippians (vv. 21 -24), and Paul offers words of assurance that he will indeed survive and be returned to the Philippians (vv. 25 -26).

Paul in v. 12 uses a rhetorical disclosure formula[52] when he says that he desires the Philippians to know (*ginōskein*) that the ordeal of imprisonment that has befallen him has actually served "to spread the gospel." When Paul says, "what has happened to me" (lit. "the things according to me," *ta kat' eme*) he refers in the first instance to his detainment. The conditions of Roman imprisonment were remarkably diverse, ranging from relatively comfortable house arrest, to a dungeon where one was surrounded by excrement, rats and lice, disease, completely unventilated, sometimes overcrowded, accompanied by beatings, squalid as it could be brutal, and where prisoners often became dishevelled and even died.[53] Yet even here affairs have "actually served"[54] the gospel's advancement. The irony of the situation would not be lost on readers. Caesar's fetters have helped the gospel spread rather than silenced it. Rather than muting the messenger, Christ has been magnified even in Paul's detainment. The progress or advance of the gospel is the key motif here and transpires in two ways.

First, "it has become known throughout the whole imperial guard and to everyone else that my imprisonment is for Christ" (v. 13). One must remember that the *praitōrion* could refer to the emperor's personal bodyguards who would be detaining Paul in the praetorian barracks in Rome, or otherwise (and more likely for us), it could designate a place, the proconsul's headquarters in Ephesus where Paul was being detained while the charges against him were investigated (*praitōrion* can refer to a military, imperial, royal, or administrative headquarters).[55] To hedge our bets somewhat, we cannot rule out the prospect that elite praetorian guards were stationed in Ephesus as part of close personal protection for the procurators who looked after the emperor's interests or to ensure the security of

---

[52] See S. E. Porter and A. W. Pitts, "The Disclosure Formula in the Epistolary Papyri and in the New Testament: Development, Form, and Syntax," in *The Language of the New Testament: Context, History, and Development* (eds. S. E. Porter and A. Pitts; Leiden: Brill, 2013), 421–438.

[53] C. S. Wansink, *Chained in Christ: The Experience and Rhetoric of Paul's Imprisonments* (Sheffield: Sheffield Academic Press, 1996), 33–43.

[54] The verb *elēluthen* ("resulted in" or "turned out") is probably stative meaning that "the gospel is in a state of continual advancement – its advance is ongoing and unstoppable" (Keown, *Philippians*, 184).

[55] See discussion in Lightfoot, *Philippians*, 99–104, although Fee, *Paul's Letter to the Philippians*, 113 n. 33 overstates the case that it must refer to the "imperial guard."

any flow of funds to and from Ephesus. In any case, the gospel has infiltrated the Roman emperor's or the Asian governor's own entourage.[56] The reference to the *praitorion* is doubly relevant since there is numismatic evidence that Philippi was colonized by a cohort of praetorians.[57] Descendants of those original colonists would have had a particular interest in any Roman *praetoriani* who were receptive to Christian faith or even converted.[58] Evidently the persons who worked in the governor's headquarters/residence, whether soldiers, slaves or servants, are said to know that Paul is imprisoned[59] on account of his devotion to Jesus Christ. What is more, it is also likely that among the imperial staff some are becoming sympathizers to this new faith and perhaps even adherents, hence the reference to saints in Caesar's household (Phil 4:22).[60]

Second, the effect of Paul's imprisonment on local believers in Ephesus is that they, "having been made confident in the Lord by my imprisonment, dare to speak the word with greater boldness and without fear" (1:14). Paul's courage under duress, far from intimidating the Ephesian believers into a cowering silence, has served to reinforce their confidence in the gospel, forced them to steel themselves, and forged a messianic mettle, so that they "are getting more and more daring in announcing the Message without any fear" (NJB). The result of Paul's imprisonment is that Christ's name is becoming known and the reputation of his followers for their devotion to Christ is becoming equally apparent.[61]

---

[56]   It is far more likely that the "whole" of the proconsul's staff in Ephesus rather than the "whole" of the 10,000 strong praetorian guard in Rome know why Paul is in chains. See too Reumann, *Philippians*, 196.

[57]   E. Krentz comments: "A series of coins from Philippi picture the goddess Victoria with the legend VIC(toria) AVG(usta) on their obverse side. The reverse [side] shows three Roman military standards ringed by a beaded 'milling,' with the legend COHOR(s) to the left and PRAE(toria) to the right, and below the standards PHIL." See F. Krentz, "Paul, Games, and the Military," in *Paul in the Greco-Roman World: A Handbook* (ed. J. Paul Sampley; Harrisburg, PA: Trinity Press International, 2003), 344–383, here 360.

[58]   Krentz, "Paul, Games, and the Military," 360.

[59]   Gk. *desmos* literally means bonds or chains, and is repeated in vv. 13, 14, and 17.

[60]   So, for example, Bockmuehl, *The Epistle to the Philippians*, 75; Fee, *Paul's Letter to the Philippians*, 112; Keown, *Philippians*, 189.

[61]   One of the debates in Pauline studies and missiology is whether Paul expected congregations to replicate his own evangelistic efforts or whether this was something reserved mostly for apostles and evangelists. See, on the one hand, J. P. Dickson, *Mission-Commitment in the Pauline Communities* (WUNT 2.159; Tübingen: Mohr Siebeck, 2003); W. P. Bowers, "Church and Mission in Paul," *JSNT* 44 (1991): 89–111; and, on the other hand, J P Ware, *The Mission of the Church in Paul's Letter to the*

The mention of the proclamation of Christ draws Paul to something of a tangential twitch[62] in vv. 15–18b against those who in his perception preach Christ from less than noble motives. Paul's comments here are very general and might refer to no more than the type of partisan polemics and preaching that characterized the Corinthian congregations (see 1 Cor 1:10–17). However, as we'll see in 3:1–11, Paul is worried that certain Jewish Christian proselytizers might arrive in Macedonia and might try to persuade the Pauline assemblies to adopt a "Christ plus" proselytism gospel. This is part of Paul's opening sally preparing the way for a later salvo of criticism against them. Paul contrasts two kinds of preachers (vv. 15–16). On the one hand, there are some (*tines*, Paul leaves the object of his disparagement unidentified) who – perhaps like the false brothers who snuck into Antioch and the agitators who entered Galatia – proclaim Christ "out of rivalry" (ESV, CSB) or "out of selfish ambition" (NIV, NRSV, CEB),[63] not sincerely but intending to increase Paul's suffering in his imprisonment. On the other hand, there are those – such as the Pauline assemblies in Ephesus and Philippi – who proclaim Christ from "goodwill," "out of love," and "knowing that I have been put here for the defense of the gospel." It is not merely Paul who is on trial, but the very gospel, and, while that should solicit support, some use it as an opportunity to encroach on Paul's apostolate and to stir up trouble for him. The difference is a matter of motives, whether one hopes to make Paul's ministry insufferable or to encourage Paul in his suffering for the gospel. Paul can see a silver lining to this cloud of division, since he rhetorically asks, "What does it matter?" (*Ti gar*). Nothing, he concludes, because either way, whether people preach from ignoble pretext or from noble principle, whether pro- or anti-Paul, in either case, Christ is proclaimed, and Paul can rejoice in that consolation (vv. 18a–b).

---

*Philippians in the Context of Ancient Judaism* (Leiden: Brill, 2005); M. Keown, *Congregational Evangelism in Philippians* (Eugene, OR: Wipf & Stock, 2009); I. H. Marshall, "Who Were the Evangelists?" in *The Mission of the Early Church to Jews and Gentiles* (eds. J. Ådna and H. Kvalbein; WUNT 127; Tübingen: Mohr Siebeck, 2000), 251–262; R. L. Plummer, *Paul's Understanding of the Church's Mission* (Milton Keynes: Paternoster, 2006).

[62]  Bockmuehl (*The Epistle to the Philippians*, 76) calls it an "unexpected excursus."

[63]  The word *epithelia* should more properly be translated as "partisan antics" or "sectarian agendas"; it is not about the ambition of a person wishing to succeed at the expense of others, but the intention to push a specific agenda roughshod over others (see Gal 5:20; Reumann, *Philippians*, 178; Hellerman, *Philippians*, 51).

## Contrast between Paul and His Competitors[64]

Paul segues from rejoicing in the proclamation of the gospel irrespective of the motives of the proclaimers (Table 1), to rejoicing at the prospect of being released from his detainment in 1:18c–20. Paul writes, "Yes, and I will continue to rejoice," because he knows that through the prayerful petition of the Philippians and with "the help[65] of the Spirit of Jesus" that events will turn out for his "deliverance" (*sōtēria*) from detainment (or worse). The interpretation of the genitives in the phrase "help of the Spirit of Jesus" is tricky. We should probably read first an objective genitive, that is, the supply that is the Spirit (see Gal 3:5); and second a genitive of source, not Jesus's own spirit, but the Holy Spirit dispensed by Jesus (see Mk 1:8; Matt 3:11; Luke 3:16; 24:49; John 1:33; 15:26; 20:22; Acts 1:8; Gal 4:6; 1 Pet 1:11). Most commentators also see here a deliberate allusion to Job 13:16 (LXX): "And this shall turn out to me for salvation" (*touto moi apobēsetai eis sōtēria*). Just as Job expressed confidence that he will be delivered from his misfortune, so too Paul affirms that as his own trial proceeds, God will rescue him all the same.[66] Richard Hays puts it well: "By echoing Job's words, Paul the prisoner tacitly assumes the role of righteous sufferer, as paradigmatically figured by Job. Awaiting his trial, he speaks with Job's voice to affirm confidence in the favorable outcome of his afflictions; thereby, he implicitly transfers to himself some of the significations that traditionally cluster about the figure of Job."[67] Paul is

Table 1 *Contrasting Paul's Competitors and Colleagues*

| Competitors | Colleagues |
| --- | --- |
| Preach the Messiah (vv. 15, 17) | Preach the Messiah (v. 15) |
| From motives of envy and rivalry (v. 15) | From motives of goodwill (v. 15) |
| And selfish ambition and pretention (v. 17) | And love (v. 16) |
| Supposing (v. 17) | Knowing (v. 16) |
| To stir up trouble for Paul in prison (v. 17) | Paul is set to defend the gospel (v. 16) |

---

[64] Thielman, *Philippians*, 61.

[65] The word *epichorēgia* is best translated as "supply" (see Eph 4:17; Col 2:19; 2 Cor 9:10).

[66] Cousar, *Philippians*, 37–38.

[67] R. B. Hays, *Echoes of Scripture in the Letters of Paul* (New Haven, CN: Yale University Press, 1989), 22.

thus seized with a confident expectation[68] and hope that whatever lies ahead of him – "whether by life or by death" – that he will not experience "shame," but instead "with daring courage that Christ's greatness will be seen in my body, now as always" (CEB). Instead, of death and shame, Paul anticipates victory and vindication.[69]

A startling point is then made by Paul in 1:21 that his deliverance does not depend upon a release from prison or even from escaping a death sentence. He states: "For to me, living is Christ and dying is gain." The parallelism and assonance of the Greek here (*Christos* ["Christ"] and *kerdos* ["gain"]) would make it an orally and aurally powerful crescendo for listeners hearing this read to them in a communal gathering. There is also an element of word play with *Zēn Christos* ("to live is Christ"), which sounds remarkably like the slogan *Zēn Chrēstos* ("life is good").[70] The notion of death as "gain" is ubiquitous in Greek thought, a "gain" understood either in terms of escape from misfortunes or release from the body.[71] Yet this is no "pious cliché";[72] neither is Paul expressing detached stoic indifference toward life or death, nor is he grandstanding like a philosophical gladiator willing to die for what he believes. Rather, Paul's confidence is based on his experience of participating in Christ's sufferings, the surety of Christ's *parousia*, the hope of sharing in Christ's resurrection (see Phil 1:6, 10; 3:10–11, 14, 20–21; cf. 2 Tim 4:18). Death is a gain because it means instant intimacy with Christ. According to Hansen, Paul defines his own prospective death by looking at Christ's cross: "That is my destiny! As Christ embraced the cross in humble obedience to God, so I desire to embrace my death as a witness to my union *with* Christ."[73]

### Bridging the Horizons: Death in Christ as Gain

Paul's statement in 1:21, "For to me, living is Christ and dying is gain" might seem to be a rather hollow platitude that offers a façade of spiritual bravado in the face of the

---

[68]   Silva (*Philippians*, 70) notes: "The word *apokaradokia* is particularly emphatic; its only other occurrence is in reference to the eager desire of creation for the final redemption, a desire also described as a groaning (Rom. 8:19, 22)."

[69]   Bockmuehl, *The Epistle to the Philippians*, 83.

[70]   Hawthorne and Martin, *Philippians*, 55.

[71]   See, for example, Bockmuehl, *The Epistle to the Philippians*, 88; Hawthorne and Martin, *Philippians*, 56; Reumann, *Philippians*, 217.

[72]   Garland, "Philippians," 204.

[73]   Hansen, *Philippians*, 89 (italics original).

tragedy and terror that is death. But this is not the case. The ancients were quite sober about the reality, inevitability, and calamity of death. The psalmist could voice anxiety about dying: "My heart is in anguish within me, the terrors of death have fallen upon me" (Ps 55:4) and the author of Ecclesiastes could lament: "No one has power over the wind to restrain the wind, or power over the day of death" (Ecc 8:8). Similarly, the Stoic philosopher Seneca said: "Most men ebb and flow in wretchedness between the fear of death and the hardships of life; they are unwilling to live, and yet do not know how to die" (*Ep.* 4.6 [LCL]) and "Death comes for us all. It presses upon our rear. Soon the battle cry will be raised: the enemy is near" (*Ad Marc.* 10.5–6 [LCL]). Paul lived in a world where death was everywhere: high infant mortality, low life expectancy, natural disasters killed without discretion of age, gender, or ethnicity, health care was primitive, disease and dysentery were especially common in squalid prisons, life was considered cheap and governing authorities had no qualms about ordering someone's death and soldiers had no inhibitions about carrying it out. Indeed, Paul could himself say at a particularly low point that "we felt that we had received the sentence of death" (2 Cor 1:9) and he even felt as if he was "being given up to death for Jesus' sake" (2 Cor 4:11). Paul knew the angst and anxiety about confronting his own mortality. Yet, whereas many Christians today seem to think that death is something that happens to other people, Paul knew very well the brutal reality of death and his pastoral remarks are neither vacuous visions of a hereafter nor pithy sayings that everything will turn out alright. Rather, Paul's confidence is that not even death "will be able to separate us from the love of God in Christ Jesus our Lord" (Rom 8:38) because in Christ's resurrection God "gives us the victory through our Lord Jesus Christ" (1 Cor 15:57). What we see in Phil 1:21–24 is not Paul's determination to face death with a kind of stoic antipathy toward it, nor Paul asking friends to dance on his grave in defiance of death. Rather, what Paul tries to explain and even embody here is how one dies in the grip of grace, how one faces death in faith, and how one finishes the race in faithfulness to God. Showing how to die Christianly, whether at the hands of persecutors or by pancreatic cancer, is something that believers offer to their friends, family, and congregation as an example for them to follow as they themselves follow in the footsteps of Christ and his holy apostles.

In 1:22–24 the read/listener witnesses Paul's inner-dialogue about which option he should prefer: remaining alive, fruitful labor, which is better for the Philippians; or, departing to be with Christ, instant intimacy with the Savior, which is better for him. He confesses, "I do not know which I prefer. I am hard pressed between the two." In rhetorical terms, this language reflects the trope known as *aporia* or *diaporēsis* where a speaker feigns perplexity to dramatize a particular predicament. The rhetorical device does not mean the conflict is less real, since Paul is hard-pressed between the prospects of death and life, and while death has its attraction, he will choose life out of fidelity to the Philippians.[74] What breaks the horns of the dilemma is his heartfelt need and the practical necessity for him to remain "in the flesh for your sake" and to be returned to the Philippians to see their progress in the faith. If given a choice, I (Gupta) argue, Paul chooses the crucified life over the noble death.[75] Paul's testament in miniature is that God's victory over the pseudo-divine and self-aggrandizing train of emperors, the powers of this present darkness, or the god of this age, is not contingent upon the perpetuation of his own mortal coil, rather, he rests in God's faithfulness to bring his own work to its appointed goal.

Paul offers words of assurance in vv. 25–26 to that effect that he will be released and be reunited to the Philippians. Paul is strongly "convinced"[76] that he will "remain and continue"[77] so that he will be able to supervise their "progress and joy in the faith" and Paul in turn will "share abundantly in your boasting in Christ Jesus when I come to you again." The use of *proskopē* ("progress" or "advance") signals an *inclusio* that links back to v. 12 and suggests that the advance of the gospel both in Paul's chains and in the Philippians' progress in the faith is a core theme. *Prokopē* was a technical term in stoicism that denotes a person's progress in moral virtue, likely familiar to anyone exposed to philosophical currents, and thus Paul hopes he can personally guide their progress by his presence.[78] Instead of mourning or grieving at Paul's death, the Philippians should expect instead to be boasting in Messiah Jesus when they see Paul again in person, much to their own benefit. Silva surmises: "Just as in prison he had become an instrument for the advance of God's word, so upon his release he will be used to bring greater spiritual health to the believers in Philippi."[79]

---

[74]  N. C. Croy, "'To Die Is Gain' (Philippians 1:19–26)," *JBL* (2003): 517–531.

[75]  N. K. Gupta, "'I Will Not Be Put to Shame': Paul, the Philippians, and the Honourable Wish for Death," *NeoT* 42 (2008): 253–267.

[76]  The perfect tense form of *pepoithōs* accentuates his state of confidence.

[77]  The expression *menō kai paramenō* is redundant, but the repetition of the *menō* sound is no doubt deliberate so as to be emphatic, most translations use "stay live," "continue," "remain," and "abide."

[78]  Reumann, *Philippians*, 194; Hellerman, *Philippians*, 42.

[79]  Silva, *Philippians*, 75.

## Closer Look: Paul and the Intermediate State

The intermediate state refers to the state and place of believers who die ahead of Christ's return and the arrival of the eschatological consummation (i.e., the kingdom of God and new creation).[80] Given that Paul refers to "being with Christ, which is better by far" (Phil 1:23), what did he think that state consisted of? What happens to believers when they die? What happens to them or where do they go? The fact is that references to an intermediate state by Paul are few and far between. Paul's eschatological discourse and exhortations focused primarily on Christ's *parousia*, the resurrection, and the final judgment. Information about an intermediate state must be inferred from Paul's scant remarks on the topic across his letters. To begin with, Paul seems to have oscillated in his own mind whether he would live to see Christ's return (Rom 13:11), or whether he would be dead when it happened (1 Cor 6:14; 2 Cor 4:14), and is perhaps deliberately ambivalent in 1 Thess 4:14–15 as to whether he considered himself part of "we who are still alive" or "those who have fallen asleep" (i.e., died) at the time of Christ's *parousia*. Yet he clearly believed some would be dead when Christ returned but they would by no means miss out on participating in the future consummation (see 1 Cor 15:29; 1 Thess 4:13–18). Thus, Paul, writing in 2 Cor 5:1–10, arguably anticipates upon death, not a spiritual resurrection, but a spiritual mode of postmortem existence, a position that is less than ideal, but still characterized by a heightened form of interpersonal communion with Christ.[81] Further, this state is clearly something that is prior to Christ's *parousia* and the general resurrection because it is ahead of the judgment of believers when their resurrection will take place (see 1 Cor 15:21–28, 51–52). Paul hopes to please the Lord in both his bodily tent and in his heavenly dwelling, knowing that he will stand before Christ at the final judgment (2 Cor 5:10; Rom 14:10). Paul is remarkably circumspect and even opaque on this subject. Perhaps, at the end of the day, the most we can say is this: For Paul, in death, we have union with Christ, which is better than terrestrial affliction and tumult (Phil 1:23), in such a state "our lives are hid with Christ in God" (Col 3:3) and is metaphorically called "a heavenly dwelling" (2 Cor 5:1–4). As a result, although we will put off our mortal coils and experience physical and biological death, we still remain "alive" to God in Christ, awaiting the final resurrection.[82] This itself is simply part of Paul's conviction that nothing – not even death – can separate believers from the love of God that

---

[80] See discussion of the intermediate state in Michael F. Bird, *Evangelical Theology* (Grand Rapids, MI: Zondervan, 2013), 312–325.

[81] M. J. Harris, *The Second Epistle to the Corinthians* (NIGTC; Grand Rapids, MI: Eerdmans, 2005), 401.

[82] See J. B. Green, *Body, Soul, and Human Life: The Nature of Humanity in the Bible* (Grand Rapids, MI: Baker, 2008), 178–180.

is in Christ Jesus (Rom 8:35–39). Polycarp understood this point when he wrote his own letter to the Philippians, exhorting them to remember "Paul himself, and the other apostles. Having confidence that none of them ran in vain, but in faith and righteousness, and that they are with the Lord in the place which they are due, who they also suffered with. For they did not love the present age, but the one who died on our behalf, and on account of us was raised up by God."[83]

### 1:27–30: THE CALL FOR PERSEVERANCE IN THE FACE OF ADVERSITY

[27] Only, live your life in a manner worthy of the gospel of Christ, so that, whether I come and see you or am absent and hear about you, I will know that you are standing firm in one spirit, striving side by side with one mind for the faith of the gospel,

[28] and are in no way intimidated by your opponents. For them this is evidence of their destruction, but of your salvation. And this is God's doing.

[29] For he has graciously granted you the privilege not only of believing in Christ, but of suffering for him as well –

[30] since you are having the same struggle that you saw I had and now hear that I still have.

Having completed his biographical update, filled as it was with pathos and confidence, Paul begins his first exhortation to the Philippians in vv. 27–30. These verses comprise a single, dense, and somewhat convoluted sentence, which nonetheless urges the conformity of their lives to the pattern of the gospel, even amidst an adversarial context. Viewed this way, this section, closely related as it is to 2:1–17, comes as close as we can imagine to the *propositio* or central thesis of the letter.[84]

There is an abrupt launch into an exhortation in 1:27, there is no inferential "Therefore" or "And also my brothers and sisters." Paul is direct: "Only,

---

[83] Polycarp, *Phil.* 9.2 (trans. R. Brannan); see R. Brannan, *The Apostolic Fathers: A New Translation* (Bellingham, WA: Lexham Press, 2018).

[84] D. Watson, "A Rhetorical Analysis of Philippians and Its Implications for the Unity Question," *NovT* 30 (1988): 65–67.

live your life in a manner worthy of the gospel of Christ." Paul begins with an adjective and adverb, literally, "Only worthily" (*monon axiōs*), which modify "live" and the underlying Greek word is *politeuomai* for "to conduct one's life as a citizen."[85] It means to live with a clear conscience before God (Acts 23:1) and it anticipates what Paul says later about possessing a "citizenship that is in heaven" (Phil 3:20; cf. Eph 2:19; *Diogn.* 5.9). Paul stresses a singular attempt to live worthily of the gospel (see Col 1:9, "you may live a life worthy of the Lord"; 2 Thess 1:8 and 1 Pet 4:17, "obey the gospel"; Gal 2:14, "walking according to the truth of the gospel"). The gospel is a royal summons to faith, trust, imitation, and allegiance in the Lord Jesus and the Philippians must ensure the congruity of their calling with their manner of life as a heavenly colony. Many inscriptions can be found urging residents to live worthily of a monarch or a city-state.[86] Thus, Paul's exhortation entails the renunciation of one way of citizenship in favor of the way of citizenship determined by allegiance to Jesus Christ that Paul will elaborate upon in Phil 2:5–8. Philippi might be a colony of Rome that enjoys the imperial patronage of *Kaisar Sebastos Kyrios* (Caesar, Emperor, Lord), but their walk and way of life should more properly be determined by the gospel of the *Kyrios Iēsous Christos* (Lord, Jesus, Christ)![87] Or, to put it paraphrastically, "Imagine you are citizens of a heavenly city called Evangelopolis, live as upright citizens and prove that you truly belong there."

---

**Closer Look: Politeuomai ("Live as a Citizen") in Context**

We have already noted that Paul's use of *politeuomai* in 1:27 is distinctive. It is the only time Paul uses this word in his letters, and in the New Testament it only otherwise appears in Acts 23:1. Therefore, it is helpful to explore further what this word means in its ancient usage. The popular translation "live" does not capture its specific meaning well, especially given its limited usage in the Greek Bible.[88] In 2 Maccabees 6:1, we learn of an Athenian attempt to force Jews to turn against

---

[85]  BDAG, 846. Paul had several ways he talked about "living." In 3:17–18 he uses his more favored term *peripateō* (cf. also 1 Thess 2:11; Gal 5:16; Rom 6:4; 8:4; 13:13; 14:15).

[86]  P. Pilhoefer, *Die erste christliche Gemeinde Europas* (WUNT 87; Tübingen: Mohr Siebeck, 1995), 137.

[87]  Cf. Bockmuehl, *The Epistle to the Philippians*, 98; Thompson and Longenecker, *Philippians and Philemon*, 51.

[88]  In the Septuagint, *politeuomai* occurs eight times, mostly in the Maccabean texts (2 Macc 6:1; 11:25; 3 Macc 3:4; 4 Macc 2:8, 23 (twice); 5:16).

their religion and to give up on *living* (*politeuomai*) by the laws of God. Here *politeuomai* refers to the way a people structure their life around certain standards (i.e., Torah; cf. 4 Macc 5:16). In Acts 23, with Paul standing before the Sanhedrin, the apostle confesses, "Brothers, up to this day I have lived my life (*politeuomai*) with a clear conscience before God" (23:1). Paul is talking about his public life, how he carries out his life with integrity in view of certain standards. C. Spicq explains how *politeuomai* is about life in relation to the *polis* (city), and this in contradistinction to *idiōteuō*, "to live as a private individual."[89] Spicq goes on to describe how Paul was calling the Philippians to "consider oneself in all of one's actions as a member of a social body, and accordingly to say nothing and do nothing that is not appropriate for a citizen of heaven."[90] To be a good citizen is to think beyond oneself, to consider the strength of the whole. The standard of the gospel of Christ probably entails conformity to the character of Christ himself as lord of his people. But in this particular context Paul appears to be placing an emphasis on the good citizen's call to unity.[91] This notion of unity for the sake of collective benefit and welfare is captured well in this statement from Aristotle on the "good citizen."

> Every state is as we see a sort of partnership, and every partnership is formed with a view to some good since all the actions of all mankind are done with a view to what they think to be good. It is therefore evident that, while all partnerships aim at some good, the partnership that is the most supreme of all and includes all the others does so most of all, and aims at the most supreme of all goods; and this is the partnership entitled the state, the political association. (*Politics* 1.1252a)[92]

The reason[93] for this gospel-worthy way of life, is that, irrespective of whether Paul is present or absent, whether he's eyeballing them in person

---

[89]   *TLNT* 3.132; cf. R. F. Collins, *The Power of Images in Paul* (Collegeville, MN: Liturgical Press, 2008), 54–56.

[90]   Collins, *The Power of Images in Paul*, 56. This fits with R. Brewer's approach to this verb, where he defines it as "obligation or allegiance to some law, order, system, or principle which imposes its requirements upon the individual, while, at the same time, maintaining an existence independent of the individual's will"; see Brewer, "The Meaning of *Politeuesthe* in Philippians 1:27," *JBL* 73.2 (1954): 76–83, at 78.

[91]   See G. Zerbe, *Citizenship: Paul on Peace and Politics* (Winnipeg, MB: CMU Press, 2012), 4. Zerbe explains that in 1:27 the language of citizenship involves a call both "to be a citizen community" and "to practice the citizenship identity" (4).

[92]   Aristotle, *Politics* 1.1252a; as cited in D. Edwards, "Good Citizenship: A Study of Philippians 1:27 and Its Implications for Contemporary Urban Ministry," *Ex Auditu* 29 (2013), 78.

[93]   In 1:27, the dependent clause (*hoti* etc) is a further elaboration of the purpose clause (*hina* etc) and explains how the Philippians live lives worthy of the gospel and its Lord.

or relying on secondhand reports from afar, he wants them to know that they "are standing firm in one spirit, striving side by side with one mind for the faith of the gospel, and are in no way intimidated by your opponents" (1:27c–d). This is in many ways a good summary of Paul's exhortation to the Philippians. He aspires for them to be gospel-centered, single-mindedly united, and persevering under adversity. The imperative command "stand firm" (*stēkete*) is a metaphor for the necessity of steadfastness and a determination to remain united, such unity being a necessary survival mechanism in the face of intense opposition. The call for unity is quite emphatic with Paul calling them to be "in one Spirit" (*en heni pneumati*) of "one mind" (*mia psychē*) as they are "striving side by side" (*synathlountes*) in the "faithfulness that advances the gospel" (*tē pistei tou euangeliou*).[94] The language co-struggling or striving together echoes military imagery of a maniple, legion, or cohort fighting together in tight formation for success or even for survival.[95] I am reminded of Josephus' vivid commendation of the Roman army, a group he praises for its perfect discipline, lock-step coordination, and pure efficiency.

This perfect discipline makes the army an ornament of peace-time and in war welds the whole into a single body; so compact are their ranks, so alert their movements in wheeling to right or left, so quick their ears for orders, their eyes for signals, their hands to act upon them. Prompt as they consequently ever are in action, none are slower than they to succumb to suffering, and never have they been known in any predicament to be beaten by numbers, by ruse, by difficulty of ground, or even by fortune; for they have more assurance of victory than of fortune. (*Wars* 3.105–106, LCL)

Paul wants to encourage a culture of cohesion and cooperation to buttress their evangelical unity in light of the powerful enemies arrayed

---

94   The translation here is by Michael F. Bird (MFB). Note: (1) *tē pistei* is a dative of advantage and implies the faith that accrues to the advantage/advancement/success/promotion of the gospel (BDAG, 964); (2) *pistei tou euangeliou* is unlikely to be a subjective genitive (in faith's gospel), which is nonsensical in context, nor an objective genitive (faith in the gospel) since progress in the faith and not initial faith is the point here. (3) More likely *pistei tou euangeliou* is either (a) a genitive of source (the faithfulness that comes from the gospel) or (b) a genitive of result (faithfulness that advances the gospel). This latter option makes sense if *tē pistei* is a dative of advantage and if advancing the gospel (1:12) is a key theme across 1:12–30.

95   Lightfoot, *Philippians*, 106; Hawthorne and Martin, *Philippians*, 93; E. Krentz, "Military Language and Metaphors in Philippians," in *Origins and Methods* (ed. B. H. McLean; JSNTSup 86; Sheffield: JSOT Press, 1993), 122–123; Garland, "Philippians," 210.

against them. Instead of standing against each other, they must stand
together; instead of being contentious, they must stand in the contest
together. Paul's words here anticipate the exhortations in Phil 2:2 about
being like-minded and united and 4:2 about avoiding division. The Philippians must contend for the gospel in their own context by not being
contentious or conceited with each other. Ultimately, as Silva comments,
"The struggles of the Christian citizen must be faced within the fellowship
of the believing community."[96]

If the Philippians stand firm, then, Paul declares in v. 28 that they can
expect to be "in no way intimidated by your opponents." In the face of
their adversaries – most likely here pagan opponents[97] – they need resolve
and resilience, which itself is a "sign" or "proof" (*endeixis*) that their
enemies will be destroyed and they themselves will be delivered. Both
destruction and deliverance are the prerogative of God and he has already
judged in their favor on account of their faith in Christ. Yet the disturbance
between the Philippians and their local critics is not civic but cosmic. The
presenting issue is not social conformity but the right of a Christian
community to exist. While the Philippians might be accused of socioreligious deviancy, they can respond with a cautionary warning of eternal
destruction and that from God.

Paul goes on to associate their present state of suffering caused by public
opposition with a confirmation of their calling and a sense of solidarity
with Paul (vv. 29–30). The reason[98] they experience persecution (most
probably in the form of ostracism, slander, discrimination, accusations of
impiety, superstition, and affronting the majesty of the Roman state and its
gods, theft of their property, verbal and physical abuse, and imprisonment,
see 2 Cor 8:1–2) is because God has "graciously granted you the privilege
not only of believing in Christ, but of suffering for him as well."[99] Suffering
in the midst of adversity is an indication of the divine favor that the
Philippians have been graciously granted (*charizomai*), not only the gift

---

[96] Silva, *Philippians*, 82.
[97] See Acts 16:20–21: "These men are disturbing our city; they are Jews and are advocating
customs that are not lawful for us as Romans to adopt or observe."
[98] Silva (*Philippians*, 83) notes: "Paul's use of *hoti* rather than *gar* makes clear that verse
29 is intended as the reason or explanation for the surprising statement in verse 28,
particularly the emphatic clause at the end, 'and this from God.'"
[99] See Oakes, *Philippians*, 89–95.

of faith, but also the gift of suffering for the sake of Christ. The proof of their election and calling, the chief symbol that they truly belong to Christ, is their faith in Christ and their suffering for the sake of the name of Christ. Just to be clear, Paul does not think that such hardship is a blip in the life of the Philippian church, where religious freedom and social favor is supposed to be normal. Much to the contrary, he thinks it is persecution and suffering that is normal. The remarks here are part and parcel of Paul's theology of the church in the world, strenuous discipleship, and suffering in faith. The inevitability and even the necessity of hardship was a distinctive theme in his instructions to the Thessalonians amidst their own misfortunes (1 Thess 2:14; 3:3–4; 2 Thess 1:4–7). In Luke's account, Paul warned the believers in Galatia that "It is through many persecutions that we must enter the kingdom of God" (Acts 14:22). Paul's instructions to the Romans announced that the path to glory always passes through the trial of suffering (Rom 8:17, 28–30).[100] Furthermore, the demonstrative proof that the Philippians have the grace-gift of faith and suffering is that they have experienced the "same struggle" that they "saw" Paul have when he was with them in Philippi (see Acts 16:19–24) and is experiencing even now in Ephesus (see 1 Cor 15:32; 2 Tim 1:18). This struggle (*agōn*) is an athletic image, often used in moral discourse of the sage striving and struggling for virtue, but which Paul has ostensible refashioned as a struggle for the gospel.[101] They have not only fellowship with Paul in the gospel, but share a common faith, and even solidarity in suffering on behalf of Christ.

---

**Closer Look: Early Christian Suffering: An Historical Model**

In his book, *Philippians: From People to Letter*, Peter Oakes offers a realistic (but fictional) scenario that demonstrates the kind of rejection and shame that early Christians faced in a city like Philippi.

Jason is a Greek of Macedonian descent. He is married to Chloe, who is also a Greek Christian. They have four young children. Jason's forebears farmed near Philippi but his own profession has been as a goldsmith, working for his cousin. He was spared any agonizing over whether to continue doing work for temples because, as soon as his cousin found out that Jason had become a Christian, he sacked him.

---

[100] See too Silva, *Philippians*, 84.
[101] Hellerman, *Philippians*, 86.

For the last eighteen months, Chloe and Jason have faced a desparate financial struggle, keeping their family alive through Jason doing casual farm-labouring, mainly for other Christians, and Chloe doing some very poorly paid work as a waitress in her second-cousin's tavern. Six months ago, Jason was involved in a fight after a discussion with some former friends. He ended up with a night in jail and, since then, has found casual labour harder to find – even from Christians. Jason thinks of himself as something of a hero. To their great regret, he and Chloe did not manage to send any money to Paul.[102]

## 2:1–4: EXHORTATION TO UNITY AND TO THE IMITATION OF CHRIST: UNITY THROUGH HUMILITY

If then there is any encouragement in Christ, any consolation from love, any sharing in the Spirit, any compassion and sympathy,

[2] make my joy complete: be of the same mind, having the same love, being in full accord and of one mind.

[3] Do nothing from selfish ambition or conceit, but in humility regard others as better than yourselves.

[4] Let each of you look not to your own interests, but to the interests of others.

The second chapter of Philippians is especially known for the regal "Christ hymn," a poem praising the self-sacrifice of Jesus in obedience to God. While there is long-standing debate about the exact purpose of 2:6–11, it is important to set that passage within its wider context in the letter. In 2:1–4, Paul transitions from talking mostly about his imprisonment (chapter one) to the present life of the Philippian community. Paul encourages them to live cooperatively and to reject any sense of rivalry or individual superiority. Paul promotes humility and service, not self-promotion and boasting. There is a sense here that the Philippians have forgotten how they experienced Christ when they became believers. They have set aside that encouragement, generosity, and other-regard, and slipped into

---

[102]   Oakes, *Philippians*, 156.

self-centered ways of engaging one another (cf. Gal 6:1–10). A. K. Grieb explains it in this way:

Living the Christ-pattern has implications for life together in community. As the church participates in the death of Christ and anticipates a resurrection like his, they are not to waste their time exalting rival leaders, setting up competitive factions, or indulging in those gifts of the Spirit that build up the individual at the expense of the community. Instead, following the crucified Lord, they are to renounce such church-destroying behaviors and to focus instead on the needs of their less powerful members, on the gifts of the Spirit that are likely to be ignored (because they are less glamorous), and to the practices that strengthen community over the long haul – such as truth-telling, generosity, forgiveness, and constancy in prayer. Because they are ambassadors of God's new creation, they are also ministers of reconciliation, proclaiming the joyful 'nevertheless' of God's surprising mercy towards those with no claim upon God whatsoever.[103]

This chapter commences with appeal to five experiences for the Philippians: encouragement, consolation, Spirit-communion, compassion, and sympathy (2:1). Two questions are raised here for the reader. Why does Paul appeal to *these specific experiences*? And *who* initiated these experiences? Rhetorically, presumably Paul wanted the Philippians to recall these earlier formative experiences, and to let such memories inform and affect their current life together. The poetic manner in which Paul phrases the beginning of this discourse is laconic in Greek.[104] *Who is doing the encouraging? The loving? Compassion and sympathy?* It could be that Paul was referring to the overall intra-communal experience, where love was given and received by the other. But there is a stronger case to make for the idea that *God* is the unnamed actor. In that case, Paul was appealing to the powerful experiences of compassion and love *from God* that initially transformed the Philippians and led them to salvation. In that case, the gracious work of God would serve as an exemplary reminder to them: If you were so inspired and changed by the gracious love of God, ought you not to imitate that same other-regard in the life you share in your community?

---

[103] A. K. Grieb, "The One Who Called You: Vocation and Leadership in the Pauline Literature," *Interpretation* 59.2 (2005): 154–165, here 163.

[104] See F. Stagg, "The Mind in Christ Jesus: Philippians 1:27–2:18," *RevExp* 77.3 (1980): 337–347, here 339: Stagg calls this unit "rhythmic and lyrical" (339).

When we look more closely at the wording of 2:1, there is no reason to differentiate the meaning of the key words; Paul strings together related terms (encouragement, sympathy, compassion) to demonstrate the gracious nature of God who cared for them through Jesus and the Spirit. The most challenging phrase here is "sharing in the Spirit." Ralph Martin is probably correct that this refers to fellowship "which comes about through his indwelling presence in the church and the Christian's personal communion with him."[105]

Paul calls the Philippians to complete his joy by coming together as one mind and soul toward one purpose (2:2). This seems to reiterate what Paul stated earlier in 1:27, and parallels the wish-prayer in 1:9 for an increase in their love. In 2:2 Paul urges them to come together as one. Scholars often point out that the language and themes that are found here (and elsewhere in Philippians) overlap with the ideals of "friendship" in the Greco-Roman world.

### Closer Look: Friendship in the Greco-Roman World and Philippians

We (Bird and Gupta) believe it is going too far to argue that Philippians is a "letter of friendship" in any technical or formal way. However, it is rather clear that friendship themes and topoi do appear in this letter. Therefore, it is helpful for the modern reader to better understand the concept of friendship in the ancient world.

Aristotle discussed the topic of friendship in his *Nicomachean Ethics* and *Eudemian Ethics*.[106] He emphasized the importance of loyalty and reliability. He taught that true friends shared life together (using the Greek word *koinōnia*) and, thus, one could only have a precious few "friends," because such commitment was comprehensive and consuming. While two people could become friends for various reasons and benefits, the highest form of friendship was the bond formed by those who united toward formation in virtue.[107] Philosophers Cicero, Plutarch, and Lucian of Samosata all wrote treatises on friendship and extolled the social values of unity

---

[105]  Hawthorne and Martin, *Philippians*, 84.
[106]  I am indebted to G. Lyons and W. Malas for the following sketch of friendship in the Greco-Roman world; see "Paul and His Friends within the Greco-Roman Context"; cf. also J. T. Fitzgerald, "Paul and Friendship," in *Paul in the Greco-Roman World* (ed. J. P. Sampley; London: Bloomsbury, 2016), 2nd ed., 1.331–362.
[107]  See *Nich. Et.* 8.3.6.

(*homoios*), partnership (*koinōnia*), equality (*isotes*), virtue (*aretē*), frankness (*parrēsia*), and loyalty (*pistis*).[108]

One can quickly see the resonances with Paul's thematic emphases in Philippians. The language of partnership/commonness is obviously a leitmotif (Phil 1:5, 7; 2:1; 3:10; 4:14–15). Paul also urges the Philippians toward unity, as if they were "one soul" (*mia psychē*). This parallels Plutarch's statement that friends must function as "one soul" (*mia psychē*) shared by two bodies, showing "agreement in words, counsels, opinions, and feelings" (*Adul. amic.* 96E).[109] Furthermore, Paul urges the Philippians to join together in agreement on mission and virtue, calling them to concentrate on the shared values of pursuing what is right, noble, and excellent (4:8).[110]

Again, as a result of some of these connections between Philippians and Greco-Roman friendship language, some scholars have argued that Paul wrote this letter with a very specific and dominant "friendship" relationship in mind.[111] But Philippians as a whole tries to accomplish a number of rhetorical aims and it is hard to limit the letter to one narrow category or construct. Aspects of familiar friendship-related themes are found throughout Philippians, but one must remember that Paul shied away from using the Greek words for friend (*philos*) or friendship (*philia*) in any of his letters.[112] The reason remains unclear, but it serves as a caution against over-reading Paul's friendship language.[113]

---

[108] Cicero, "On Friendship"; Plutarch, "How to Tell a Flatterer from a Friend"; Lucian, "Toxaris, or Friendship." Cicero defines friendship as "nothing else than an accord in all things, human and divine, conjoined with mutual goodwill and affection" (*Amic.* 6.20); as cited in L. T. Johnson, "Making Connections: The Material Expression of Friendship in the New Testament" *Interpretation* 48 (1994): 158–171, here 160.

[109] Philo similarly writes that a true friend is so near to oneself that he is "equal to the soul" (*isos tē psychē sou*). This bears strikingly close resemblance to the way Paul describes Timothy as one who is *isopsychon* ("equal in soul"; Phil 2:20). For a discussion of this comparison, see A. Batten, *Friendship and Benefaction in James* (Atlanta, GA: SBL Press, 2017), 43.

[110] Cicero taught that friends shared a special union of "thought and inclination" (Cicero, *Planc.* 2.5); as cited in Hansen, *Philippians*, 9.

[111] See J. T. Fitzgerald, "*Philippians, Epistle to the*," ABD 5.313–326; S. K. Stowers, "Friends and Enemies in Politics of Heaven: Reading Theology in Philippians," in *Pauline Theology, vol. 1: Thessalonians, Philippians, Galatians, Philemon* (ed. J. M. Bassler; Minneapolis, MN: Fortress, 1991), 105–121.

[112] Bockmuehl, *The Epistle to the Philippians*, 18; cf. J. P. Heil, *Philippians: Let Us Rejoice in Being Conformed to Christ* (Atlanta, GA: SBL Press, 2010), 8, n 13. One explanation may be that he was far more concerned with familial language (brothers and sisters) than that of "friends"; see Alexander, "Hellenistic Letter-Forms."

[113] Note, for example, that other New Testament writers felt more comfortable with the language of "friend" (*philos*) (John 15:13–15; Acts 27:3; James 2:23; 4:4; 3 John 1.15).

Each of the key words in 2:2 is important to Philippians as a whole, and thus this verse (like 1:27) functions as another kind of master statement. First, Paul underscores what brings him joy. It is not the removal of his prison chains *per se*, but ultimately it is seeing his converts embody Christ-like humility, deference, and harmony. Second, twice in this verse he focuses on unity of *mind*. The verb *phroneō* refers to a comprehensive way the mind "sees" reality and shapes the life and will toward this vision.[114] This verb and related cognates are found throughout Philippians (1:7; 2:2–3, 5; 3:15, 19; 4:2, 7). Obviously, Paul makes much of *how one sees the world*, one's outlook or perspective. Paul was concerned that the Philippians were not properly understanding the purpose and value of his and their suffering, and ultimately what it meant to glory in Christ and not seek glory according to worldly standards. Thus, he calls them repeatedly in this letter to come together in outlook and life to remember their heavenly calling and citizenship so to "represent" that identity in their earthly lives.

Third, Paul highlights the centrality of love. To have *the same love* is to show care and compassion for the other (see 2:4). While this word for love (*agapē*) does not occur frequently in Philippians, not only was it promoted in chapter one (1:9), but the Christ Hymn itself demonstrates Christ's devotion ("love") to God and his self-sacrifice for mortals (2:6–11). Timothy and Epaphroditus are also presented as models of love; Paul flags up Timothy's selfless compassion (2:20) and Epaphroditus' deep affection for the Philippians (2:26). And it should not be ignored that Paul himself is a model for love; indeed, this letter of comfort and encouragement itself could be called a "letter of love." At the beginning of chapter four, he explicitly states how much he loves and misses them, and that they are his pride and joy, so to speak (4:1). Furthermore, one of his favored titles for the Philippians is "my beloved" (2:12; cf. 3:13; 4:8).

In 2:3–4, Paul sets up a contrast between a self-centered way of living and the way of generosity and love, a carnal perspective and a spiritual one. The NRSV offers the following translation "Do nothing from selfish ambition or conceit" (2:3a). It is difficult in English to convey the meaning of Paul's Greek wording in its context. He was not criticizing ambition or

---

[114] Fowl defines *phroneō* as a "pattern of thinking and acting"; see *Philippians*, 82; Flemming, *Philippians*, 99.

even pride. One has to get a sense for the competitive nature of acquiring honor in Paul's world to capture his sentiment here. As Joseph Hellerman explains,

Individuals in Philippi's highly stratified honor culture were deeply embedded in patronage networks that operated across the social classes. An ambitious local aristocrat would expect support form his friends, clients, and persons in his extended household. Preoccupation with one's own social advantage naturally led, therefore, to factions and rivalry.[115]

That is to say, honor was the most prized commodity and it was conceived of as a limited good, which bred fierce competition.[116] But in Philippians Paul speaks out strongly against any kind of honor conflict that brings down the other person. The first word Paul uses in 2:3a, *eritheia*, refers to a self-seeking spirit of competitiveness. The second term, *kenodoxia*, literally means "empty praise" or "vainglory," but carries this sense of seeking fame for fame's sake ("that kind of 'empty glory' that only the self-blessed can bestow on themselves"[117]).[118] Philo's use of *kenodoxia* I find very insightful. In a discourse on Joseph, Philo notes that the patriarch was a shepherd, which providentially prepared him well for a later life in Egyptian politics. Philo took Joseph's "coat of many colors" as an allegorical representation of the politician who must be versatile, that is, able to show many colors. But Philo warns of the demagogue who, when he stands on the tribunal platform, is sold off (like Josephus was!) to his obsession for recognition and status, virtually becoming a slave with countless masters. Just as Joseph was supposedly torn to shreds by wild beasts, so too the politician can be ravaged by *kenodoxia*, a blood-thirsty beast that masterfully consumes its prey.[119] Put simply, *kenodoxia* involves this elusive quest for fame that has no real substance and leaves the pursuer with nothing but more enemies.

---

[115] Hellerman, *Philippians*, 99; Oakes, *Philippians*, 181–182.

[116] See J. E. Lendon, "Roman Honor," in *The Oxford Handbook of Social Relations in the Roman World* (ed. M. Peachin; Oxford: Oxford University Press, 2011), 377–403.

[117] Fee, *Paul's Letter to the Philippians*, 187. Witherington comments: "it refers to someone who thinks too highly of himself but paradoxially must continue to self-promote as there is a sense of insecurity about his importance and honor" (*Philippians*, 128).

[118] This word is found in a vice list in 4 Macc 2:15 next to *philarchia*, which means "lust for power," and followed later by "arrogance" (*megalauchia*).

[119] Philo, *On Joseph*, 36.

Alternatively, Paul extols humility (*tapeinophrosynē*), a quality not trad-itionally appreciated by ancient Romans and Greeks.[120] While they valued things like moderation and even gentleness and clemency, Romans associ-ated "humility" with shabbiness and low status.[121] Jews, however, respected humility. The Lord favors the humble (Ps 18:27; 37:11), and calls his people to show grace to them (Prov 14:21) and they ought to aspire to identify with the lowly (Prov 16:19).

Paul was not calling the Philippians to force themselves into a humble station (by becoming homeless or poor *per se*); *tapeinophrosynē* here refers to a humble attitude (e.g., a "lowness mind-set"). What this involves Paul explains – "regard others as better than yourselves" (NRSV). The NRSV translation here does not quite capture what Paul is getting at. Paul was not really saying that one should treat others as *better*. There is a typical Greek word for "better" (*kreitton*) and he does not employ it here. Rather, he uses *hyperechō*, which means *superior*, as in, *higher in status*. Keeping in mind the honor-conscious and class-conscious nature of Roman social life, Paul was trying to undermine the cultural value system that focused on honor value and social rank. To be "humble" for Paul meant (1) that one did not dwell on their *own* high status, and (2) one did not judge or favor others based on *their* status. If *everyone* treated the other as superior in status (and vice versa), then this subverts the entire system.

So Paul explains furthermore, "Let each of you look not to your own interests, but to the interests of others" (2:4).[122] By and large, Roman culture was deeply self-interested. As Horace satirically stated, "Vanity [Glory] drags all, bound to her glittering chariot, the unknown no less than the well known."[123] Luke Timothy Johnson perfectly captures how

---

[120]   For an important historical study, see K. Wengst, *Humility: Solidarity of the Humiliated* (Philadelphia: Fortress, 1988).

[121]   Epictetus associated "humility" with being "slave-minded" (*Diatr.* 1.9.10; 3.24.56); as noted in L. T. Johnson, *Reading Romans* (Macon, GA: Helwys, 2001), 195.

[122]   Here it is worth observing that it is unclear whether or not the original Greek text included an "also" (*kai*) after the "but": "look not to your own interests, but [also] the interests of others." The inclusion of the "also" would emphasize that it is not inappropriate to attend to one's affairs, only that one is obligated to care for others as well. Still, whether the "also" is present or not, the meaning is essentially the same. A truly *Christian* mind-set places an essential and high value on regard and care for the other. On the text-critical matter, see Reumann, *Philippians*, 316–317.

[123]   Horace, *Sat.* 1.6.23–24 (Fairclough, LCL), as cited in Hill, *Servant of All*, 82.

concern for the other (2:4) is a central feature of humility: "Having humility means placing oneself appropriately within the life of the community. Indeed, it begins with a sense of otherness, a sensitivity to what is different from oneself."[124]

Bridging the Horizons: Humility and Self-Concern

When Paul explains to the Philippians that they should not look to their own interests or concerns (for the sake of humility and love), this could easily be misunderstood to mean that believers are not allowed to care for themselves or advocate for their own rights or needs. But that is a form of "doormat humility" that Paul would never endorse. Humility does not mean that you cannot attend to your own needs, and it certainly does not mean that you cannot ask for help. The main point that Paul is getting at is that believers, in imitation of Lord Jesus Christ, ought to be preoccupied with the needs and concerns of the other. Note the wording of the famous love command: "love your neighbor as yourself" (Rom 13:9). It is not "love your neighbor *instead* of yourself." The love command recognizes that instinctually we look out for ourselves – as we should. So, we ought to feel that same protective instinct for others. Paul makes explicit a communal ideal that each person (including self) is cared for equally (2 Cor 8:1–15). I find resonant the famous adage, "humility is not thinking less of yourself, its thinking of yourself less."[125]

## 2:5–11: EXHORTATION TO UNITY AND TO THE IMITATION OF CHRIST: THE MIND OF CHRIST

[5] Let the same mind be in you that was in Christ Jesus,

[6] who, though he was in the form of God, did not regard equality with God as something to be exploited,

[7] but emptied himself, taking the form of a slave, being born in human likeness. And being found in human form,

[8] he humbled himself and became obedient to the point of death – even death on a cross.

---

[124] Johnson, *Reading Romans*, 195.
[125] This quote is often misattributed to C. S. Lewis; its origins are not exactly clear.

[9] Therefore God also highly exalted him and gave him the name that is above every name,

[10] so that at the name of Jesus every knee should bend, in heaven and on earth and under the earth,

[11] and every tongue should confess that Jesus Christ is Lord, to the glory of God the Father.

There are few texts over which more academic ink has been spilled than this passage, which includes the so-called Christ Hymn (2:6–11).[126] It admittedly deserves close attention and careful study due to its attractive poetic features, and the way that it draws together several themes in Philippians through the narration of the story of the humility and obedience of Jesus.

An earlier generation was preoccupied with certain questions about this passage related to its nature and background. First, there is the issue of the origins and "pre-history" of the text. Was it a piece of early Christian tradition that predated Philippians (and, thus, was a pre-Pauline composition)? In the past, this seemed to be a firm conclusion,[127] but nowadays it is widely questioned and refuted.[128] Not only does it fit perfectly into the rhetorical flow of Philippians, but other than its poetic quality there is no reason to believe that Paul himself did not compose it. Furthermore, even if he borrowed it, we have no way of knowing if and to what degree he changed it. I resonate strongly, also, with Todd Still's comment about whether a pre-Pauline origin is relevant to its interpretation: "I fail to see the pressing need, be it theological, stylistic, or lexical, to identify the author(s) of this passage as one(s) other than Paul, especially given the

---

[126]  Key bibliographical items include R. P. Martin, *Carmen Christi: Philippians ii:5–11 in Recent Interpretation and in the Setting of Early Christian Worship* (SNTSMS; Cambridge: Cambridge University Press, 1967); idem, *A Hymn of Christ: Philippians 2:5–11 in Recent Research and Interpretation* (Downers Grove, IL: InterVarsity Press, 1997); R. P. Martin and B. J. Dodd, eds., *Where Christology Began: Essays on Philippians 2* (Louisville, KY: Westminster John Knox, 1998); J. T. Sanders, *New Testament Christological Hymns: Their Historical Religious Background* (SNTSMS; Cambridge: Cambridge University Press, 2004), 9–11, 58–74. G. P. Fewster offers a helpful discussion of cross-currents in recent scholarship on this passage; see Fewster, "The Philippians 'Christ Hymn': Trends in Critical Scholarship," *CBR* 13.2 (2015): 191–206.
[127]  See E. E. Ellis, *The Making of the New Testament Documents* (Leiden: Brill, 2002), 103.
[128]  For an up-to-date review of the academic discussion, see M. Gordley, *New Testament Christological Hymns* (Downers Grove, IL: InterVarsity Press, 2018), 79–110.

apostle's proven ability to write with poetic profundity on any number of matters relative to the gospel."[129]

More important for a study of Philippians is the discussion of this passage's conceptual background and influences. Famously, Ernst Käsemann argued that the Christ Hymn evokes a Greek Gnostic redeemer myth that offered an analogy to the Christ event.[130] But Käsemann's view has been thoroughly rejected today because the character of this Gnostic myth has proven anachronistic, and the proposed connections tenuous. Morna Hooker (and others) have suggested that the Christ Hymn compares Jesus Christ to Adam,[131] where the first Adam, in the image of God, rebelled and disobeyed God, but the second Adam (Christ) humbled himself and became fully obedient. Looking for Adamic resonances holds some merit, but there seem to be too few concrete (especially linguistic) links to Old Testament and early Jewish Adam texts to make an open-and-shut case. Others have proposed that the Hymn relates to Jewish wisdom traditions, specifically personified Wisdom (see Prov 8; Wis 6–9; Sir 1, 24), that benevolent agent of God who is called upon to visit and bless the earth (Wis 9:9–10). Or perhaps the Isaianic Suffering Servant passages may have influenced the Christ Hymn. More recently, we have seen imperial interpretations of the Christ Hymn comparing the status and nature of Jesus Christ to Roman emperors. In this frame, the Christ Hymn establishes Christ as a lord/emperor like Caesar (*isa theos* [Phil 2:6], equal in status to the divine, as emperors were thought to be), but a different kind of ruler, not lording it over others with his power, but serving and aiding them in humility and generosity.[132] All of these proposed allusions/associations have some merit and make for interesting discussions and debates, but in reality what the variety of these ostensible resonances tell us is that the Christ Hymn has an open quality that makes it relatable not only to various elements of Jewish tradition, but also to Greco-Roman cultures as well. It cannot be tethered exclusively to any one background or

---

[129] T. D. Still, *Philippians* (SHBC; Macon, GA: Smyth & Helwys, 2011), 66.

[130] E. Käsemann, "A Critical Analysis of Philippians 2:5-11." *JTC* 5 (1968): 45–88.

[131] Morna Hooker, "Philippians 2:6-11," in *Jesus und Paulus: Festschrift für W. G. Kümmel* (eds. E. E. Ellis and E. Grässer; Göttingen: Vandenhoeck & Ruprecht, 1975), 151–164.

[132] See E. M. Heen, "Phil 2:6-11 and Resistance to Local Timocratic Rule: Isa Theō and the Cult of the Emperor in the East," in *Paul and the Roman Imperial Order* (ed. R. A. Horsley; London: Continuum, 2004), 125–154.

framework, but has become one of the most treasured parts of Scripture for its ability to inspire the imagination and identify with multiple biblical and non-biblical legends, themes, and types.

When it comes to analyzing the *form* of the Christ Hymn, we enter another thicket of confusion and contention. Should 2:6–11 be labeled a *hymn*, a *poem*, or something else (e.g., stylistic prose)? Of course, this depends on how we define what a hymn or poem is, and in what context. Liturgical and poetical qualities are evident, but I believe Matthew Gordley is correct to simply describe this passage as an encomium.[133] He observes that Paul's discourse here shares with traditional Greco-Roman and early Jewish encomia the emphasis on a figure's origins, praiseworthy deeds, divine favor, and special honors (cf. Sir 44–50). We might go one step further and refer to the Philippian Hymn as something like a "mythic encomium" (or "parabolic encomium"). Adding the word "mythic" is not meant to imply it is not true – certainly Paul believed it had rhetoric power *because* of Christ's real supremacy. Rather, by "mythic" I mean that Paul retells the Christ story in a myth-like or legendary manner for vividness and literary effect. It is as if Paul generated a special parable to poetically capture the tale of Christ. Analogously, Revelation 12 narrates the story of Mary and Jesus in an apocalyptic frame:

A great portent appeared in heaven: a woman clothed with the sun, with the moon under her feet, and on her head a crown of twelve stars.[2] She was pregnant and was crying out in birth pangs, in the agony of giving birth.[3] Then another portent appeared in heaven: a great red dragon, with seven heads and ten horns, and seven diadems on his heads.[4] His tail swept down a third of the stars of heaven and threw them to the earth. Then the dragon stood before the woman who was about to bear a child, so that he might devour her child as soon as it was born.[5] And she gave birth to a son, a male child, who is to rule all the nations with a rod of iron. But her child was snatched away and taken to God and to his throne;[6] and the woman fled into the wilderness, where she has a place prepared by God, so that there she can be nourished for one thousand two hundred sixty days. (Rev 12:1–6)

Some of what is said here reflects the historical portrait given in the Gospels: a pregnant woman gives birth, Satan is threatened, Jesus is raised, and so on. But the story is infused with this cosmic symbolism. In Phil

---

[133]   Gordley, *New Testament Christological Hymns*, 99; see also A. Y. Collins, "Psalms, Hymns, and the Origins of Christology" *BibInt* 11.3 (2003): 361–372.

2:6–11, Paul utilizes an overall narrative framework of extreme abnegation and subsquent exaltation to depict a Christ-like *phronesis* and obedience that the Philippians should praise and emulate.

Having established in 2:1–4 the idea that the Philippians ought to respond with communal deference and love to the care given to them by Christ and the Spirit, Paul stops here to address more directly the power of a transformed *phronesis*. English translations might mislead readers regarding the force and scope of this statement from Paul. The NRSV renders the first part of this as "Let the same mind be in you." But taking into consideration the use of the imperative, as well as the plural verb and object of the preposition, it conveyed something more like: "Think this way together for your corporate benefit." That is, *all of you – shape the way you think for the benefit of your community*. Perhaps more than any other Pauline letter (other than 2 Corinthians), Philippians repeatedly points to the significance of a *transformed epistemology and imagination* in order to properly detect the ways of God in the world. And here, in 2:5, Paul links that to Jesus Christ. But scholars have long disagreed about *how* to interpret the second portion of this verse. The RSV and NRSV helpfully lay out the options:

Have this mind among yourselves, which is yours in Christ Jesus. (RSV)

Let the same mind be in you, that was in Christ Jesus. (NRSV)

The reason why there is translational and interpretive disagreement about 2:5b is due to the absence of a verb in the relative clause. That is, a rough literal translation of the Greek text would read: "Think this among yourselves *which also in Christ Jesus*." Here is the question – should it be understood as *which also belongs to you because you are in Jesus Christ*"? Or, *which was also found in Christ Jesus?* The first option (RSV) reads the relative clause as clarifying how or why they can have this mind(-set); that is, it is because of Christ, and it is because they are a community of Christ. The second approach (NRSV) focuses more on emulation: *imitate the mind-set of Christ*. From a syntactical standpoint, either reading is feasible, but given what follows I find the second approach (NRSV; emulation) more convincing.[134] John Chrysostom associates this verse (and the whole

---

[134] M. J. Gorman proposes a third option, which focuses on participation in Christ and the transformation of the community: "Cultivate this mind-set – this way of thinking,

of 2:5–11) with 2 Cor 8:9: "For you know the generous act of our Lord Jesus Christ, that though he was rich, yet for your sake he became poor so that by his poverty you might become rich."[135] Here Paul was using the story of Christ as a model to convince the Corinthians to show generosity toward the recipients of his relief efforts. So, similarly, in Philippians it makes good sense that Jesus Christ serves as a master story of intrepid obedience toward God, which leads to humility and self-sacrifice, ultimately ending in exaltation.

### Closer Look: Ethical Model or Cosmic Doxology?

There is a long-standing debate in scholarship regarding whether the Philippian "Christ Hymn" (2:6–11) is meant to be interpreted primarily as an ethical model for the Philippians to imitate, or if it is meant to tell the story of the incarnation and exaltation of Christ, not as a person to emulate, but so that they may learn to live properly under his Lordship. One can see how this debate is related to the translation issues of the introductory statement in 2:5. Is Paul framing the Hymn as the example of a proper mind-set (NRSV), or is it demonstrating how Christ has uniquely established a new state of affairs into which they must live (RSV)?

E. Käsemann was emphatic that Paul did not treat Jesus Christ as someone that mortals can emulate – his person and work are inimitable.[136] R. P. Martin points out further that Paul does not promise exaltation for the Philippians, so this would leave the latter half of the Hymn irrelevant. The Hymn ends with supreme worship of Christ.[137]

On the other hand, the vast majority of scholars today see Paul as calling the Philippians to adopt the humble mind-set of Christ, even if in a general way. I (Gupta) cannot help but come to this conclusion when seeing the focus on *phroneō* ("I think") in 2:5, and then the appeal to the *consideration* (*hēgeomai*) of Christ in 2:6.[138]

---

acting, and feeling – in your community, which is in fact a community in the Messiah Jesus."; see *Participating in Christ: Explorations in Paul's Theology and Spirituality* (Grand Rapids, MI: Baker, 2019).

[135] Chrysostom, *Hom. Phil.* 6 on Philippians. See www.newadvent.org/fathers/230206.htm.

[136] See E. Käsemann, "Kritische Analyse von Phil. 2,5–11," *ZThK* 47 (1950): 313–360; English translation by A. Carse, "A Critical Analysis of Phil. 2.5–11," in *God and Christ: Existence and Providence* (ed. R. W. Funk; New York: Harper & Row, 1968), 45–88.

[137] Martin, *Carmen Christi*, 63–96.

[138] See Fowl, *Philippians*, 89–90.

Scholars often refer to the "V-shaped" trajectory of the Christ narrative, from high glory, down to humble earthly existence, down lower even to death on a cross – and then super-exaltation to the highest place where he receives knee-bent worship and confession from all kinds of creatures, wherever they are.[139] But Paul does not simply recount these "movements." He underscores Christ's thought-process, in particular his selflessness, his orientation toward obedience to God, and his humility. Verse six begins with the subject (Jesus Christ) in a privileged position – namely equal with God (*isa theō*).[140] He is also described as being in the "form of God" (*en morphē theou*). This phrasing has been the subject of intense scrutiny and fierce debate for hundreds of years. While it was once assumed to refer to the divine nature of Christ, it has become more widely recognized that the word *morphē* does not really carry the meaning of (internal) "nature." Rather, scholars like Markus Bockmuehl are correct when they describe it in reference to the way something appears from an external perspective.[141] Stephen Fowl argues that we ought to relate the language of form here to the Old Testament notion of glory: "In the LXX the visible form of God is often described as in terms of God's [*doxa*], God's glory and splendor, by which the majesty of God is made manifest to humanity."[142] And we can go one step further and say that the more glorious the form of a being, the more honor and respect it deserved. Put simply, Paul describes the honoree of this encomium as having nothing less than divine glory.

Again, when it comes to the language of *morphē*, it has long been assumed or argued that here this word means "nature" or "character."[143] But the actual usage of *morphē* in the Greek Bible does not seem to bear this out. For example, LXX Isa 44:13 uses *morphē* in reference to an idol made in the *form* of a human. Fourth Maccabees talks about how children look *in form* like their parents (15:4). Joseph Hellerman is no doubt correct

[139]  See Reumann, *Philippians*, 334; also Hooker, "Philippians," 502–503.
[140]  Some scholars (e.g., E. Heen) have tried to draw out (anti-)imperial resonances with this language, as sometimes emperors were praised as being equal to the divine; see Heen, "Phil. 2:6–11 and Resistance to Local Timocratic Rule."
[141]  Bockmuehl, *The Epistle to the Philippians*, 127–128.
[142]  S. Fowl, "Christology and Ethics in Philippians 2:5–11," in *Where Christology Began* (eds. R. P. Martin and B. J. Dodd; Louisville, KY: Westminster John Knox, 1998), 140–153, here 142.
[143]  Fee defines *morphē* as "*that which truly characterizes a given reality*"; *Paul's Letter to the Philippians*, 204; hence "nature"; cf. similarly, Witherington, *Philippians*, 140.

when he concludes that in general, and specifically in Philippians 2:6, this word refers "to visible appearance, with no indication, one way or another, of any corresponding inward quality."[144] Hellerman reads the "form" language in the Christ Hymn in relation to honor and status, rather than nature and inner character. What Phil 2:6 communicates is that, at the beginning of this story, the hero enjoys the highest glory and status of heaven.

While Christ experienced this exalted glorious status, he did not *regard* (*hēgeomai*) it as *harpagmos*. It is not an exaggeration to say this word presents one of the most perplexing interpretive challenges in the New Testament.[145] The basic meaning of *harpagmos* is "robbery" or "loot." The confusion lies with the fact that this exalted figure did not treat his equal-to-God status as *robbery*. *How could he rob (or loot) something he already had?* The most sensible conclusion is that, if "loot" is something someone tends to protect tightly, here it means that Christ was not unwilling to relinquish this glory for the right reason.[146] Ben Witherington articulates well how this portion of the Christ Hymn would have fit within Paul's overall rhetorical aims of Philippians:

A deity has certain privileges, powers, and prerogatives and a status, a standing, a rank above all others. In status-conscious Philippi, Paul is trying to stress that Christ stripped himself of his divine privileges and status and took on the responsibilities, limitations, and status of a human being.[147]

So Christ did not treat this status as a possession to protect at all costs. Again, v. 6 establishes the initial state of exaltation before the movement downward. And it bears repeating that Paul underscores Christ's *attitude* (*hēgeomai*). This is an important verb for Paul in Philippians – it is found only eleven times in the Pauline corpus, six times in Philippians alone.

---

[144] J. Hellerman, "Μορφῇ θεοῦ as a Signifier of Social Status in Philippians 2:6," *JETS* 52 (2009): 779–797, here 784; Hellerman, *Philippians*, 110; see too Bockmuehl, *The Epistle to the Philippians*, 127–129.

[145] See R. W. Hoover, "The Harpagmos Enigma: A Philological Solution," *HTR* 64 (1971): 95–119.

[146] See B. Fisk, "The Odyssey of Christ: A Novel Context for Philippians 2:6–11," in *Exploring Kenotic Christology* (ed. C. S. Evans; Oxford: Oxford University Press, 2006), 45–73, esp. 64–65.

[147] Witherington, *Philippians*, 143; cf. D. P. Moessner, "Turning Status 'Upside Down' in Philippi: Christ Jesus' 'Emptying Himself' as Forfeiting Any Acknowledgement of His 'Equality with God,'" *HBT* 31 (2009): 123–143.

Thus, Paul makes much of what we might call a Christoform epistemology, *conformity to the way Christ thinks.* Just as Paul had counseled the Philippians in 2:3 to *consider* (*hēgeomai*) others as higher in status, so in 2:6 he puts forth the model mind-set of Christ who did not *consider* (*hēgeomai*) his high status as something to hoard.

In the next verse (2:7), we immediately encounter a strong contrast – he is worthy of highest honor, *yet* he "emptied himself." The verb here (*kenoō*) is the focal point for so-called kenotic Christology conversations,[148] but Pauline interpreters ought to be careful to determine Paul's precise meaning here based on the context. The verb *kenoō* means "to become empty," like when drink is poured out of a cup (see LXX Jer 15:9; 1 Cor 1:17). *But what is the "content" that is emptied?* Certainly Paul had no specific ontological element in mind (e.g., "divinity"). It is crucial that the reader connects *kenoō* here back to 2:3 where Paul had warned the Philippians not to be driven by **kenodoxia**, "empty-glory." This is a rather transparent wordplay in Greek – too many people seek a fame that is empty or hollow, but Christ, full of glory, chose to make himself "nothing," so to speak. His becoming nothing is demonstrated in his self-abnegation, "taking the form of a slave." Now, in true fact, Paul knew that Jesus of Nazareth never *actually* served as a slave (*doulos*). Rather, it appears that Paul was trying to communicate here that the great distance that Christ moved from high glory to lowly mortal existence is like a king becoming a slave.[149] This is a word-picture representing Christ's deep humility and absolute concern for obedience to God and love of others. In Paul's language of slavery here, there is also a sense of giving up or giving over of his life to save others. As C. F. D. Moule explains, "A slave, as property sold to another, scarcely belonged to himself . . . [and] Jesus so completely

---

[148] See, for example, Evans, *Exploring Kenotic Christology*, esp. chs. 1–4 (pp. 1–111).

[149] It is worthwhile also to pick up Martin Hengel's observation that Paul may have explicitly mentioned the slave-like nature of Christ's incarnation because crucifixion was generally known to be a punishment commonly inflicted on troublemaking slaves: "Anyone who was present at the worship of the churches founded by Paul in the course of his mission, in which this hymn was sung, and indeed any reader of Philippians in ancient times, would inevitably have seen a direct connection between the 'emptied himself, taking the form of a slave' . . . and . . . 'he humbled himself and was obedient to death, even the death of a cross'. Death on the cross was a penalty for slaves, as everyone knew: as such it symbolized extreme humiliation, shame and torture"; *Crucifixion in the Ancient World and the Folly of the Message of the Cross* (Philadelphia: Fortress, 1977), 62. See more later on 2:8 for more on crucifixion.

stripped himself of all rights and securities as to be comparable to a slave."[150]

Also, here it is stated that he was born "in human likeness" (*en homoiōmati anthrōpōn*). For all intents and purposes, it appears that the word "likeness" (*homoiōma*) is a synonym for the word "form" (*morphē*) used in 2:6. Certainly the reader should not conclude that "likeness" carries any sense of false appearance, as if Christ wasn't *really* human. Rather, Paul was focusing on the diminished appearance and status of Christ, descending from heavenly glory to mundane earthly appearance. Karl Barth has done well to draw out the way Paul used "likeness" language to demonstrate how appearances can be deceiving. While many with a mundane perspective would have been repulsed by Christ's meek human form, those with eyes to see and ears to hear, so to speak, could perceive of his unique majesty.

He [Christ] puts himself in a position where only he himself knows himself in the way that the Father knows him. In the unknowability into which he enters, it is now certainly the Father's part to reveal him. But the step that brings him into that unrecognizable condition, into the *incognito*, is grounded entirely in himself alone . . . [H]e exists in such a way that any direct, immediate way of regarding him – e.g., to the historical and psychological approach – he does not present the picture of his proper, original, divine Being, but solely the picture of a human being.[151]

The last clause of this verse (2:7d: "And being found in human form") essentially repeats what has already been said, but with yet again another

---

[150] C. F. D. Moule, "Further Reflections on Philippians 2:5–11," in *Apostolic History and the Gospel* (eds. W. W. Gasque and R. P. Martin; Exeter: Paternoster, 1970), 265–276, here 268. I find that Cyril of Alexandria presents a cogent interpretation of the language of "form" of "emptying" in the Christ Hymn: "[I]t is not that one has ascended to the fullness from a state of emptiness, but rather that he has lowered himself from divine exaltation and ineffable glory. It is not that he was a lowly man who has been glorified and exalted, but rather that in his freedom he assumed the form of a slave. It is not that, being a slave, he leaped up into the glory of freedom: the one who was in the form of the Father, and his equal, came to be in human likeness, rather than being a man who has been enriched by participation in the likeness of God"; see *On the Creed*, 15, as cited in M. Edwards, ed., *We Believe in the Crucified and Risen Lord* (ACD 3; Downers Grove, IL: InterVarsity Press, 2009), 116.

[151] Barth, *Philippians*, 63; similarly H. C. G. Moule: "The Lord was (a) man not only in nature but in look, patent to all; and He was (b) more than met the eye: the true and manifest Manhood was the veil of Godhead"; see H. C. G. Moule, *The Epistle to the Philippians* (Cambridge: Cambridge University Press, 1893), 40.

word (*schēma*) for "form." It functions as a transition from v. 7 to v. 8, but it is worth observing Paul's use of the word "found" – it is not *just* that Christ came into the likeness of mortal humanity, but also that this is how he was recognized and treated by other humans. It is rather reminiscent of what would be written later in the Gospel of John: "He came to his own people [whom he created], but [even] his own [fellow Jews] did not accept him" (John 1:11). Both in John and Philippians, the authors tease out a sense of irony. Here he is, a glorious being worthy of high praise, and in his noble condescension he is rejected and treated far lower than his worth.

As we consider further the downward movement of Christ in this passage, v. 8 takes him to the absolute nadir. But Paul is clear that Christ was not an unwitting victim of circumstance, or an unwilling victim of Rome. Rather, he humbled *himself*; the Greek word *tapeinoō* was often used at the time in the sense of "humility" (which we consider a virtue today), but it more straightforwardly pointed to lowering in a vertical sense.[152] Paul chose this word to capture the humble self-lowering of Christ. In the Roman world, lowliness was not respected or prized, as it implied degradation; and, truth be told, people did not tend to humble *themselves*, but humbled *others*. Early Jews had an understanding that mortals ought to humble themselves before God (Sir 3:18; LXX Dan 10:12; cf. 1 Pet 5:6; Jas 4:10), but never did they refer to God *humbling himself*. And yet here Paul refers to glorious Christ's intentional self-lowering.

Along the way in chapter two of Philippians, we have been noting wordplay resonances between the Christ Hymn (2:6–11) and the beginning of this chapter (esp. 2:1–4). And again here we have the connection between the self-lowering/humility of Christ (*tapeinoō*) and Paul's call for humility/lowness mind-set (*tapeinophrosynē*) in 2:3. Christ is the model for true obedience to God, true fellowship and partnership with others, and genuine humility and inclusion over and against vanity, self-centeredness, and competition. Christ here is presented as a living example of the similar counsel that Paul gives to the Romans: "Live in harmony with one another; do not be haughty, but associate with the lowly; do not claim to be wiser than you are" (Rom 12:16).

---

[152] For example, John the Baptist prophesied the filling of valleys and leveling (*tapeinoō*) of mountains at the Eschaton (Luke 3:5).

Next, Paul describes Christ's attitude and behavior (in this self-emptied, servile, and humble stature) as *obedient* (*hypokoos*) – but, obedient to *whom?* Presumably God the Father. God is described as Father in 1:2 and 4:20, and also in the Christ Hymn itself (2:11). While Jesus is not explicitly called God's Son in Philippians, the earliest Christian readers would easily have inferred this (cf. 1 Thess 1:9–10; Gal 4:4). And the language Paul chose here seems to bear this out. Prov 4:3 (LXX) states, "I became a son and I am obedient (*hypokoos*) to my father." While it is difficult to prove any direct link, I cannot help but make a connection between Phil 2:8 and the Jesus tradition recounting Christ's humble obedience to God in prayer in the Garden of Gethsemane. According to Mark's Gospel, in his hour of desperation, Jesus throws himself on the ground and prays, "Abba, Father, for you all things are possible; remove this cup from me; yet, not what I want, but what you want" (14:35–36). Just as Mark narrates, Jesus ultimately humbles himself and conforms to the will of the Father in deferential obedience. He accepts the cup of suffering and death, even death on a cross.

Up to this point, the Christ Hymn has carried a generic quality, timeless and ethereal. But at the end of 2:8 it crashes into vivid historical reality with the word "cross" (*stauros*). It is no longer "timeless," but fixed into the ancient Roman world, and a punishment and shame-mechanism that indelibly marked the story of Jesus and his followers. It is well-documented, inside and outside of the New Testament, that Rome punished criminals and troublemakers with crucifixion to demonstrate the ultimate penalty for deviance and sedition. We can estimate that over 30,000 people were crucified in the Roman era.[153] No type of person was absolutely exempt (e.g., women, soldiers, citizens), but from the extant evidence we learn that the overwhelming majority of crucified persons were slaves. J. G. Cook explains that the most common crimes or reasons associated with crucifixion were brigandage, political sedition, participation in slave revolts, disobedience of slaves, insubordinate behavior of soldiers (especially treason), and piracy.[154] It is also crucial to recognize

---

[153]   Much of the information about crucifixion that follows is indebted to the research of J. G. Cook, "Roman Crucifixion: From the Second Punic War to Constantine," *ZNW* 104 (2013): 1–32.

[154]   Cook, "Roman Crucifixion," 32.

that Rome engineered crucifixion to function, not so much as a punishment of pain (although certainly it was agonizing), but as a public display of shame. Crosses were erected on thoroughfares as spectacles.[155] When Spartacus' army was crucified, the 6,000 condemned were positioned on crosses along the way from Capua to Rome – a length of 200 kilometers. As another example of the way crucifixion was treated as a spectacle, we can refer to Nero's wanton execution of Christians as recounted by Tacitus:

> And as they perished, mockeries were added, so that, covered in the hides of wild beasts, they expired from mutilation by dogs or, fixed to crosses and made flammable, on the dwindling of daylight they were burned for use as nocturnal illumination. (Tacitus, *Ann.* 15.44.4)[156]

It is necessary to keep this historical context of crucifixion in mind as we read Paul's ode to Christ in Philippians 2:6–11. The mind-set and choice of humility and obedience of Christ (as narrated in 2:6–8) leads him to the cross – what Cicero called the "tree of shame" (*Rab. perd.* 4.13). One detects in the Greek text at the end of 2:8 a sense of horror or shock: *thanatou de staurou – not just death, but (gulp!) death on a cross!* When one looks at the record of how crucifixion is mentioned in the literary sources, it is almost always presented this way:

(a) [Y] was crucified
    OR
(b) [X] crucified [Y]

But here in Philippians Paul presents Christ as *willingly* going to his death on the cross *as a choice*, an act of obedience. There is absolutely nothing of this kind in the historical accounts of crucifixion during or prior to the time of Jesus. And certainly Paul serves as one of the first people to write about a crucified person in such a way as to parody the crucifixion by associating it with the person's virtue, nobility, and exaltation.[157]

---

[155] So Quintilian famously commented that "Whenever we crucify the guilty, the most crowded roads are chosen, where the most people can see and be moved by this fear. For penalties relate not so much to retribution as to their exemplary effect" (*Decl.* 274); as cited in Hengel, *Crucifixion*, 50 n. 14.

[156] Cook, "Roman Crucifixion," 17.

[157] See the important article, J. R. Marcus, "Crucifixion as Parodic Exaltation," *JBL* 125.1 (2006): 73–87. This came to be an important way for Christians to "redeem" the shame of crucifixion; note the comment of Bishop Methodius (CE 270–311): "For the Word

The "V"-shaped story that Paul tells in the Christ Hymn turns from the low point to divine promotion. If one were to trace the trajectory of this story following conventional Roman values, the cross would be the end of the tale – there is no recovery from that, no sign of hope, no vindication or restitution. But for Paul, not only is there an "afterlife" for Jesus beyond death by crucifixion, but *supreme* exaltation. And this not in spite of the cross, but precisely because Jesus was fully obedient to God and dared to believe this act of respect for God would be worth the immediate consequences.

Paul chose his words very carefully here. In response to Jesus' obedience, God lifted him up – the nature of the verb *hyperupsoō* carries the sense of not just an exaltation, but a *super-exaltation*; not merely a raising up, but a lifting up to a high position.[158] Paul may have intended here an ironic twist to the "lifting up" that happens with crucifixion. Rome "lifted" Jesus up on a cross as a public-shaming mechanism to lower or extinguish his dignity. But, from God's perspective, his crucifixion as an act of obedience leads to an even *higher* raising up. While the Gospel of John obviously postdates Philippians, it may be interesting to note here how John plays off of the related verb *hypsoō* when Jesus says: "when I am lifted up (*hypsoō*) from the earth, I will draw all people to myself" (cf. John 8:28). But the main point that Paul makes here is that the one God puts his stamp of approval on Jesus and honors him with a supreme position and status. He overrules, as it were, Rome's (and, symbolically, the world's) damnation of Jesus.

Paul professes also that God bestowed on him a supreme name. Before we review options for what that name is, it behooves us to pause and examine Paul's word for "gave" here (*charizō*); it is related to the Greek word for grace (*charis*). Paul probably means here that God was pleased with Jesus and poured out favor on him by exalting him highly and

---

suffered, being in the flesh affixed to the cross, that he might bring humankind, who had been deceived by error, to it [sic?] supreme and god-like majesty, restoring to it that divine life from which it had been alienated"; *On the Cross and Passion of Christ*, ANF 6:400; as cited in Edwards, *We Believe in the Crucified and Risen Lord*, 120; cf. also D. W. Chapman, *Ancient Jewish and Christian Perceptions of Crucifixion* (Grand Rapids, MI: Baker, 2010), 252–253.

[158]  While the verb *hypsoō* is rather common in the NT, *hyperupsoō* is only found in Phil 2:9. In the LXX and early Jewish liturgical works, this verb (*hyperupsoō*) tends to be used for worship of a supreme or exalted deity (LXX Ps. 96.9; *Odes* 8.52–88; *Prayer of Azariah* 1.29–66).

bestowing on him this special name. This same verb Paul used in 1:29 in reference to God graciously bestowing on the Philippians not only the privilege of believing in Christ, but also suffering in identification with him – not unlike the privilege a soldier might have of serving a king and having the honor of suffering in battle as a representative of that leader.

Now, the most exercising exegetical question presented by this verse pertains to the "name" that is given by God. In 2:9, Paul does not explicitly state what this "name" is. Reumann presents several viable options: (a) Jesus, (b) Christ, (c) Son, (d) God, (e) Lord.[159] The problem with the first two of these (Jesus or Christ/Messiah) is that Jesus already had these names *before* his exaltation. As for (c), this also appears to be something one could have said about the earthly Jesus; and it is not really a uniquely supreme title. When it comes to (d), Paul does not attribute this title to Jesus in a direct way elsewhere in his letters.[160] Option (e), "Lord," makes the most sense for several reasons. First and foremost, the word Lord (*kyrios*) is explicated as the focal point of confession in 2:11 ("every tongue should confess that Jesus Christ is Lord (*kyrios*)"). Second, there are obvious intertextual links between the Christ Hymn (esp. Phil 2:9–11) and Isa 45:20–25 (see later). While this text repeatedly refers to singular worship of (the one and only) God (LXX: *theos*), we also find interspersed throughout this section and surrounding passages affirmation that "I am the LORD, and there is no other god besides me" (Isa 45:5; cf. "I am the Lord God" Isa 43:15, 3, 5, 6). While it appears that Paul identifies Jesus *with* the one Lord God (YHWH, the God of Israel), he does not presume they are exactly the same – this much is obvious from the Christ Hymn itself (e.g., 2:6, 8, 9). Somehow, Jesus shares in the "oneness" of God, claiming the supreme title "Lord" (see 1 Cor 8:6).[161] This is why the "name" that Paul refers to here is probably "lord" (*kyrios*), but the "name" could

---

[159] It is very important to recognize that the Greek word for "name" (*onoma*) is not categorically limited to personal names, and can also refer to titles (see, e.g., Rev 19:16).

[160] On the relevance of Rom 9:5, see J. D. G. Dunn, *Romans* (WBC; Dallas, TX: Word, 1988), 2.528–535.

[161] For recent discussions of Paul's Christology, see L. W. Hurtado, *Lord Jesus Christ: Devotion to Jesus in Earliest Christianity* (Grand Rapids, MI: Eerdmans, 2003); C. Tilling, *Paul's Divine Christology* (Grand Rapids, MI: Eerdmans, 2015); D. B. Capes, *The Divine Christ: Paul, the Lord Jesus, and the Scriptures of Israel* (Grand Rapids, MI: Baker, 2018).

be the full phrase *Lord Jesus Christ*, reflecting back on the confessional phrase of Phil 2:11.[162]

Paul makes it clear that this new "name" is a title fitting with a supreme position, such that "every knee should bend, in heaven and on earth and under the earth, and every tongue should confess that Jesus Christ is Lord" (2:10–11a). The act of people kneeling represents acknowledgment that someone else is superior in authority and status (cf. Matt 15:25; 3 Macc 2:1). It is a symbolic gesture of humility and deference. For example, in Matthew's Gospel, the Magi come and bow down before the child messiah (Matt 2:11). Ironically, this genuflectic act is bookended near the end of the gospel by the soldiers who put a crown of thorns on Jesus' head and kneel down before him, confessing, "Hail, King of the Jews" (27:29). Paul paints a picture of every single creature humbled before the crucified and exalted Lord Jesus Christ – even the most powerful cosmic beings wherever in the stratosphere or nether-regions they might be found.

Paul also writes that every tongue will confess the preeminent lordship of Jesus (Phil 2:11a). Confession involves a public proclamation of a fundamental truth. It often pronounces a particular value. When it involves "confessing" God, it includes a sense of respect, praise, and thanksgiving (Matt 1:25; Rom 15:9). And this will all serve to bring praise and glory to God (Phil 2:11b). Why does Paul close out the Christ Hymn with this mention of God (the Father)? Probably for two reasons. First, it reinforces a key theme of the Hymn, namely that Christ lives and serves, not to glorify himself *per se*, but to respect and obey his Father (2:8). Second, associating Jesus with the cross would naturally have led to feelings of shame. Paul seeks to reframe the crucifixion of Jesus, not as a public mark of degradation, but the context for Christ's passionate obedience to God, whatever the cost. Ultimately, then, the resurrection and lordship-nomination of Jesus serves as God's stamp of approval of Jesus' deference to God. This is Paul's way of expressing what is later written in the Gospels – the Father is well-pleased with his Son (Matt 3:17). His self-sacrifice honors God, it does not deny or shame him.

---

[162]  The Greek text does not include the word "is" in the confession in 2:11 (Jesus Christ "is" Lord); English translations add this because it is assumed in Greek, or perhaps it is better to think of the confession as "Lord Jesus Christ" (*kyrios Iesous Christos*).

2:12–18: EXHORTATION TO UNITY AND TO THE IMITATION OF
CHRIST: HOW SALVATION IS WORKED OUT

<sup>12</sup> Therefore, my beloved, just as you have always obeyed me, not only in my presence, but much more now in my absence, work out your own salvation with fear and trembling;

<sup>13</sup> for it is God who is at work in you, enabling you both to will and to work for his good pleasure.

<sup>14</sup> Do all things without murmuring and arguing,

<sup>15</sup> so that you may be blameless and innocent, children of God without blemish in the midst of a crooked and perverse generation, in which you shine like stars in the world.

<sup>16</sup> It is by your holding fast to the word of life that I can boast on the day of Christ that I did not run in vain or labor in vain.

<sup>17</sup> But even if I am being poured out as a libation over the sacrifice and the offering of your faith, I am glad and rejoice with all of you –

<sup>18</sup> and in the same way you also must be glad and rejoice with me.

This passage is tied closely to both the Christ Hymn (2:5–11) and the section before it (1:27–2:4). Beginning in 1:27, Paul called the Philippian believers to live a life that modeled good citizenship of the kingdom of God in Messiah Jesus. Under the threat of persecution and opprobrium, Paul still held them responsible for coming together as a whole body-politic, like-minded in honor and virtue, each one looking out for the other (2:3–4). The Christ Hymn adds to that directive both the *model* and *ministry* of Jesus Christ. He is their example of one who had the right mind-set: regardless of his grand status, he humbled himself and gave himself up for others in obedience to God the Father (*model*). Having been awarded the highest name and status, he now leads and empowers others, including the Philippians, to serve the gospel commonwealth and to be a light to the world (*ministry*).

The Christ Hymn then transitions into exhortations and commands, beginning at 2:12. First, Paul calls attention to their past obedience (*hypē-kousate*, echoing the submission of Jesus to God in 2:8, *hypokoos*), reinforcing their right attitude and behavior as they followed God before this period of difficulty and suffering. But now Paul prompts them to keep the faith, so to speak, and to "work out your own salvation." We will return later to the interpretive challenges posed by Paul's language here, but for now we can address the matter of context. *Why does Paul give these exhortations in 2:12–16? Are they simply general moral exhortations, or are they aimed at a specific problem or concern in Philippi?*[163] Paul appears to be addressing the present circumstance of his absence (2:12) and probably also the specter of his potential demise (2:17). Undoubtedly, these factors could have led to doubt, discouragement, in-fighting, and even despair in the Philippian church. Imagine a unit of soldiers in the throes of battle, and their general is captured – what happens to the troops? Without strong leadership, fear and chaos can easily take over. Philippians 2:12–18 has the marks of a kind of farewell speech spurring the others to march on, as it were.

Fred Craddock has argued that Paul needed to challenge the Philippians to trust and obey God – and to know God's presence and empowerment – in the apostle's own absence. Craddock writes,

There is no question but that Paul's presence *personally* made a difference in the life of the church. There is no question but that Paul's presence *apostolically* made a difference in the life of the church. Paul knows that, but he also knows that he must not tie their conduct directly to his presence. Otherwise, the Philippian congregation is a cult, not a church. Paul wishes to set them, in his absence, in God's presence with fear and trembling.[164]

In a way, Paul apostolically serves as an intermediary between the Philippians and God – he coached and directed them, and modeled what it meant to follow God and please him. Here now he enjoins them to trust God more directly and to carry on in faith. In Phil 2:14–16, Paul moves in the direction of painting their walk with God in the colors of Israel's wandering. In the wilderness, it is all too easy to lose your way, grumble and complain, and even give up hope. Paul encourages resilient faith, integrity, and even boldness and courage.

---

[163] See N. K. Gupta, "Mirror-Reading Moral Issues in Paul's Letters," *JSNT* 34.4 (2012): 361–381.

[164] F. Craddock, *Philippians* (Interpretation; Louisville, KY: Westminster John Knox, 1985), 44. Craddock compares Phil 2:12–18 with Moses' farewell speech in Deuteronomy (31:24–32:3), but he observes that, while Moses pointed to Israel's inevitable waywardness, Paul expresses hope and joy in view of his converts' faith and obedience; see Craddock, *Philippians*, 44–45.

We may now examine this passage more closely. Paul commences not with a harsh rebuke, but with warmth and grace – "my beloved" (2:12a). Statistically, Paul *does* use this term of endearment at transition points in his letters when he gives counsel (e.g., Rom 12:9; 1 Cor 15:58), but it is not merely a rhetorical device. Paul firmly believed that the love of God is a deep comfort (Phil 2:1), and Paul reaffirms his love and concern for the Philippians in 4:1: "my brothers and sisters, whom I love and long for, my joy and crown."

After affirming their past obedience and respectful submission to the will of God, Paul offers a master command that arches over the whole of 2:12–18: "work out your own salvation with fear and trembling." From the start, it ought to be clear that Paul was not telling the Philippians to *earn* their own personal eternal salvation. If they were already feeling timid and doubt-filled, imagine what *that* kind of message would do to their faith! Both the Greek words *katergazomai* ("work out") and *sōteria* ("salvation") need to be properly understood *in this context*. Let's start with *sōteria*. In the undisputed letters, Paul uses this noun only fourteen times. Most occurrences do seem to relate to eschatological and eternal "salvation" (e.g., Rom 1:16; 1 Thess 5:9). But there are two factors that make this meaning less apropos when it comes to Phil 2:12. First, it is unclear why Paul would be talking about eternal salvation in a passage about persever- ance, obedience, and responsible behavior. Second, it makes good sense to link the use of *sōteria* in 2:12 with Paul's earlier use of this word in 1:19. Seemingly in reference to his restrictive and bleak situation in prison, Paul expresses hope that God will see to Paul's *salvation* (NRSV: "deliverance"). In that situation, Paul was not necessarily referring to either freedom from imprisonment (see 1:20), or to future salvation. The use of *sōteria* in 1:19 carried the sense of *things working out according to God's will for the best, whatever that best may be.* Paul was able to come to terms with letting God work things out and learning to trust and obey his ways and will. What seems to be happening in 2:12 is that Paul urges the Philippians not to get bent out of shape due to the present difficult circumstances, but to carry on in faith and hope, anticipating that God will work things out *for their best, whatever that best may be.*

That Paul was probably harking back to 1:19 is indicated by his use of *heautōn* ("your own") in 2:12. Here Paul does not use the basic word for your (*hymōn*), but rather the reflexive pronoun *heautou*, which carries the

sense of "your *own*" or "*for yourselves.*" This implies something like:
*I (Paul) have figured out how to trust in God's own way of working things
out for the best, and now I call upon you to figure it out <u>for yourselves</u>.*[165]

What about Paul's use of the language of "work[ing] out?" Admittedly, it
is a bit strange to find Paul talking about *sōteria* being worked out or
produced. To be clear, though, *katergazomai* is not a verb of earning, but
one of making. To make their own "salvation" (or overall harmony with
God and the world) refers to lifestyle and obedience.[166] When it comes to
Paul's use of salvation language here, we might find a helpful analog in
1 Pet 2:2: "Like newborn infants, long for the pure, spiritual milk, so that by
it you may grow into salvation." While 1 Peter clearly attests that only God
can save (1 Pet 1:3–5, 2:10), in 2:2 the author can talk about growing up in
salvation, becoming more mature in line with the more perfect ways of
God. In the same way, the Philippians were being exhorted to live their
lives in humility, unity, and obedience, counting on God to see them
through the hard times.

Paul's qualification that they ought to obey and work this out "with fear
and trembling" is not a scare tactic. Rather, this language tends to be used
when one is especially concerned to respect the will of God, even in spite of
how God-pleasing decisions might not be socially or culturally favorable
(cf. 1 Cor 2:2–3; 2 Cor 7:15).

In 2:13, Paul encourages the Philippians that they are not alone in
working all of this out. Despite the apostle's lamentable absence, *God is
there*, and he is invisibly but powerfully at work in their midst, and he will
see to their well-being. Here is a call to faith that the outside appearance of
things does not tell the whole tale.

*All that is gold does not glitter,*
*Not all those who wander are lost;*
*The old that is strong does not wither,*

[165] See Reumann's rendering of *sōteria* here as "what salvation means" (*Philippians*, 386);
H. C. G. Moule is not too far off with "our whole 'saving' from evil, in union with
Christ" (*Philippians*, 45). M. D. Hooker underscores the important point that the "your
[own]" in 2:12 is plural, not singular, indicating that Paul is talking about a corporate
experience, not an individual one (see "Philippians," 512).

[166] Note the use of *katergazomai* in 1 Pet 4:3 where it involves the actions, habits, or lifestyle
that arises out of the will; on Philippians 2:12, see Fee, *Paul's Letter to the
Philippians*, 255.

*Deep roots are not reached by the frost.*
*From the ashes a fire shall be woken,*
*A light from the shadows shall spring;*
*Renewed shall be the blade that was broken,*
*The crownless again shall be king.*

> Bilbo Baggins (J. R. R. Tolkien)

I am struck here by Tolkien's language of *wandering* and *light/darkness*, because Paul seems to develop some of these images himself in Philippians (2:14–16). Paul was urging the Philippians not to see only with their eyes, but to "look" for the work of God by faith. Paul spells out the dark side of this journey by calling upon them to work and live without "murmuring or arguing" (Phil 2:14). Undoubtedly, Paul was echoing the misbehavior of Israel in their wilderness period, where they grumbled against the inconvenient way the Lord delivered them and provided for them (see Exod 16:7–12). This led not only to impiety, but also division within Israel. Fee is surely right, then, when he explains that Paul was rebuking the Philippians' "posturing and bickering – selfish ambition, empty conceit, complaining, arguing" that had eroded their "united front for Christ" as they buckled under outside threat and pressure.[167]

An attitude and habit of dwelling on self-pity and blaming others sets a powerful trap of stagnancy. Instead, Paul pointed the Philippians toward a path of integrity, purity, and unity (2:15–16). In v. 2:15, it becomes clear that Paul was warning the Philippians *not* to act like Israel when they sinned against God in the wilderness. Note the similarities between Phil 2:14–15 and Deut 32:4–5:

Do all things without murmuring and arguing, that you may be blameless and innocent, children of God without blemish in the midst of a crooked and perverse generation, in which you shine like stars in the world. (Phil 2:14–15)

The Rock [God], his work is perfect, and all his ways are just. A faithful God, without deceit, just and upright is he, yet his degenerate children have dealt falsely with him, a perverse and crooked generation. (Deut 32:4–5)

Paul does not allude to Deut 32 out of any sort of animosity toward Jews or Judaism. Early Jews and Christians alike could point back to the era of

---

[167] G. D. Fee, *Philippians* (IVPNT; Downers Grove, IL: InterVarsity Press, 2003), 158.

Israel's wilderness wandering as a negative example (e.g., Ps 78:17–63; Sir 46:7; *Pirke Aboth* 5.7; Josephus, *Ant.* 4.1f; Acts 7:39–40; 13:18; Heb 3:8). Not all Israelites were always sinful during that time, but Jews remembered a wider pattern of waywardness and idolatry (*4 Esdras* 7.107).[168] We must remember that in the highly agonistic Roman world, competing with one another was a "normal" way of showing superiority (cf. Rom 12:10; 1 Cor 1:10f). Paul was undercutting this, by reinforcing their unity and integrity. Their eyes should not be on point-scoring or winning favor in view of popular opinion, but on the God who judges all (cf. Phil 2:16; cf. 1:10).

As *individuals*, they ought not to draw attention to themselves (as superior or "right"), but as a *corporate family of God* they should be a beacon to guide others. Many scholars detect here an allusion to Dan 12:3, which foretells a resurrection age where the wise "will light up like the luminaries of heaven, and those who strengthen my words will be as the stars of heaven forever and ever" (NETS). If Paul did have this text in mind, he may have been thinking about how believers living in light of the resurrection bear witness to the pure and powerful light of God that radiated from the face of Christ (2 Cor 4:6). This contrasts with the dark minds and dark behavior of this "crooked and perverse generation" – but who are the people that comprise this "generation" that Paul refers to? Paul was not talking about Jews in general, because the Philippian believers were certainly not hanging around Jewish communities on a regular basis (see Introduction). It would appear that Paul had his eye on the troublemaking Jewish Christians who were provoking the Philippian church (see 3:2–16).[169] They do *not* shine like stars because they have not fully understood or assimilated the death and resurrection of Jesus. But Paul refers to the Philippians as luminaries in the *world*, so his overall intention is to challenge them to be an example to *all* (cf. 1 Thess 4:11–12).

Paul urges the Philippians furthermore, in 2:16, to "[hold] fast to the word of life that I can boast on the day of Christ that I did not run in vain or labor in vain." That is, this is how these believers shine like stars. The clause "holding fast to the word of life" has generated extensive debate

---

[168] Cf. *4 Esdras* 9.32: "But though our ancestors received the law, they did not keep it and did not observe the statutes; yet the fruit of the law did not perish – for it could not, because it was yours" (NRSV).

[169] Silva, *Philippians*, 125.

about the exact meaning of the verb (*epechō*). Some argue that it means "hold fast," others that it means "hold forth." The former has to do with grasping (commitment), the latter with giving (witness). In my own (Gupta's) examination, I see no clear or convincing evidence for the second option.[170] The general meaning of *epechō* is "hold tightly," and when it is used more figuratively it pertains to being fixated on something. Hence, Ben Sira writes, "Do not be *occupied* with your money" (Sir 5:1a; cf. 16:3). So Paul tells the Philippians to be *fixated on* or *occupied with* the "word of life." The phrase "word of life" is not typical for Paul (he prefers "word of God"/"word of the Lord"). Here he may have chosen this language to give the Philippians assurance that God was looking after their lives and infusing them with joy and salvation, but to fully receive these things they must obey God's "word." This "word" (*logos*) is not a specific text *per se*, but a reference to the gospel, which promises eternal life, and this embodied in Jesus Christ (cf. 1 John 1:1).

Ultimately, Paul directs their attention to the "day of Christ," which involves judgment. It would be very uncharacteristic for him to talk about judgment as if it were a matter of earning salvation, weighing good versus bad deeds. So why does he raise this matter? I find that it is helpful to appeal to Jesus' teaching on watchfulness as a framework for early Christian thought. According to Matthew (24:42–51), Jesus called upon his disciples to live faithfully and vigilantly in view of the Lord's return. He gives the analogy of the wise and loyal slave who was put in charge of the household in the absence of his master: "blessed is that slave whom his master will find at work when he arrives" (Matt 24:46). We cannot be absolutely certain Paul himself knew of such a teaching of Jesus, but I find it likely given that Paul's lesson on vigilance and faithfulness in 1 Thess 5:1–11 bears remarkable similarities.

Twice in Philippians Paul refers to the "day of Christ" – eschatological language connected to the return of the Lord and the "day of the Lord" (1 Cor 5:5: 2 Cor 1:14).[171] This is conceived of by Paul as a great day of

---

[170] See the discussion in Reumann, *Philippians*, 394.

[171] For helpful background information, see J. Plevnik, *Paul and the Parousia: An Exegetical and Theological Investigation* (Peabody, MA: Hendrickson, 1997), 3–44; more recently, E. Adams, "The Coming of God Tradition and Its Influence on New Testament Parousia Texts," in *Biblical Traditions in Transmission* (eds. C. Hempel and J. M. Lieu; Leiden: Brill, 2006), 1–19.

reckoning. Paul considered the "day of Christ" to be a transformative day of illumination where all things are revealed for what they truly are; as Paul writes, "Therefore do not pronounce judgment before the time, before the Lord comes, who will bring to light the things now hidden in darkness and will disclose the purposes of the heart. Then each one will receive commendation from God" (1 Cor 4:5). In Philippians, Paul wants the believers to know that their attention should be fastidiously devoted to honor and integrity before the Lord Jesus Christ – all this would bring Paul himself and his ministry great honor (cf. Gal 2:2).[172]

The mention of Paul's ministry in 2:16 leads him to reflect again on his own situation and the possibility of his death in 2:17–18. He considers that his life may come to an end soon. It was crucial that Paul frame his potential fate for the Philippians. In the Roman world, honor was everything, and they might have viewed Paul's imprisonment (and execution) as shameful (see Phil 1:20).[173] All along in this letter, Paul has been teaching the Philippians how to think about value and honor with new eyes, with the mind of Christ. Here too he reinterprets his own potential death, not as if he were a pariah, but as an offering pleasing to God. Before we look at Paul's cultic metaphor here more closely, it is worth noting that Paul's positioning of his suffering as noble aligns in general with some ancient moralist ideas that attempted to conceive of suffering as simply part of proving one's strength and resolve (e.g., Rom 5:3–5).

For example, Seneca once wrote, "Mucius was tested by fire, Fabricius by poverty, Rutilius by exile, Regulus by torture, Socrates by poison, Cato by death. It is ill fortune alone that reveals these great examples" (Seneca, *Prov.* 3.4). While Paul was not a Stoic philosopher, he would have shared with them a sense that difficulties in life can be responded to in powerful and positive ways.[174] In order to communicate this message, Paul draws on

---

[172]  On Paul's ministry priorities and how we viewed his calling in view of final judgment, see J. W. Thompson, *Pastoral Ministry according to Paul* (Grand Rapids, MI: Baker, 2006), 31–60.

[173]  On Roman views of death, see C. Barton, *Roman Honor: The Fire in the Bones* (Los Angeles: University of California Press, 2001), 29–130; V. Hope, *Roman Death: The Dying and the Dead in Ancient Rome* (London: Continuum, 2009), 50–55; idem, *Death in Ancient Rome: A Sourcebook* (London: Routledge, 2007), 39–46.

[174]  For a comparison of Paul and Seneca, see N. K. Gupta, "Fighting the Good Fight: The Good Life in Paul and the Giants of Philosophy" in *Paul and the Giants of Philosophy* (Downers Grove, IL: InterVarsity Press, 2019), 95–105; for a critical analysis that lays out

a cultic image of drink offerings and sacrifice. This metaphor would have conjured up a vivid picture in the reader's imagination, because ancient drink offerings were often wine, and its pouring out resembled the spilling of blood (*Sib. Or.* 8.388; Josephus, *Ant.* 2.66). Paul's (possible) death should not be seen as a life wasted or cut short, but a beautiful and acceptable offering to God (cf. Phil 4:18; Rom 12:1–2). Paul mentions not only his own situation, but how his ministry was connected to *their* lives. Even at a distance, in prison, he was not alone, because he could co-offer his gift to God with the "sacrifice" (*thysia*) and "service" (*leitourgia*) of the Philippians' faith. All of the challenges and persecutions they are facing (the Philippians and Paul) are not for nothing. In the midst of all that pressure, they can show their faith (*pistis*). Paul's use of faith language here is not about "belief" *per se*. It refers to the whole of one's orientation toward God in thought, trust, and faithfulness.[175]

If the first readers were not unsettled enough by now at Paul's reference to his potential demise, he concludes this section by talking about *joy* (2:17b–18). Paul mentions that he feels joyful and enters into the joy that they ought to feel (2:17b); and likewise they should share in *his* joy. To be frank, at least some of the Philippians would have found this notion absurd. When someone is experiencing suffering, hardship, rejection, and alienation – jubilation, gladness, and celebration are not the natural reactions. And yet this is precisely why Paul goes out of his way to make an important theological statement that ought to have deep meaning for the life of his readers.

### Bridging the Horizons: Christian Joy

The basic sense of "joy" is gladness, delight, or happiness. Miroslav Volf refers to joy as the "affective component of the good life."[176] Volf points out that joy-language is

---

the differences, see C. K. Rowe, *One True Life: The Stoics and Early Christians as Rival Traditions* (New Haven, CT: Yale University Press, 2016).

[175] See N. K. Gupta, *Paul and the Language of Faith* (Grand Rapids, MI: Eerdmans, 2019); M. W. Bates, *Salvation by Allegiance Alone* (Grand Rapids, MI: Baker, 2017); T. Morgan, *Roman Faith and Christian Faith* (Oxford: Oxford University Press, 2015); cf. also Collins, The Power of Images in Paul, 61.

[176] M. Volf, "What Is Good? Joy and the Well-Lived Life," *Christian Century*, July 1 (2016): 1–10, here 10.

used not just for good feelings *per se*, but specifically feeling good *about* something good; in that sense, it is a *reactionary emotion*.[177] Emotions are interesting things. They can be involuntary (like crying during a movie), but there is also a way to look at them as indicators of values or virtues. Greek biographer Diogenes Laertius mentions the perspective of Zeno. Zeno stressed the importance of emotional control. He mentions three examples: joy, caution, and wishing. The first, joy, is a form of disciplined elation (as opposed to wanton pleasure). The second, caution, involves careful avoidance (rather than terror). The third, wishing, is yearning under restraint, rather than craving that borders on addiction.[178] Plutarch tells us that the philosopher Epicurus typically preached that one should seek one's own happiness, and yet he confesses that a deep joy comes from bringing happiness to others (*Mor.* 778).[179]

These Greco-Roman authors, and Jewish ones as well (e.g., Isa 65:19), use "joy" as an indicator of human fulfillment. Why is this so? Joy is associated not only with pleasure, but harmony, good fortune, a sense that things are good, right, and that one is "in sync" with the world, as it were. With this in mind, communities could urge their people to either commit themselves to rejoicing, or refrain from it, in order to align with certain values or virtues. Prov 24:19 says, "Do not *rejoice* over evildoers, nor envy sinners." According to Matthew, when Jesus teaches about the values of the kingdom of God, he calls them "blessed" who are persecuted for his sake; they should "rejoice and be glad" because they will receive a special reward in heaven (Matt 5:12).

Paul's call for the Philippians to "rejoice," then, is about having the same mindset as Christ, seeing their situation with the eyes of faith, and celebrating what God is and will do in their midst – in spite of what seems like unfair and unbearable circumstances. You can imagine a situation where someone is dying and their friends are justifiably despondent. But she might say, "When I die, don't be sad, celebrate my life." This is similar to Paul's sentiment. *Don't look at Paul's incarceration and (their own) suffering as weakness, defeat, or futility. Quite the opposite, human suffering matters to God, and it sometimes demonstrates a life lived faithfully to God in worship and for the good of the world.* There is also a key eschatological point in the subtext of Paul's statement: present trials, sufferings, and persecutions mean all the more that that a heavenly glory and joy is yet ahead (2 Cor 4:17).

---

[177] For example: "The kingdom of heaven is like treasure hidden in a field, which someone found and hid; then in his joy he goes and sells all that he has and buys that field" (Matt 13:44). Note here the joy is an assumingly sudden response to the discovery of the treasure.

[178] See Diogenes, *Lives* 7.116.

[179] "For chiefest joy doth gracious kindness give"; note the similarities here to Jesus' dictum, "it is more blessed to give than receive" (Acts 20:35).

Within the thought-world of early Christianity, 1 Peter probably articulates this eschatological dimension most overtly: "rejoice insofar as you are sharing Christ's sufferings, so that you may also be glad and shout for joy when his glory is revealed" (4:13).

Similarly, Paul told the Thessalonians to "rejoice always" (1 Thess 5:16). By this, Paul did not mean that they ought to "put on a happy face" over their suffering and grief. Rather, Paul was saying, intentional joy in the Lord is a form of trust in the God who has promised to right wrongs, to vindicate the innocent, and to vanquish evil. Because of God's great promises, even if they pertain to a future not yet fully realized, one can rejoice *now*. Think of it like getting a message that a friend of yours has sent you a birthday present, something very special. You haven't received the present yet, but you feel jubilance and eagerness in anticipation of it. So it is with Christian joy, Paul urges.

In Phil 2:17b–18 Paul writes (paraphrasing a bit), *I join in celebrating your joy – congratulations! And please also celebrate my joy.* Again, the language borders on paradox here. Only Christian faith and hope could celebrate in the midst of suffering, he urges; what prevents it from being sheer madness is trust in God. The Philippians were to rejoice just as the Apostles did – according to Acts – when they counted themselves privileged to suffer dishonor "for the sake of the name [of Christ]" (Acts 5:41).

## 2:19–30: NEWS ABOUT TIMOTHY AND EPAPHRODITUS

[19] I hope in the Lord Jesus to send Timothy to you soon, so that I may be cheered by news of you.

[20] I have no one like him who will be genuinely concerned for your welfare.

[21] All of them are seeking their own interests, not those of Jesus Christ.

[22] But Timothy's worth you know, how like a son with a father he has served with me in the work of the gospel.

[23] I hope therefore to send him as soon as I see how things go with me;

[24] and I trust in the Lord that I will also come soon.

[25] Still, I think it necessary to send to you Epaphroditus – my brother and co-worker and fellow soldier, your messenger and minister to my need;

²⁶ for he has been longing for all of you, and has been distressed because you heard that he was ill.

²⁷ He was indeed so ill that he nearly died. But God had mercy on him, and not only on him but on me also, so that I would not have one sorrow after another.

²⁸ I am the more eager to send him, therefore, in order that you may rejoice at seeing him again, and that I may be less anxious.

²⁹ Welcome him then in the Lord with all joy, and honor such people,

³⁰ because he came close to death for the work of Christ, risking his life to make up for those services that you could not give me.

Beginning with 2:19, we can sense a clear transition of subject. On the most basic level, Paul moves from the exhortations toward obedience, integrity, faithfulness, and testimony to "news" about Timothy, Epaphroditus, and Paul himself. In that sense, Fee is correct that "this is the stuff of which real letters are made."[180] One expects in personal correspondence that the senders will talk their well-being, that of the readers, and sometimes also of mutual friends. But his discussion of these matters at *this* juncture in his letter to the Philippians is undoubtedly strategic with respect to his rhetorical aims. Timothy and Epaphroditus were being sent by Paul as representatives and "go-betweens," but Paul also commends them as models of godliness and good partners in ministry. Given what we have discussed earlier, though, regarding the Philippians' attachment to *Paul* in particular I (Gupta) believe Paul is also showing them that their faith can and should be supported by many other competent colleagues and partners, not just the "big man" (Paul) himself. This, no doubt, is part of Paul's overall concern in this letter to prompt the Philippians to have a disposition and mind-set of seeking the good of the other and the group first and foremost, and learning to set aside any sense of self-seeking (whether for self-glorification, or out of fear). In terms of how this section is structured, first Paul commends Timothy as Paul's proxy (2:19–24; and Paul ends this passage with a tantalizingly brief mention of his own hope of visiting them; 2:24). Then he commends Epaphroditus, explaining his near-death situation and how they should welcome him with due honor and respect for his exemplary service to Paul and the gospel (2:25–30).

---

[180]  Fee, *Philippians*, 259.

This passage serves an important role in this letter for at least two reasons. First, Paul presents Timothy and Epaphroditus as case studies or models of obedience to God and the gospel of Jesus Christ that is marked by humility and unity. This letter constantly plays on the light and shadow sides of living in relation to the gospel (1:27). Not only does Paul describe the life of faith and obedience, but sets up a virtual gallery of types and anti-types.[181]

## Gospel-Worthy Lifestyles

Second, it is striking how much we see the language of emotional inter-connectedness in this section (2:19–30). Paul hopes to be "cheered" when he receives news of their well-being (2:19). Timothy is deeply "concerned" with them (2:20). Epaphroditus "longs" for them (2:26). Paul was spared deep grief when Epaphroditus survived his near-death experience (2:27). For Paul, this is not mere sentimentalism, but an expression of lives intertwined in such a way that they share the ups-and-downs of life (cf. Rom 12:15). This would have been an important message for the Philippians because, under the circumstances, they may have settled into factions and provoked one another (cf. 2:3–4; 4:2–3). When such divisions exist, groups put up walls and snap judgments are often made about the other. What Paul models here is a network of persons (i.e., Paul, Timothy, Epaphroditus, and the Philippians) whose lives are intertwined, and they inevitably share each other's joys and sorrows. After all, it is hard to hate someone you care about – or, put another way, it is easy to hate someone you *don't* care about.

Turning now to a closer look at the verses, Paul begins this section with his plan to send Timothy to them. Timothy, a travel companion of Paul, is also mentioned in the prescripts of 2 Corinthians, Philemon and Colossians. According to 1 Thess 3:1–6, more than once Timothy was entrusted with the role of being a ministry proxy for Paul when he could not visit his converts. The implication from Phil 2:19 is that Timothy would go to Philippi, encourage the believers, learn more about their situation and how they are coping, and return to Paul to share the news with the hopes

---

[181]  See R. A. Culpepper, "Co-workers in Suffering: Philippians 2:19–30," *Review & Expositor* 77 (1980): 349–358, here 353; P.-B. Smit, *Paradigms of Being in Christ* (LNTS; London: T & T Clark, 2013), 113–115.

Table 2 *Modeling Gospel-Worthy Lifestyles*

| Text | Model | Anti-type |
|---|---|---|
| 1:15–17 | Benevolent proclamation of Christ | Duplicitous proclamation of Christ |
| 2:1–11 | The obedience and humility of Christ | |
| 2:19–24 | The pure intentions and dedication of Timothy | |
| 2:25–30 | The courageous ministry of Epaphroditus | |
| 3:1–4 | | Beware of those who focused on the flesh |
| 3:7–16[182] | Paul's freedom from boasting and union with Christ | |
| 3:18–19 | | Many (believers) live as "enemies of the cross of Christ" |
| 4:2–3 | Euodia, Syntyche, and Clement model bold action for the sake of the gospel | |

of lifting his spirit and giving him strength and encouragement in prison. Paul expresses in 2:19b that good news of their resilient faith and perseverance would be a great encouragement (Table 2).[183]

Paul then digresses from his discussion of "travel plans" to commend Timothy. First, he identifies Timothy as someone who is unique in his affection and concerns for them (Phil 2:20). When Paul says he has no one like him (Phil 2:20a), he uses the adjective *isopsychos*, which literally means "equal in soul." This appears to be conventional friendship language (cf. LXX Ps 54:14), and Paul's point would be that sending such a close confidant as Timothy would be *virtually* like Paul himself visiting – *I have full confidence that he will minister to you and see to your welfare exactly as I would.*

---

[182] Paul goes as far as calling upon the Philippians to imitate him in 3:17.

[183] Paul uses an uncommon verb here, *eupsycheō*, which the NRSV translates as "cheered." From the few occurrences of this word in ancient Greek literature, and the use of cognates like *eupsychos*, it is not so much a feeling of cheeriness as it is of heart and will emboldened (see 1 Macc 9:14; 2 Macc 7:20; 14:18; 3 Macc 7:18; 4 Macc 6:11; 9:23; Josephus, *Ant.* 11.241). The upshot to this insight is that Paul would be flipping the dynamic of his relationship with the Philippians; instead of him being the one to encourage them *per se*, Paul was calling upon them to "be brave" to help him "be brave" (cf. LXX Prov. 30:29–31 [*eupsychos*]).

Paul then steps further away from their specific circumstances to put forth his friend Timothy as an anti-type to the many selfish and greedy people out there who are wolves in sheep's clothing: "For everyone looks out for their own interests, not that of Jesus Christ" (Phil 2:21, NIV). Paul appears to indulge in some cynicism here; he no doubt experienced harm and animosity from other believers who pretended to have pure motives (cf. Phil 1:15–17). Perhaps he was also worried about such people preying upon the Philippians (cf. Phil 3:18). Thus, Paul clearly had a dual purpose for commending Timothy, both to promote him as a suitable proxy for Paul himself, and to hold him up as a Christ-like example of other-regard.[184] The original auditors of the letter would hear Paul identify Timothy as an example of 2:4: "Let each of you look not to your own interests, but to the interests of others."

In Phil 2:22, Paul further compliments Timothy by comparing him to a son who wraps himself up entirely in his father's business, the father in this image being Paul. The point is not that Timothy obeys Paul, but that Paul's junior colleague Timothy has unreservedly devoted himself to the work of the gospel, just as Paul has. The language Paul uses for Timothy's service is strong (*douleuō*); this verb literally refers to the work of a slave. What Paul intends in this is to represent Timothy as single-heartedly devoted to serving the gospel mission. Again, to have the leadership presence of Timothy would be *as good as* having Paul himself in the flesh.[185] Cousar sums up well the intent of Paul's extended admiration of Timothy.

Paul's heartfelt approbation of Timothy indicates . . . that he is more than a trusted colleague. He models the type of life the apostle wants to see embodied in Philippi. He cares about others and exhibits in his own life the *phronesis* that Paul has encouraged the Philippians to demonstrate.[186]

With v. 23, Paul resumes his discussion of travel plans, repeating again his desire to send Timothy soon. Looking back to 2:17 (and before that to 1:20), Paul had already hinted at his possible demise. But here he shows some optimism (if that is the right word) about the potential of his release such

---

[184]  On this subject in general, see D. G. Horrell, *Solidarity and Difference: A Contemporary Reading of Paul's Ethics* (London: T&T Clark, 2015), 204–245.

[185]  Philo also compares the son's work for the father to that of a slave (for a master); there Philo was referring to the work of a priest "serving" Father God (*Spec.* 1.57; cf. LXX Jer 3:22).

[186]  Cousar, *Philippians*, 65.

that he might come in the flesh, as it were. What does all this have to do with Timothy? Hawthorne and Martin propose that Paul still needed to consult with Timothy regarding his defense, and *then* he would be dispatched.[187] They also point out that Paul talks directly about needing to focus on *his own affairs* (*ta peri eme*) – the sort of thing he criticized earlier in the letter (2:4; 2:21). But probably here he is demonstrating that it is not unchristian to address or handle one's own affairs; rather, the problem is when we are so preoccupied with our own concerns (and success) that we neglect the needs and concerns of others.[188]

Just as soon as he boldly states his intent to come in person "soon" (2:24), he adds that he feels the need to also send the Philippian Epaphroditus back to them (2:25ff.).

---

### Closer Look: Who Was Epaphroditus?

Epaphroditus is only mentioned by name in Paul's letters in Philippians (2:25; 4:18), although a short form of the same name, Epaphras, also occurs (Col 1:7; 4:3; Philm 23). Because the person called Epaphras is noted as a Colossian (Col 4:12), it is not assumed to be the same person as in Philippians. "Epaphroditus" was a common Greek name, associated with the goddess Aphrodite, and it is fair to speculate that he may have been a follower of the cult of Aphrodite before following Jesus Christ.[189] Eduard Verhoef notes that both the name-versions (Epaphroditus and Epaphras) appear on extant Latin inscriptions found in regions close to Philippi.[190] In terms of Epaphroditus' status and function in the Philippian church, we know that they entrusted him with the important task of sending their aid and gifts to Paul (Phil 2:25). Furthermore, there is good reason to believe Epaphroditus was also the person who delivered Paul's letter to the Philippians.[191]

---

[187]  Hawthorne and Martin, *Philippians*, 156.
[188]  Hawthorne and Martin, *Philippians*, 156.
[189]  There is evidence that a cult of Aphrodite was prominent in Roman Philippi; see J. R. Harrison, "Excavating the Urban and Country Life of Roman Philippi and Its Territory," in *The First Urban Churches 4: Roman Philippi* (eds. J. R. Harrison and L. L. Welborn; Atlanta, GA: SBL Press, 2018), 1–62, 27; Pilhofer, *Philippi*, 2.681.
[190]  Verhoef, *Philippi*, 40.
[191]  E. R. Richards notes that since Epaphroditus was the Philippians representative who delivered the church's gifts and aid to Paul, he would naturally have expected (upon completion of his service to Paul) a "thank-you note," as it were; see *Paul and First-Century Letter Writing* (Downers Grove, IL: InterVarsity Press, 2004), 207.

Much like his commendation of Timothy (2:19–24), Paul's description of Epaphroditus is extensive and effusive. He predicates about Epaphroditus five things in 2:25 alone.

*Brother.* The mention of Epaphroditus as Paul's "brother" is somewhat natural, as this was a common way to refer to a fellow Christian (e.g., 1 Cor 8:13; cf. Philm 16). But on this occasion in particular I (Gupta) wonder if there is more to it than that. Looking at Paul's letters, he has a tendency to refer to Timothy as "brother Timothy" (2 Cor 1:1; Col 1:1; 1 Thess 3:2; Philm 1). This almost appears to be a kind of title nickname for Timothy. Perhaps Paul was going out his way to commend Epaphroditus to the Philippians on par with Timothy.

*Coworker.* Along those same lines, Paul attributes to both Timothy and Epaphroditus the title of "coworker" (*synergos*; applied to Timothy, see 2 Cor 8:23). When Paul calls someone a "coworker," this tends to imply the person: (1) exercised some form of leadership alongside Paul and (2) became a kind of public representative of the faith such that they inevitably had to endure persecution.[192]

*Fellow soldier.* A much less common title that Paul attributes to his coworkers in the gospel is that of "fellow soldier" (*systratiōtes*). While battle imagery *is* regularly found in Paul,[193] he only names another believer as a co-soldier in Philemon (2, applied to Archippus). It should not go unnoticed, though, that occasionally Paul would refer to someone as a fellow "prisoner-of-war" (*synaichmalōtos*; Rom 16:7; Philm 23; Col 4:10). This is not the typical word for "prisoner" (*desmios*). The word *synaichmalōtos* refers to people who are *captured* and *imprisoned*, usually in reference to captured enemy combatants (cf. Luke 21:24).

The description of Epaphroditus as a "fellow soldier" may have been a rhetorically strategic commendation of someone who was being sent home prematurely. It is conceivable that, if Epaphroditus was meant to have

---

[192] He uses this language for: Prisca and Aquila (Rom 16:3); Urbanus (Rom 16:9); Timothy (Rom 16:21); Apollos and Cephas (1 Cor 3:9–22); the household of Stephanas (1 Cor 16:15); Titus (2 Cor 8:23); Euodia, Syntyche, and Clement (Phil 4:3); Tychicus, Onesimus, Aristarchus, Mark, and Jesus called Justus (Col 4:11).

[193] See, for example, Krentz, "Military Language," 105–127; idem, "Paul, Games, and the Military," 344–383. Josephus also uses this word in relation to a speech Moses gives to Israel before they enter into the land of Canaan: "O you Israelites and fellow soldiers (*systratiōtai*), who have been partners with me in this long and uneasy journey" (*Ant.* 4.177).

stayed with Paul "to the end," that when he fell ill and was now returning to Philippi, he might be seen as something less than discharging his duties fully and successfully. Paul presents him as a good soldier who not only served on the front lines, as it were, but even risked his life (to aid Paul) such that he nearly died – courage was the single most important virtue of a Roman soldier, and this is precisely what Paul approves of in Epaphroditus.

*Apostle/messenger.* Paul refers to Epaphroditus as *apostolos*. In early Christianity, this term sometimes had a specialized meaning in reference to an authoritative office (e.g., Paul and Peter as part of *the* Apostles). Here it should be clear that Epaphroditus was not considered by Paul an "Apostle" in that sense. Most English translations render *apostolos* here as something like "messenger" (NIV, NRSV). The most basic meaning of *apostolos* is indeed "messenger" (cf. John 13:16), but the Greek Bible tends to use the word *angelos* when this meaning is intended. That raises the question of whether or not Paul intended something more specific than "messenger" in the context of Philippians. In 1 Corinthians, Paul refers to roles in the Church such as "apostles," "prophets," and "teachers" (also including healers, assistants, leaders of various kinds; see 1 Cor 12:28). It *could*, then, be the case that Epaphroditus served the Philippian church in a more official capacity as a representative leader "sent out" (as the root of the word implies) to do ministry on their behalf (cf. 2 Cor 8:23). In that case, it may be best to translate it here as (lower-case) "apostle." It is important to note at this point that Paul switches the focus from activities that Epaphroditus carried out that mirror the work of Paul (e.g., soldier), and observes how he was someone doing work on behalf of the *Philippians* (*your* apostle, *your* servant).

*Servant.* The fourth and final title used of Epaphroditus in this verse is *leitourgos*, often translated "minister" or "servant." The English word "minister" can be confusing and anachronistic, because Paul certainly did not intend the meaning here of "pastor" or "ordained minister" in the modern sense. As for "servant," Paul had many terms at his disposal that more generically meant this (e.g., *hyperētēs, diakonos*). The word *leitourgos* could carry one of two connotations here. One possibility is that Paul was using language familiar in the Greco-Roman political sphere in reference to persons who carried out some kind of public service – we would call them "civil servants." Note in Rom 13:6 how Paul refers to government leaders as "servants of God" (*leitourgoi theou*).[194] However, Jews were accustomed to using *leitourgos* (and its cognates) in relation to the priestly service in the temple (hence Phil 2:17, *thysia kai leitourgia*).[195] Scholars disagree about which context this word comes from in this circumstance, but perhaps the line between these two is too artificial. Either nuance communicates that the *leitourgos* provides a representative service for the good of the people.[196]

After these vivid descriptions and titles, Paul delves into further details about Epaphroditus' circumstances (2:26–28). We can gather the following information from these verses (and Phil 4:18):

- Epaphroditus was sent to Paul from Philippi to deliver the church's gifts and aid (4:18).
- Along the way to Paul, Epaphroditus fell ill (2:26b) – the circumstances are lost to history. A sensible presumption is that the journey was unkind to him and he wound up with a sickness or injury far worse than he imagined.
- Paul explains that the problem was so severe Epaphroditus almost died (2:27a).[197]
- Epaphroditus made a physical recovery (2:27b), which was a relief to Paul (2:27c).
- Epaphroditus became homesick and longed to return to his Philippian community (2:26a), both to lift his own spirit and also to comfort any among them who were worried about him (2:28).

By all accounts, Paul goes out of his way in the letter to the Philippians to recognize and honor Epaphroditus. Some scholars see this as only the apostle Paul lifting up Epaphroditus as a model of courage, faith, and perseverance.[198] M. Silva thinks that the Philippians expected Paul to send

---

[194] Cf. TLNT 2.378–387.
[195] See Philo, *Mos.* 2.276; *Somn.* 2.231; cf. Josephus, *Ant.* 13.55.
[196] See A. Clarke, *A Pauline Theology of Church Leadership* (LNTS; London: T & T Clark, 2004); N. K. Gupta, *Worship that Makes Sense to Paul* (BZNW; New York: de Gruyter, 2010), 141.
[197] Culpepper notes that the Greek text could be rendered into English as "he was death's neighbor" (*paraplesion thanato*); see "Co-workers in Suffering," 356.
[198] For example, Fee, *Philippians*, 273. Also, Flemming: "Epaphroditus had willingly taken the way of the cross-publicly identifying himself with Caesar's prisoner, putting his own life on the line in service to others" (*Philippians*, 150). Smit goes as far as arguing that

*Timothy* to them, but Paul was now sending Epaphroditus *first* because of these unexpected circumstances, and his commendation of Epaphroditus would ensure a warm welcome.[199] Another perspective is that the Philippians expected Epaphroditus to stay with Paul *longer* and when he returned early he may have been met with disrespect, as if he did not faithfully and fully discharge his representative role.[200]

Without more contextual information, it is hard to make a choice, but I (Gupta) slightly favor the last option, in view of the extent to which Paul goes to insure a respectful reception of Epaphroditus, the detailed explanation of his risk-taking and recovery as valiant ("for the work of Christ"; 2:30a), and as something that Epaphroditus took upon himself, whereas the rest of the Philippians remained safe and free from danger (2:30). Paul's own emotional attachment to Epaphroditus (2:27c) signals a meaningful ministry that he had toward Paul, even if for a shortened period.

Looking back again at this whole passage (2:19–30), it is clear that, while Paul appreciates the value that the Philippians placed in his leadership, he wanted to point to the effective and admirable ministries of some of his coworkers such as Timothy and Epaphroditus, perhaps in part to help the Philippians begin to imagine a world without him. Thompson and Longenecker wisely observe that Paul's exalting of these men would have been countercultural in the Roman world: "While ancient people gave honor to those who made major donations or achieved recognition for military success, the church honors those who, often behind the scenes, sacrifice for the benefit of others."[201]

### 3:1–4A: WARNING AGAINST JEWISH CHRISTIAN PROSELYTIZERS

Finally, my brothers and sisters, rejoice in the Lord. To write the same things to you is not troublesome to me, and for you it is a safeguard.

[2] Beware of the dogs, beware of the evil workers, beware of those who mutilate the flesh!

Paul's portrayal of Epaphroditus risking his life (2:30) parallels Christ's self-sacrifice (2:6–8); see *Paradigms of Being in Christ*, 113–114.
[199] Silva, *Philippians*, 159.
[200] For example, see Culpepper, "Co-workers in Suffering," 356; Bockmuehl, *The Epistle to the Philippians*, 173–174; Witherington, *Philippians*, 174–175.
[201] Thompson and Longenecker, *Philippians and Philemon*, 89.

³ For it is we who are the circumcision, who worship in the Spirit of God and boast in Christ Jesus and have no confidence in the flesh –

⁴ even though I, too, have reason for confidence in the flesh.

The letter next takes an "intriguing turn."²⁰² After the exhortations toward unity and humility and the commendations of Timothy and Epaphroditus, we now encounter some of the most rancorous polemics in the Pauline corpus (Phil 3:2–4a), a profoundly christological interpretation of Paul's life and conversion (3:4b–11), plus some memorable exhortations about striving in faithfulness, imitation, and attaining resurrection (3:12–21). The whole chapter is striking for its acute mixture of polemics and *pastoralia*, the stark renouncement of privileges and performance in favor of the hope for resurrection, and the text reaches something of a dramatic crescendo in the description of Christ as Savior of a commonwealth of believers. At a rhetorical level, Paul utilizes his own biography, acute irony, several comparisons, chiasmuses, wordplay, denunciations, alliteration, repetition, and deep pathos to communicate his message. Paul propels his audience to revile the enemies of the cross as much as to rejoice in the surpassing worth of knowing Christ.

Paul begins with some opaque transitional remarks (v. 1) before engaging in deviant labeling against Jewish Christ-believing proselytizers²⁰³

---

²⁰² Fee, *Philippians*, 285.

²⁰³ Paul's Jewish Christian opponents are routinely called "judaizers," but this is a misnomer. Strictly speaking, only Gentiles can judaize, that is, adhere to Jewish customs for which circumcision was generally the climax (Josephus, *War* 2.454 records how Metilius promised to "judaize to the point of circumcision"). Accordingly, someone who compels Gentiles to judaize to the point of circumcision is not a "judaizer," but is more properly called a "proselytizer" since they are desiring to make Gentiles into Jewish proselytes, that is, converts to Judaism. Put simply, Jews proselytize and Gentiles judaize. While this might seem like an insignificant qualification or distinction, and I (Bird) feel like I'm in an uphill battle to convince people of the terminology, in reality a lot rides on it, for a start, how do we name and conceive of Paul's Jewish Christ-believing opponents, and how it is Gentiles who are the ones who adopted a judaized way of life as opposed to a Hellenized one. On judaizing, see Mark D. Nanos (*The Irony of Galatians: Paul's Letter in First-Century Context* [Peabody, MA: Hendrickson, 2002], 116) writes: "While judaizing is something that Gentiles seeking Jewish status may engage in, it is not appropriate for describing Jews who may be involved with initiating the interest in or facilitating this process among Gentiles. The verb is intransitive, so that the terms *judaizing* and *Judaizers* refer to Gentiles who choose, at various levels and in various ways, to become or to live like Jews." See similarly J. D. G. Dunn, *New Perspective on Paul* (Grand Rapids, MI: Eerdmans, 2008), 470 n. 4.

while simultaneously valorizing his differences from them and reinterpret-
ing Israel's markers of prestige to pertain to Gentile Christ-believers (vv.
2–4b). Paul's point is relatively clear, the opponents are outsiders, who are
malevolent and malicious, predatory and pernicious, who would harm the
Philippians in terms of their relationship with Christ and even physically
harm the genitals of the male congregants. Gentile Christ-believers already
have what the proselytizers seek to cajole them with: covenant-belonging
(but without circumcision), worshipping God (but without the temple
cultus), and cause for boasting in Christ Jesus (but without fleshly effort
or excision of any part of one's flesh). Paul is attempting to reinforce a
socioreligious partition between the Gentile-majority Philippian assemblies
on the one hand and these Jewish Christ-believing proselytizers with their
pro-circumcision and pro-Torah views on the other hand. Paul is worried
that these proselytizers may arrive in Macedonia and will try to trouble the
Gentile believers there just as they tried to, or successfully did, in Antioch
and Galatia.[204] Paul's remarks here are charged with sectarian rhetoric,
certainly not unknown between Jewish sects, and he seeks to differentiate
the proselytizers from his own vision of believing and belonging to Christ.
Paul achieves this by denigrating their version of Christ-faith, which entails
conversion to Judaism and adherence to Torah and by warning against
their perversion of the gospel of Jesus Christ. This in turn lays the ground
work for Paul to begin a reinterpretation and reestimation of his own
Jewish heritage vis-à-vis God, Messiah, faith, and Spirit in Phil 3:4–11.

Virtually all English translations begin with "Finally" (*to loipon*) in v. 1a,
which would make it oddly appear that Paul is beginning his conclusion
halfway through the letter. On top of that, the mood changes abruptly from

---

[204] Thus we disagree with several scholars who suppose that there are no real opponents in
view (e.g., Garland, "Philippians," 241, 247; idem, "The Composition and Unity of
Philippians: Some Neglected Literary Factors," *NovT* 27 (1985): 166–167; cf. D. A.
deSilva, "No Confidence in the Flesh," *TrinJ* 15 [1994]: 29–32; Thompson and
Longenecker, *Philippians and Philemon*, 94–97, 100; S. Grindheim, *The Crux of
Election* (WUNT 2.202; Tübingen: Mohr/Siebeck, 2005), 121–122), whereby the
primary point is that just as Christ did not exploit his privileged status as equal to
God, just as Paul did not exploit his privileged Jewish status, and, unlike the Jews who
wrongly boast in their privileged status, the Philippians are called to "let go of the
Roman cultural advantage and abandon the power and status of the Roman Empire." I'd
(Bird) aver that: (1) At stake is not just Paul's personal example, but the challenge of
potential intruders (Gnilka, *Philippians*, 188); and (2) As Phil 3:17–18 makes clear, Paul's
exhortation about example and enemies are not mutually exclusive.

3:1 to 3:2, from "eirenical calm" to "violent hysteria."[205] This is why, quite understandably, many commentators treat 3:1 as the end of one letter that belongs after 4:1 with 3:2–21 as a fragment of a separate letter that has been interpolated at this point.[206] That thesis is plausible in some respects, but ultimately it raises more textual questions that it solves, and there are perhaps better alternatives that support a unified approach to the letter.

First, there are so many verbal and thematic correlations across the letter that renders a compilation thesis untenable. Consider the following:[207] (1) There is something of an *inclusio* with the exhortation to "stand firm" (1:27; 4:1); (2) Similarly, the motif of citizenship brackets the central section of the letter (1:27; 3:20); (3) There are manifold verbal connections between 2:6–11 and 3:7–11, 20–21;[208] (4) Paul's claim that "to live is Christ, to die is gain"(1:21) is matched by "gain Christ" (3:8); (5) The eschatological texture of the letter evident at 1:6 and 2:16 is continued in 3:12–16, 20–21; (6) Plus, we have to ask, why stitch multiple letters together in the first place, and, if you did, why not smooth out the awkward seams? Bockmuehl is on the money: "The biblical critic's wielding of the scalpel is generally more dangerous to the patient than the application of Ockham's razor to the critic's hypothesis."[209]

Second, looking at lexical data, on the one hand, yes, Paul can indeed end a letter with *loipon* as he does in 2 Cor 13:11. But on the other hand, we should remember that in 1 Thess 3, Paul provided a travel itinerary for Timothy, just as he does for Timothy and Epaphroditus in the second half of Philippians 2, before remarking "finally" (*loipon*) in 1 Thess 4:1, and then embarking on some lengthy and detailed moral exhortations and

---

[205] J. H. Houlden, *Paul's Letters from Prison* (Philadelphia: Westminster, 1970), 41.

[206] See, for example, Gnilka, *Philippians*, 8–10.

[207] See Garland, "Composition and Unity of Philippians"; Fee, *Philippians*, 285–286; and esp. Keown, *Philippians*, 2.69–71.

[208] See, for example, Garland, "Composition and Unity of Philippians," 158–159; A. Lincoln, *Paradise Now and Not Yet: Studies in the Role of the Heavenly Dimension in Paul's Thought with Special Reference to His Eschatology* (SNTSMS; Cambridge: Cambridge University Press, 1981), 87–89; Hansen, *Philippians*, 277; Thompson and Longenecker, *Philippians and Philemon*, 91–92, V. Koperski, *The Knowledge of Christ Jesus My Lord: The High Christology of Philippians 3:7–11* (Kampen: Kok Pharos, 1996), 324; Oakes, *Philippians*, 30; M. S. Park, *Submission within the Godhead and the Church in the Epistle to the Philippians* (London: Continuum, 2007); 57–62; H. Wotjtkowiak, *Christologie und Ethik im Philipperbrief* (Göttingen: Vandenhoeck & Ruprecht, 2012), 176.

[209] Bockmuehl, *The Epistle to the Philippians*, 176; similarly Silva, *Philippians*, 143; Fee, *Philippians*, 187

assurances about the dead not missing out on participating in Christ's second coming across 1 Thess 4–5. That makes perfect sense because, as Margaret E. Thrall notes, *loipon* can "be used as a transitional particle, to introduce either a logical conclusion or a fresh point in the progress of thought."[210] Thus, in places such as Phil 3:1, 4:8, 1 Thess 4:1, and 1 Cor 7:29, *loipon* signifies not a conclusion, but a transition to a new subject.[211] So *loipon* would be better translated here as something like "Furthermore" or "In addition."

Third, the abruptness of Paul's change of topic between 3:1a and 3:1b–21 is perhaps best accounted for by his jittery train of thought, ebbing and flowing as it does between exhortation, affectionate remarks, and stern reminders. While Paul's arguments can be carefully structured and rhetorically fine-tuned, like any human author, he can abruptly change topic (Gal 2:21–3:1), suddenly return to things he's forgotten (1 Cor 1:14–17), or else engage in an extemporaneous digression (2 Cor 2:14–17; 6:3–13). An awkward transition or clunky seam in the letter is not unusual for Paul's style, so it is not necessarily evidence for multiple sources haplessly stitched together.

Therefore, I'd suggest that *loipon* in v. 1a does not mark the end of a letter, but serves to signify the end of one discussion about house-church unity and the travel plans of his companions by rehearsing, again, the theme of rejoicing.

Paul urges the "brothers and sisters" (see 1:12) to "rejoice in the Lord" (*chairete en kuriō*) in v. 1a. This is not a concluding salutation equivalent to "farewell in the Lord" (as per 2 Cor 13:11), but recaps a major theme of joy in the letter (Phil 1:18, 2:17–18, 28–29; 4:4 10). Paul stresses joy because it is joy that characterizes those united with Christ and united with each other even in the midst of adversity. For Paul, faith is more than belief, it is joy and celebration, the eschatological outpouring of gladness in God that accompanies God's redemptive acts just as the Scriptures promised (see, e.g., Ps 14:7; 53:6; Isa 25:9; 65:19; Jer 31:13). Paul's gospel is good news, glad

---

[210]   M. E. Thrall, *Greek Particles in the New Testament* (Leiden: Brill, 1962), 28, cited in Garland, "Philippians," 238; See meanings listed in BDAG, 603; and J. T. Reed, *A Discourse Analysis of Philippians: Method and Rhetoric in the Debate over Literary Integrity* (JSNTSup 136; Sheffield: Sheffield Academic Press, 1997), 239–265.

[211]   Porter, *Idioms*, 122; Hellerman, *Philippians*, 168.

tidings, and joyous proclamation, yielding eschatological celebration among its beneficiaries.

The apostle does change topic from a reminder to rejoice in v. 1a to a reminder about some further instructions in v. 1b for which he is about to communicate in vv. 2–21.[212] He states, "To write the same things to you is not troublesome to me." Paul is unlikely here to be providing an explanation for the reminder to rejoice in v. 1a since joy is ubiquitous across the letter, it's hard to imagine the command to rejoice as a "safeguard," and Paul supplies the rationale for repeating himself in v. 18 in the context of giving a warning. As such, the rationale for Paul's reminder in v. 1b must be to introduce the new material that immediately follows in vv. 2–21.[213]

The style of language used in v. 1b is a typical trope in ancient letter writing to introduce a topic that possesses some import, while insisting that it is part of time-tested wisdom.[214] The adjective *skneros* means "pertaining to being bothersome."[215] As such, Paul is not perturbed in discussing matters germane to church unity, warning about proselytizers, and showing himself as the example of one who has renounced his inherited or acquired privileges. That is because, "for you it is a safeguard." The adjective *asphales* means "pertaining to a state of safety and security, and hence free from danger,"[216] with the implication that Paul's exhortations are a way to establish their stability in the faith. What Paul means by "the same things" (*ta auta*) is not immediately obviously. It could refer to matters he instructed them about in previous letters or else, and more likely, he now puts into writing (*graphein*) warnings about intruders (Gal 1:6–9; 2 Cor 11:4; Acts 20:29–32) and exhortations pertaining to his own pattern of life (1 Cor 4:17; 11:1) that he previously instructed them about in

---

[212] So too, for example, Cousar, *Philippians*, 68; Osiek, *Philippians*, 80; Witherington, *Philippians*, 187.

[213] Rightly, Fee, *Philippians*, 292–293; Silva, *Philippians*, 152; Cousar, *Philippians*, 68; Hellerman, *Philippians*, 169; Keown, *Philippians*, 2.95–96; contra, for example, Lightfoot, *Philippians*, 125; George B. Caird, *Paul's Letters from Prison* (Oxford: Oxford University Press, 1976), 132; Bockmuehl, *The Epistle to the Philippians*, 180; Hansen, *Philippians*, 213–214.

[214] Cousar, *Philippians*, 68; Witherington, *Philippians*, 184; Hansen, *Philippians*, 213; Hellerman, *Philippians*, 169. Reed (*Discourse Analysis of Philippians*, 264–265) calls it an "epistolary hesitation formula" that marks a shift from the positive exhortations in 2:28–3:1 to the negative exhortations in 3:2–21.

[215] LN 22.8.

[216] LN 22.10.

person. Thus, this "safeguard" is necessary given the possibility of Jewish Christ-believing rivals arriving in Macedonia and Paul's response is to remind them of the very things he instructed them about: beware of different gospels with a different Jesus and remember the cruciform and resurrectiform pattern of life that Paul himself modeled before them.

Paul thrice repeats his abrupt warning, "Watch out!" in v. 2. The verb *blepete* is a second-person plural imperative and is a corporate admonition for the entire Philippian assembly to take heed to his warning.[217] After each "Watch out," Paul describes something of the persons he is warning them about with three rhetorically charged images.[218] In other letters, Paul certainly did not shy from, shall we say, vigorous denunciation of persons who in his mind compromised the gospel or sought to corrupt his Gentile converts (see Gal 1:8–9; 5:12; 6:12–13; 2 Cor 11:13–15; Rom 16:17–18). Here in v. 2 we find much of the same thing, albeit with a certain level of jarring intensity as Paul does more than throw some shade on dislikeable colleagues; rather, he drops some rhetorical napalm on existentially menacing adversaries.

---

[217]  Many commentators follow G. D. Kilpatrick ("*Blepete*, Philippians 3:2," in *In Memoriam Paul Kahle* [eds. M. Black and G. Fohrer; Berlin: Töpelmann, 1968], 146–148) by arguing that when the verb *blepete* is followed by a direct object in the accusative case that it is not a warning, but pointing to an example, and it might be translated as "consider" or "take due heed" (see, e.g., Mk 4:24; 1 Cor 1:26; 10:18; 2 Cor 10:7; Col 4:17). This leads Caird (*Paul's Letters from Prison*, 131) followed by Garland (*Philippians*, 234–235) to claim that Paul was not attacking Jewish Christ-believers, but warning the Philippians not to adopt the boastful ways of the Jews. In which case, Paul would not be warning about Jewish Christ-believing proselytizers, as much as pointing to them and to the Jews more generally as a bad example of people who boast in their privileged status. The problem with that view is that: (1) It is the need for a safeguard and security (*asaphales*) in v. 1b that launches Paul's remarks in v. 2, in which case, it is context and semantics not syntax, that makes *blepete* into a warning; (2) The opponents described in vv. 2, 18–19 are not merely a bad example, but clearly rivals to Paul, and potential perverters of the gospel as the parallels to Galatians, 2 Corinthians, and Romans make clear. (3) That 3:2 was understood as a warning is apparent in our earliest copy of Philippians in 𝔓⁴⁶, which adds *blepete* at Phil 3:18 "*Watch out for* the enemies of the cross." See Reed, *Discourse Analysis of Philippians*, 245–246; Bockmuehl, *The Epistle to the Philippians*, 185; Fee, *Philippians*, 293 n. 36; Witherington, *Philippians*, 190–191; Thurston, *Philippians and Philemon*, 112–113; Silva, *Philippians*, 153; Hansen, *Philippians*, 215–217; Reumann, *Philippians*, 470–471; Hellerman, *Philippians*, 170; Keown, *Philippians*, 2.99–100.

[218]  There is a case of assonance in Paul's negative designation of these persons with k-sounding words: *kynas, kakous ergatas, katatomēn*.

First, Paul calls them "dogs" (*kynas*). To call someone a "dog" was an insult that transcended Mediterranean cultures.[219] In Jewish tradition, dogs were considered to be unclean since unclean things were thrown to dogs (Exod 22:31; *m. Ned.* 4.3), Israel's leaders were once likened to insatiable dogs (Isa 56:10–11), dogs refers to sinners returning to their sin like a dog returning to its own vomit (Prov 26:11; 2 Pet 2:22), the designation was an opprobrium against Gentiles (Mk 7:27–28; Matt 15:26–27; *m. Bek.* 5.6), the Matthean Jesus taught against giving "holy things" to "dogs," meaning Gentiles (Matt 7:6), and John of Patmos ranks dogs with all things opposed to God's holiness, "Outside are the dogs and sorcerers and fornicators and murderers and idolaters, and everyone who loves and practices falsehood" (Rev 22:15). The irony is that these Jewish Christ-believing proselytizers are, declares Paul, the symbol and summit of all things unclean before God. Whereas the proselytizers sought to impose Mosaic standards of clean and unclean upon Gentiles in order to cleanse them of their contamination by pagan idolatry and immorality, Paul taught that God had purified Gentiles by faith, baptism, and the Spirit of God, which is why they did not need Torah observance (see Acts 15:9, "He did not discriminate between us and them, for he purified their hearts by faith," cf. Gal 2:15–16; Rom 15:16; 1 Cor 1:2; 6:11; Eph 5:26; Tit 2:14; Heb 10:22; 1 John 1:7, 9).

Second, Paul describes them as "evil workers" (*kakous ergatas*), words that mean far more than "bad hombres," but is a sectarian term for those who are actually anti-God and anti-God's law. Judas called Maccabbeus embarked on a violent purge of Judea and hunted down Hellenizing Jews, as a result: "Lawbreakers shrank back for fear of him; all the evildoers (*hoi ergatai tēs anomias*) were confounded; and deliverance prospered by his hand" (1 Macc 3:6). Paul attacked the so-called super-apostles who traveled to Corinth as "deceitful workers" (*ergatai dolioi*, 2 Cor 11:13), indicating his willingness to use such language against Jewish Christ-believing opponents. Whereas these Jewish Christ-believing proselytizers believed that they were doing God's work by getting Gentiles to obey God's Torah, Paul says that this is a wicked work, contrary to God. Paul is perhaps also echoing the language of the Psalms about those who do lawless or unrighteous works (e.g., Ps 5:6; 6:9; 13:4; 27:3; 35:13; 52:5; 57:3; 58:3, 6; 63:3; 91:8, 10) or the

---

[219]  L3J 1013.

wicked-doers destined for destruction in wisdom literature and the prophets (Prov 10:29; Sir 27:3, 10; Mic 2:1; Hos 6:8). Paul himself uses such language for persons destined for judgment (Rom 2:9; 13:4; 2 Cor 11:13–15). This language ordinarily describes people who are outside of God's covenant people and are active opponents of God's own purposes. Paul thus implies that the proselytizers are on the wrong side of redemptive history, working against what God requires of his people, and they are even opposed to the plans and purposes of God. By their efforts to force Christ-believing Gentiles to enter the Sinaitic covenant, they have alienated themselves from the God of the covenant.

Third, the harshest insult Paul casts against these Jewish Christians is to call them the "mutilation" (*katatomē*). A cognate word is used in the LXX for Israelite priests being forbidden to flay their flesh as pagan priests do (Lev 21:5) and for pagan slashes to the body as part of their rituals (1 Kgs 18:28). The rites of the Cybele cultus required devotees to engage in self-flagellation and even castration.[220] This language also recalls Paul's forceful remarks in Gal 5:12 where he says, "I wish those who unsettle you would castrate themselves!" Paul normally calls Jewish Christ-believers in favor of circumcising Gentiles the *peritomē* party or "circumcision group/advocates" (Gal 2:12), but he can also define circumcision or being unforeskinned as so distinctive of Jews that it constitutes a metonym for being Jewish (see Gal 2:7–8; Rom 15:8; Col 4:11; Tit 1:10). The reason for the change is paronomasia, a polemical play on words.[221] The proselytizers might think of themselves as committed to *peritomē* ("circumcision") when in fact they are advocates of *katatomē* ("mutilation"), pagan religious slashing! This is like calling your local Baptist congregation "the drowners!" or the Methodists "the meth lab!"

In sum, Paul draws on Jewish anti-Gentile tropes and intra-Jewish sectarian polemics and provocatively applies them to his adversaries. They are Gentile dogs, the Hellenizing law-breakers, pagan priests who flay the flesh, they are the real outsiders! Or, as Thielman paraphrases v. 2: "beware of the curs, the criminals, the cutters."[222]

---

[220] L. Adkins and R. A. Adkins, *Handbook to Life in Ancient Rome* (Oxford: Oxford University Press, 2002), 289.

[221] See Lightfoot, *Philippians*, 144.

[222] Thielman, *Philippians*, 167.

To appreciate the proselytizer's argument, they probably reasoned that the Messiah perfected rather than dismantled the covenantal architecture of Israel's faith. Abraham was circumcised as the first Gentile convert to Israel's ancestral religion (Gen 17:9–14, 23–24), Moses required circumcision as the *sine qua non* of being in the covenant for males (Lev 12:3; 1 Macc 1:15), circumcision was the condition of Gentiles joining Israel (Gen 34:14–24; Exod 12:44, 48; Jdth 14:10; Esth 8:17; Josephus, *Ant.* 13.257–258; 20.38, 44–45; Josephus, *War* 2.454), it's called the "covenant of circumcision" for a good reason (Acts 7:8), Jesus was circumcised (Luke 2:21), circumcision is good for one's personal hygiene and virility (Philo, *Spec. Leg.* 1.3–7), circumcision keeps God's people separate and even pagans know that it's the sign of being one of the covenant people (Josephus, *Ant.* 1.192; 1 Macc 1:60–61; Tacitus, *Hist.* 5.5.2; Juvenal, *Satires* 14.99; Petronius, *Satyricon*, 102.14; Suetonius, *Dom.* 12.2). Circumcision was regarded by Jews, and by extension some Jewish Christ-believers, as the rite of passage for Gentile converts to join the covenant people who would be saved in the end-time (see Acts 15:1–5; Gal 2:4–5; 5:1–6; 6:12–15).[223] As a result, in Paul's mind, the potential agitators who might come to Macedonia taught that belonging to Jesus entailed a mixture of messianic faith and mutilated flesh!

Paul's response across his letters to those advocating circumcision is threefold: (1) Abraham had faith before he had circumcision, circumcision was the seal of the righteousness he had by faith, not the means for attaining righteous or any covenant standing (Rom 4); (2) The Torah brings curses for disobedience, so if you get circumcised then you have to obey the Torah, and then end up coming under its curses (Gal 3); and (3) While circumcision is not a bad thing that God has dispensed with (Rom 3:1), ultimately circumcision is not the instrument for salvation or the identity marker for belonging to God's people, for what matters is not circumcision, but Christ, faith, Spirit, obedience, and the new creation (Gal 5:6; 6:11–16; 1 Cor 7:19; Rom 2:25–29).[224]

Paul's subsequent explanatory clause ("For," *gar*), followed quickly by three participle clauses in v. 3, justifies why he is right to take such a hard

---

[223] M. F. Bird, *Crossing Over Sea and Land: Jewish Missionary Activity in the Second Temple Period* (Grand Rapids, MI: Baker, 2009), 17–43.

[224] M. F. Bird, *An Anomalous Jew: Paul among Jews, Greeks, and Romans* (Grand Rapids, MI. Eerdmans, 2016), 79–81.

stand and why he may use such harsh language against his Jewish Christ-believing rivals. He does so by way of reference to aspects of Jewish heritage that are inherited by Christ-believers in a transformed way according to the dispensation of Christ and the Spirit.[225]

First, Paul says, speaking inclusively of both himself (a Jewish Christ-believer) and the Philippians (Gentile Christ-believers),[226] "We are the circumcision."[227] On the one hand, in the Old Testament, circumcision referred to the slicing or excision of the male foreskin as a sign of belonging to Israel in its covenant with YHWH (Gen 17:9–14; Lev 12:3; Josh 5:1–9). Circumcision was not entirely unique to Israel, as circumcision was also practiced by Egyptian, Syrian, and Arab tribes (Josephus, *Ant.* 1.214; 8.262; *Apion* 1.169–171; Philo, *Spec. Leg.* 1.2), however, circumcision was certainly distinctive of Israelite males, and, in the face of aggressive Hellenization, circumcision was regarded as a sign of allegiance to the Judean way of life (see 1 Macc 1–2). In fact, Greeks and Romans who mentioned the practice referred to circumcision with a mixture of confusion and revulsion, thus circumcision became symbolic for Jewish "otherness."[228] On the other hand, the Old Testament also treats the ritual act of circumcision as symbolic for an inward devotion unto God, hence the call to "circumcise your hearts" (Deut 10:16; 30:6; Jer 4:4; 9:25–26; Ezek 44:7), which Jewish authors exposited further (*Jub* 1.23; 1QpHab 11.13; 1QS 5.5; Philo, *Spec. Leg.* 1.305). This is why one of the most polemical charges one Jew could make against other Jews was to call them "uncircumcised in hearts" (Lev 26:41; Jer 9:26; Acts 7:51). This image of circumcised hearts lent itself to a

---

[225]  Fee (*Philippians*, 302) detects an "implicit Trinitarianism" here with serving God, worshipping by the Spirit, and boasting in Christ Jesus.

[226]  Lightfoot (*Philippians*, 143) adds the gloss, "we – you and I – Gentile and Jew alike." Cf. Bockmuehl, *The Epistle to the Philippians*, 191; Fee, *Philippians*, 298; Keown, *Philippians*, 2.107–108. Contra L. J. Windsor (*Paul and the Vocation of Israel* [BZNW 205; Berlin: de Gruyter, 2014], 53–55) who thinks the "we" refers to only Paul and Timothy, while D.W. B. Robinson ("We are the Circumcision," *ABR* 15 [1967]: 30–31) restricts it to Jewish Christians.

[227]  Strictly speaking, the position of the article (*hē*) before "circumcision" (*peritomē*) makes it the subject of the sentence, literally, "The circumcision is us" (N. T. Wright, *Justification: God's Plan and Paul's Vision* [Downers Grove, IL: InterVarsity Press, 2009], 149; Reumann, *Philippians*, 463; NLT: "For we who worship by the Spirit of God are the ones who are truly circumcised").

[228]  J. J. Collins, "A Symbol of Otherness: Circumcision and Salvation in the First Century," in *'To See Ourselves as Others See Us': Christians, Jews, and 'Others' in Late Antiquity*, (eds. J. Neusner and D. S. Frerichs; Chico, CA: Scholars, 1985), 163–186.

metaphorical or allegorical interpretation of circumcision. Philo affirmed the necessity of physical circumcision against those who wanted to treat it exclusively as an allegory (*Migr. Abr.* 89–94), but Philo also gave a philosophical interpretation of circumcision to exposit its true meaning. For example, Philo refers to "a circumcision of circumcision and a purification of purification" (*Somn.* 2.25), he sees circumcision as "a symbol of the excision of the pleasures which deceive the mind" and "a symbol of a person's knowing himself, and dispensing with that terrible affliction, the ignorant opinions of the soul" (*Spec. Leg.* 1.9–10). Elsewhere, Philo claims that what makes a Gentile a proselyte is not physical circumcision, but submission to God "because the proselyte is one who circumcises not his uncircumcision but his desires and sensual pleasures and the other passions of the soul" (*Quaest. in Ex.* 2.2). Somewhat analogously, Paul demonstrates in Romans that he knows that circumcision is a sign of Jewish males belonging in the covenant, with obedience as the way a Jew is meant to appropriate his covenantal belonging. But then Paul substitutes covenant obedience for the covenant sign of circumcision. As a result, covenantal disobedience nullifies a Jew's circumcision as a sign of covenant status, while uncircumcised Gentiles can have their obedience regarded as/substituted for/imputed as physical circumcision. Hence Paul's remarks:

> Circumcision indeed is of value if you obey the law; but if you break the law, your circumcision has become uncircumcision. So, if those who are uncircumcised keep the requirements of the law, will not their uncircumcision be regarded as circumcision? Then those who are physically uncircumcised but keep the law will condemn you that have the written code and circumcision but break the law. For a person is not a Jew who is one outwardly, nor is true circumcision something external and physical. Rather, a person is a Jew who is one inwardly, and real circumcision is a matter of the heart – it is spiritual and not literal. Such a person receives praise not from others but from God. (Rom 2:25–29)

Paul, despite his reputation, did not forbid circumcision for Jews (Acts 21:21), in fact, he affirmed the role of circumcision in Israel's sacred history (Rom 3:1); he encouraged circumcised Jews to continue as they were without seeking epispasm, that is, a reversal of circumcision (1 Cor 7:18; cf. 1 Macc 1:15; Josephus, *Ant.* 12.241); he believed Abraham was the father and forebear of both the circumcised and uncircumcised who have faith in Christ (Rom 4:12); and Paul had Timothy circumcised, albeit for pragmatic missional reasons (Acts 16:3). Even so, Paul battled fiercely against anyone who would try to coerce his Gentile converts to be circumcised (Gal 2:3; 6:12–13). He could disparage physical circumcision as pertaining only to the "flesh" and as something, like making idols, "made by human hands" (Eph 2:11). Paul doesn't repudiate circumcision, but he does relativize circumcision in light of Christ and the Spirit, because for Paul what circumcision signifies is greater than the mark of circumcision itself. What truly matters is not circumcision, but "faith working through love" (Gal 5:6), the "new creation" (Gal 6:15), "a circumcision not done with hands, by putting off the body of flesh, in the circumcision of the Messiah" (Col 2:11, CSB), a new person where there is "no longer Greek and Jew, circumcision and uncircumcision" (Col 3:11). A point that was to be repeated in Christian literature in the coming centuries (see *Ep. Barn.* 9:1–9; Justin, *Dial.* 12.3; 15.7; 19.3–6; 20.1–3; 92.4).[229] Circumcision, as the sign of allegiance to the Judean way of life, and a sign of the covenant, is supplanted by baptism as the sign of allegiance and belonging to God through Jesus Christ (Rom 6:4–6; Gal 3:27–29; Col 2:11–12).

When Paul says, "We are the circumcision!" (v. 3) he is not suggesting that Gentile Christ-believers have taken the place of the Jews in some kind of crass supersessionism.[230] However, the coming of the Messiah and the gift of the Spirit, this does not leave Israel intact, as if things for the Jews can continue as normal with Gentiles now able to enter the doors of the local synagogue with some kind of "Judaism-lite" option for those who cannot bear having their Gentile genitals interfered with thanks to the local chapter of "Jews for Gentiles for Jesus." No, Paul is staking a claim here that the boundaries of God's election, the identity of his people, his "Israel," is now drawn around Messiah and the Spirit, so that Israel is

---

[229]  See further on circumcision A. Blaschke, *Beschneidung: Zeugnisse der Biblel und verwandter Texte* (TANZ 28; Tübingen: Francke, 1998); N. E. Livesey, *Circumcision as Malleable Symbol* (WUNT 2.295; Tübingen: Mohr Siebeck, 2010).

[230]  Contra Lightfoot, *Philippians*, 6. Even worse is John Chrysostom: "The Jews are no longer children" (*Phil. Hom.* 10). Dunn (*New Perspective on Paul*, 473) calls this "an unjustified reading." Holloway (*Philippians*, 156) rightly warns of the "religious prejudices of Paul's Christian interpreters." Note Keown (*Philippians*, 2.109) who asserts that Paul does not envisage a new Israel, a replacement of Israel, or a supersession of Israel, "but the continuity and extension of the remnant Israel by faith with those who accept Israel's Messiah and so are integrated into historical Israel by faith in the Messiah." See D. J. Harrington, "Did Paul Disavow Judaism? A Closer Look at Philippians 3:2–11," *TBT* 45 (2007): 295–300; Bockmuehl, *The Epistle to the Philippians*, 191.

enlarged to include the Gentiles who prove by their faith, allegiance, and obedience that they belong to God's covenant people, which, Paul would say, is precisely what God's promises to Israel always pointed toward (Gal 3:13–14; Rom 15:8–12).[231] Paul's words, "We are the circumcision," is an affirmation that God's election, adoption, covenant, and call belongs to Gentiles, once far off from God, but now brought near by Christ.

Second, Paul says that Christ-believers are those "who worship in the Spirit of God" (v. 3). The Spirit of God (*oi pneumati theou*) here is the domain of worship (dative of sphere) or the instrument for worship (dative of agency).[232] Although both options are true in their own way since a distinguishing and striking claim of Christian devotion was to worship/ serve God in and by the Spirit (Rom 1:9; 12:1; John 4:23–24). The word *latreuō* generally means "serve," but its usage in the Greek literature, the LXX, and NT has religious connotations of carrying out religious duties usually of a cultic nature, which renders fitting the translation of "worship" (ESV, KJV, NRSV, NJB, NASB).[233] Importantly, Paul is not saying that the Jews do not worship God, because Paul elsewhere can announce the privileges of the Jews in possessing "the adoption, the glory, the covenants, the giving of the law, the worship, and the promises" (Rom 9:4) and the Lucan Paul was certainly willing to engage in cultic acts in the temple as a demonstration of his Jewish piety (Acts 21:22–26; cf. 24:14). Paul's point is, as Bockmuehl notes, a contrast between "the true circumcision whose service is empowered by and directed towards the Spirit of God, and those whose service is narrow-mindedly focused on their 'works of the Law' as defining their service and status before God."[234] Worship in the Spirit is the true circumcision for Paul because it enables true worship of God and defines the true people of God. As Ambrosiaster put it: "It is evident that those who are faithful are circumcised in their own hearts. By cutting away the cloud of error, they see and recognize the Lord of creation. This is what it means to 'serve in the Spirit' and 'glory in the Lord Jesus Christ.'"[235]

A further characteristic of this redefined "circumcision" group is that they "boast in Christ Jesus and have no confidence in the flesh" (v. 3). Paul

---

[231] This is a key theme across *PFG*, part III.
[232] See Hellerman, *Philippians*, 173 for options.
[233] BDAG, 587.
[234] Bockmuehl, *The Epistle to the Philippians*, 192.
[235] Edwards, *Galatians, Ephesians, Philippians*, 267.

implicitly rules out any inappropriate confidence (*peithō*)[236] in the "flesh" (*sarx*) with "flesh" conceived here not as a synonym for the "self," but as a mixture of ancestral pride, a self-assured attitude, and human weakness (validated by what Paul says in vv. 3–6). For Reumann, "Flesh becomes the base for operations for Sin, the bastion for human pride and improper boasting."[237] One could even regard *sarx* as describing life before and outside of Christ.[238] The (stereo-)typical boasting of the Jews to establish one's status above Gentiles and before God – whether based on ethnicity or effort, whether founded upon election or built upon zeal for Israel's holiness against pagan contamination – are ruled out.[239] Boasting is in itself okay (see Jer 9:23–24; Philm 1:26; 2:16), but only on the appropriate basis, which is "exulting" (*kauchaomai*)[240] in Messiah Jesus. In other words, rather than boast in one's self, that is, exhibit a haughty confidence and make a claim for divinely favored status based upon one's inherited privileges as a Jew and how it plays out with Torah-practice (vv. 4–6), Paul claims that the only acceptable boasting is that which makes much of Jesus. Precisely what Paul himself exemplifies: "May I never boast of anything except the cross of our Lord Jesus Christ, by which the world has been crucified to me, and I to the world" (Gal 6:14); "For I will not venture to speak of anything except what Christ has accomplished through me to win obedience from the Gentiles" (Rom 15:18) and "I will boast all the more gladly of my weaknesses, so that the power of Christ may dwell in me" (2 Cor 12:9).[241]

In other words, Paul is saying that the sign of belonging to God is not the standard Jewish measures of circumcision, cultus, and confidence in Israel's forthcoming triumph over the pagans. Instead, the currency of covenantal belonging is true obedience (circumcision), being a

---

[236] The perfect participle *pepoithotes* heightens the prominence of the action and has a present force, "relying, trusting, depending, having confidence" (Hellerman, *Philippians*, 174).

[237] Reumann, *Philippians*, 465.

[238] Fee, *Philippians*, 301–302; Silva, *Philippians*, 149; Hellerman, *Philippians*, 174.

[239] See S. J. Gathercole, *Where Is the Boasting? Early Jewish Soteriology and Paul's Response in Romans 1–5* (Grand Rapids, MI: Eerdmans, 2002). Barclay's comment (*Paul and the Gift*, 509), although speaking of Romans, just as well applies to Phil 3: "If the only legitimate 'boast,' the only ground of worth, is in the work of God in Christ … those who reconceptualize themselves 'in Christ' are divested of every claim to superiority, attributed or acquired."

[240] According to BDAG, 536: "boast, glory, pride oneself, brag."

[241] See too 1 Cor 1:28–31; 10:17; 2 Cor 1:14; Eph 2:9.

Spirit-person (worship by the Spirit), and boasting in the Messiah's deeds (no confidence in the flesh).

---

### Closer Look: Jewish Sectarian Polemics

The context in which to understand Paul's combative remarks against Jewish Christ-believing rivals in 3:2–4 is not the tradition of *adversus Israel* literature that one finds in Melito of Sardis, Justin Martyr, the *Epistle to Diognetus*, and the *Epistle of Barnabas*, nor even the bitter attacks leveled against the Jews given by bishops Ignatius and John Chrysostom, but as a species of discourse related to intra-Jewish sectarian polemics. Paul can indeed speak with hostility against his fellow Jews (1 Thess 2:14-16), lament their unbelief (Romans 9–11), even as he aspires for their conversion to Christ (1 Cor 9:20; 2 Cor 3:16; Rom 11.26–32), but here in Phil 3 his target is fellow Jewish Christ-believers, making his remarks an intra-Christian affair akin to other species of intra-Jewish polemics. Consequently, we should not read the text here as a salvo of confrontational interfaith attacks by a Christian against the Jews. Rather, we are best to understand Paul's statements as part of the internecine and sectarian rivalry within a Jewish movement, largely over the matter of continuity and discontinuity between the Abrahamic, Sinaitic, and messianic epochs, as well as pertaining to the status of Gentiles in the Church and the requirements laid upon them for inclusion in the Church. It is within the debate and polemics in places like Phil 3 that Paul arguably attempts to forge a distinctly Christ-believing identity for both himself and his congregations.[242] Because of the intra-Christian nature of the discourse – and by "Christian" we mean here "Jewish Christian" – it is useful and illuminating to observe some of the things that some Jewish groups said about other Jewish groups. This provides us with a context in which to understand Paul's polemical remarks against other Jewish Christians.

---

| | | |
|---|---|---|
| For they [i.e. the Pharisees] had sought flattery, choosing travesties of true religion; they looked for ways to break | But really they [i.e. the Pharisees] consume the goods of the poor, saying their acts are according to justice while in fact they are | In secret places underground was their [i.e. some Judean priest] lawbreaking, provoking (him [God]), son involved |

---

[242] On which, see N. Nikki, *Opponents and Identity in Philippians* (NovTSup 173; Leiden: Brill, 2019). Also, deSilva ("No Confidence in the Flesh," 30) points to the German proverb: "Sage mir, mit wem du streitest, und ich sage dir, wer du bist" ("Tell me with whom you fight, and I will tell you who you are") with the result that, "The references to enemies clarify and strengthen commitment to the κοινωνία of the Christian community."

the law; they favored the fine neck. They called the guilty innocent, and the innocent guilty. They overstepped covenant, violated law; and they conspired together to kill the innocent, for all those who lived pure lives they loathed from the bottom of their heart. So they persecuted them violently, and were happy to see the people quarrel. Because of all this God became very angry with their company. He annihilated the los of them because all their deeds were uncleanness to him. (CD 1.18–2.1 [trans. from Wise, Abegg, Cook).

simply exterminators, deceitfully seeking to conceal themselves so that they will not be known as completely godless because of their criminal deeds committed all the day long, saying, 'We shall have feasts, even luxurious winnings and dinings. Indeed, we shall behave ourselves as princes.' They, with hand and mind, will touch impure things, yet their mouths will speak enormous things, and they will even say, 'Do not touch me, lest you pollute me in the position I occupy. (T.Mos 7.5–10 [trans. J. Priest])

with mother and father with daughter; everyone committed adultery with his neigbor's wife; they made agreements with them with an oath about these things. They stole from the sanctuary of God as if they were no redeeming heir. They walked on the place of sacrifice of the Lord, (coming) from all kinds of uncleanness; and (coming) with menstrual blood (on them), they defile the sacrifices as if they were common meat. There was no sin they left undone in which they did not surpass the Gentiles. (Pss. Sol. 8.9–13 [trans. R. Wright])

He [i.e., the high priest Jason] took delight in establishing a gymnasium right under the citadel, and he induced the noblest of the young men to wear the Greek hat. There was such an extreme of Hellenization and increase in the adoption of foreign ways because of the surpassing wickedness of Jason, who was ungodly and no true high priest, that the priests were no longer intent upon their service at the altar. Despising the sanctuary and neglecting the sacrifices, they hurried to take part in the unlawful proceedings in the wrestling arena after the signal for the discus-throwing, disdaining the honors prized by their ancestors and putting the highest value upon Greek forms of prestige. (2 Mac 4:12–15, NRSV)

I know the slander of those who say they are Jews [of Asia Minor] and are not, but are a synagogue of Satan . . . Take note! I will make those from the synagogue of Satan, who claim to be Jews and are not, but are lying – note this – I will make them come and bow down at your feet, and they will know that I have loved you. (Rev 2:9; 3:9, CSB)

3:4B–6: PAUL'S INHERITED JEWISH PRIVILEGES

If anyone else has reason to be confident in the flesh, I have more:

⁵ circumcised on the eighth day, a member of the people of Israel, of the tribe of Benjamin, a Hebrew born of Hebrews; as to the law, a Pharisee;

⁶ as to zeal, a persecutor of the church; as to righteousness under the law, blameless.

The mention of putting "confidence" in the flesh (participle form of *peithō*) in v. 3 provides the springboard for Paul to discourse about his own former "confidence" in the flesh (noun *pepoithēsis*) in v. 4a and the confidence anyone else might assert (infinitive *pepoithenai*) in v. 4b.²⁴³ Paul's aim in vv. 4–6 is to crush such confidence! Paul shifts from censuring those who put confidence in the flesh, to warning as to why putting confidence in the flesh is a bad option. What Paul does here is lay out his former confidence in the flesh as expressed in his inherited Jewish privileges (see 2 Cor 11:22; Rom 11:1; Acts 23:6).²⁴⁴ Not only his "national righteousness," but also his claim to a salient and superior status based on how he performed and perfected those privileges as a zealous Pharisee. Paul knows this path, he knows it from the inside and out, in his thinking back then, he didn't just practice Torah, he practically perfected it!²⁴⁵ But

---

²⁴³ We see clear wordplay, as noted by Holloway, *Philippians*, 157 n. 10.

²⁴⁴ The term "inherited privileges" goes back to Lightfoot, *Philippians*, 143.

²⁴⁵ Helpful here is P. T. O'Brien, "Was Paul Converted?" in *Justification and Variegated Nomism* (eds. D. A. Carson, M. A. Seifrid, and P. T. O'Brien; Grand Rapids, MI: Baker, 2001–2004), vol. 2, 372–375, who rightly notes that it is not just Jewish privileges, but also personal achievement in those privileges that is in view. This points somewhat away from E. P. Sanders' view that "my righteousness" means nothing performative but "the peculiar result of being an observant Jew which is in and of itself a good thing" (*Paul, the Law, and the Jewish People* [Philadelphia: Fortress, 1985], 44–45). Similarly, N. T Wright suggests what is at issue is not "How might I earn God's favour," but "What are the signs that I am a member of God's people?" (*PFG*, 987, 991). On reflection, I think these two questions of ethnicity and effort dovetail together, as O'Brien shows. As proof of that, Wright goes on to argue that Phil 3:4-6 is about "national or ethnic status," but also "demonstrating through Torah-practice, one's covenant membership as per the previous six categories" (*PFG*, 988–989) – thus ethnicity and effort or privilege and performance are two sides of the same coin! Dunn's mature work on the topic (*New Perspective on Paul*, 480) admits that Paul's words here go "well beyond confidence in ethnic status" and "there is an element of self-achievement and of pride in self-achievement in both Gal. 1.14 and by implication in Phil. 3.6." P. M. Sprinkle (*Paul & Judaism Revisited: A Study of Divine and Human Agency in Salvation* [Downers Grove, IL: InterVarsity Press, 2013], 247) offers a good summary: "While it is true that Saul the

now, looking back upon his former way of life in Judaism from the vantage point of faith (see Gal 1:13), through the lens of a Messiah-shaped perspective (see 1 Cor 2:16), he knows such confidences are a dead-end, a false confidence, a stumbling block, and, in comparison to Christ, they are worthless (see Gal 2:15–21; Rom 9:30–10:4).[246]

Paul attacks not merely Jewish ethnocentrism (the view that God has limited his grace to the Jews) nor a type of Jewish nomism (the view that Torah observance obtains salvation), but something of a hybrid. Paul critiques an ethnocentric nomism,[247] where salvation is enclosed within the boundaries of Jewish communities and dependent on the rites of entry to join the Jewish community, measures of righteousness and fidelity within the Jewish community, and contingent upon scales of attainment weighed ahead of the eschaton.[248] In contrast, Paul dismantles traditional Jewish categories of constructing worth based on the recalibration of values brought by the advent of Christ.[249] This is designed, first, to warn the Philippians against being seduced into adopting Jewish scales for calculating and establishing one's worth before God, which certain Jewish Christ-

---

Pharisee was certainly not trying to pull himself up by his moral bootstraps and earn his way to heaven, his life was devoted to triggering God's end-time salvation through torah devotion and the violent purification of Israel. More than just a call to a new vocation, Paul's Damascus road encounter would entail a rereading of salvation history – a transposition of the divine and human dynamics in bringing eschatological salvation into the present through the death and resurrection of the Messiah." See too Gathercole, *Where Is the Boasting?*, 181–182; Hansen, *Philippians*, 239; Grindheim, *The Crux of Election*, 133–134.

[246]   What we find in Phil 3:6 is proof that Paul's conversion to Christ-faith was not borne of a guilt-stricken conscience searching for a merciful God like an Augustine or Martin Luther. Further, Rom 7:7–25 is best understood as a retrospective view of Paul's pre-conversion life from the standpoint of faith in Christ. According to G. Theissen (*Psychological Aspects of Pauline Theology* [trans. J. P. Galvin; Philadelphia: Fortress, 1987], 235): "The thesis defended here . . . is that Phil. 3:4–6 reflects the consciousness of the pre-Christian Paul, while Romans 7 depicts a conflict that was unconscious at the time, one of which Paul became conscious only later."

[247]   M. F. Bird, *The Saving Righteousness of God: Studies on Paul, Justification, and the New Perspective* (Milton Keynes: Paternoster, 2007), 19–35, esp. 116–117.

[248]   See further M. F. Bird, "What If Martin Luther Had Read the Dead Sea Scrolls? Historical Particularity and Theological Interpretation on Pauline Theology: Galatians as a Test Case," *JTI* 3 (2009): 118.

[249]   J. M. G. Barclay, *Paul: A Very Brief History* (London: SPCK, 2017), 77; idem, *Paul and the Gift*, esp. 356–387, 426, 439. Similarly, Garland ("Philippians," 237) comments: "Faith in Christ creates a new self-understanding that destroys delusions of grandeur built on fleshly categories. Glorifying in Christ means looking away from the self to Christ, on whom one relies solely for salvation."

believing proselytizers might attempt to foist upon them. Paul endeavors to prove that "faith in Christ places Gentile believers on the same footing before God as Jewish believers, co opting them into the Abrahamic covenant which circumcision symbolizes."[250] Then, second, Paul might also want the Philippians to reflect on their own resident scales of worth, such as honor, prestige, and glory, either ascribed by birth or acquired by achievement – parallel to Paul's Jewish privileges and accomplishments[251] and urge "his readers to resist accommodation to the social verticality and pride of honors which so indelibly left their mark on public life in Philippi, by radically redefining, vis-à-vis the dominant culture, the kind of behaviour to be honoured among member of the Christian *ekklēsia*."[252]

Paul declares in v. 4b not merely the fact of his former confidence in the "flesh," a metonym for his former Jewish way life, but his superlative and superior grounds for having such confidence: "If anyone else has reason to be confident in the flesh, I have more." Paul boldly declares that if confidence in the flesh is currency in covenantal righteousness, then, "I have more" (*egō mallon*). The adverb *mallon* means to a greater and higher degree.[253] Paul can not only claim equal confidence in the flesh as his imagined interlocutors, but he can claim it to an even superior degree than they can. Paul had greater claim for confidence in his Jewish heritage and more license for hubris than his Jewish Christ-believing rivals because of how he lived out his Judaism as a zealous Pharisee. He can out-righteous them in any of the indices that they are using to determine righteousness.

First, when it comes to parentage and pedigree, Paul is proudly Jewish (v. 5). He was "circumcised on the eighth day,[254] a member of the people of

---

[250] Bockmuehl, *The Epistle to the Philippians*, 191.
[251] Pilhofer (*Philippi*, 1.122–127) notes Roman equivalents to Paul's inherited privileges found in inscriptions and writings:

| | |
| --- | --- |
| Circumcised on the eighth day | *Toga virilus* (taking on the Toga as a coming of age ceremony) |
| From the ethnic group of Israel | *Civis Romanus* (Roman citizenship) |
| From the tribe of Benjamin | *Tribu Voltinia* (an ancient Roman tribal line common in Philippi) |
| Hebrew from Hebrews | *Cai Filius* (sons of Cai, a family name) |

[252] Hellerman, *Philippians*, 128, esp. 121–128.
[253] BDAG, 613.
[254] See Gen 17:12, "every male among you shall be circumcised when he is eight days old." Cf Lev 12:3; Luke 2:21; *Jub.* 15.11–14.

Israel, of the tribe of Benjamin, a Hebrew born of Hebrews." Paul lays out various prestige labels such as "circumcision," "Israel," "tribe of Benjamin," and "Hebrew born of Hebrew" to valorize himself as a Jewish male. Paul signals the integrity of his Jewish identity and his fully fledged Israelite ancestry by stressing the purity of his Jewish lineage. Paul is not a half-Jew, not the son of a proselyte, and not a proselyte himself. Paul has a Hebrew mother and claims that Hebrew is his mother-tongue. Paul is not like those returning Judean exiles who "could not prove by their ancestral houses or lineage that they belonged to Israel" (Ezra 2:59; Neh 7:661; 1 Esdr 5:37). He belongs to the Jewish commonwealth as one of the sons of covenant and he has a claim for full membership in Israel's ethno-religious tradition. Paul's background means he has "platinum membership" in the elect people.[255] This naturally reminds one of how Josephus set out his Jewish family credentials: "The family from which I am born is not an insignificant one, but has descended from a long line of priests; and as nobility among several people is of different origin, so with us to be of the sacerdotal dignity, is a proof of the glory of my family ... By my mother I am of a royal bloodline, descended from the Hasmoneans, a family that possessed both the office of the high priesthood and the dignity of a king combined together."[256]

Second, Paul adds, "as to the law, a Pharisee" (v. 5). Paul asserts that when it comes to the Torah that he adopted the halakah of the Pharisees, their precise manner of interpretation and the pattern of life that went with it. Importantly, we should not think of the Pharisees as merely emblems of religious externalism and legalistic hypocrisy. Jesus was closer to the Pharisees than to any other sect (Mk 12:18–27) and many Pharisees joined the early Church (Acts 15:5). Pharisaism was a Judean faction that had a long history as a political force and a religious renewal movement. The Pharisees were known for their scrupulous observance[257] and their separation from others.[258] The Pharisees were arguably concerned with transmitting their "tradition" to the people to cultivate a priestly level of purity that sought to avoid cultic and moral contamination and would usher in

---

[255] Grindheim, *The Crux of Election*, 128.
[256] Josephus, *Life* 1–2 (3–9 is about Josephus' heritage) (trans. MFB).
[257] Note the use of the word *akribeia* ("exactness" or "precision") in Acts 22:3; 26:5; Josephus, *War* 1.108–109; 2.162; *Ant.* 20.200–201; *Life* 191.
[258] See, for example, Mk 2:16; 7:5; Acts 11:3; Gal 2:11–14.

the renewal of the nation (see Mk 7:3–5; Gal 1:14; Josephus, *Ant.* 13.288, 297–298, 408; 18.15).[259] The Pharisees also had a zealous wing that hoped for and were willing to fight for the purification of Israel from Gentile domination, particularly in the Pharisaic school associated with Rabbi Shammai. Paul sounds like the Pharisees whom Josephus describes as being skilled in interpretation of the Jewish tradition, believed themselves to be favored by God, opposed to pagan rulers, refused to take an oath of loyalty to the Roman emperor, and given to sedition (Josephus, *Ant.* 17.41–42; 18.4).[260]

Third, Paul connects his former Pharisaism with a particular ethos that was willing to engage in holy violence to protect the sanctity of the Jewish people and their worship of God, which is why he says about himself, "as to zeal, a persecutor of the church" (v. 6).

Importantly, "zeal" here (*zēlos*) doesn't mean merely bucket loads of enthusiasm, but connects to a well-known tradition whereby one engaged in fervent devotion to God by performing zealous acts of violence to protect God's honor and Israel's holiness.[261] In the Torah, God himself has a particular zeal or jealousy for his worship – aniconic monolatry to be exact – by Israel (Exod 20:5; 34:14; Deut 4:23–24; 5:9; 6:14–15; 32:21). Elijah exercised zeal in his destruction of the Baal prophets (1 Kg 18:40; 19:10, 14; 1 Macc 2:58). Phinehas burned with zeal and turned back God's wrath by killing an Israelite man who married a Midianite woman (Num 25:6–13), and Phinehas was subsequently remembered as the paradigmatic holy zealot for Israel's holiness and God's reputation (Ps 106:28–31; Sir 45:23–24; 4 Macc 18:12; Josephus, *Ant.* 4.152–155). In a Jewish novella, the

[259] See J. P. Meier, *A Marginal Jew: Companions and Competitors* (ABRL; New York: Doubleday, 2001), 289–388; R. Deines, "The Pharisees between 'Judaisms' and 'Common Judaism,'" in *Justification and Variegated Nomism*, (eds. D. A. Carson, M. A. Seifrid, and P. T. O'Brien; Grand Rapids, MI: Baker, 2001), 2 vols., 1.443–504; J. D. G. Dunn, *Jesus Remembered* (Grand Rapids, MI: Eerdmans, 2003), 266–270; B. Chilton and J. Neusner, eds., *In Quest of the Historical Pharisees* (Waco, TX: Baylor University Press, 2008); N. T. Wright, *New Testament and the People of God* (Minneapolis: Fortress, 1992), 187–197; *Jesus and the Victory of God* (Minneapolis: Fortress, 1996), 377–382; *PFG*, 80–89; 177–196.

[260] Wright (*PFG*, 85–90) sees Paul as a Shammaite Pharisee, whereas J. Neusner (*The Rabbinic Traditions about the Pharisees before 70* [Leiden: Brill, 1971], 1.341–376) identifies Paul as belonging to a separate school associated with Gamaliel.

[261] See J. D. G. Dunn, *Beginning from Jerusalem* (CITM; Grand Rapids, MI: Eerdmans, 2009), 342–346; *PFG*, 80–90.

widow Judith called upon God to aid "your beloved children who burned with zeal for you and abhorred the pollution of their blood and called on you for help" against the Assyrians (Jdth 9:4). The Maccabean insurgency began when a Judean priest named Mattathias saw a fellow villager in Modein come forward to offer a sacrifice upon a pagan altar. Consequently, "He burned with zeal and his heart was stirred. He gave vent to righteous anger; he ran and killed him on the altar. At the same time he killed the king's officer who was forcing them to sacrifice, and he tore down the altar. Thus he burned with zeal for the law, just as Phinehas did against Zimri son of Salu" (1 Macc 2:24–26; cf. 2 Macc 4:2; Josephus, *Ant.* 12.270–271). We can also mention Philo who referred to myriads of vigilantes who were zealous for the Judean laws and were willing to visit violence upon anyone known to break those laws (Philo, *Spec. Leg.* 2.253). During the time of the Judean rebellion against Rome, a party called "zealots" emerged who were known for their holy violence (Josephus, *War* 2.651). According to Lionel Windsor, such zeal "manifests itself chiefly in the exclusion of idolatry and immorality and in the violent removal of any foreigners who are tempting Israel towards such idolatry and immorality" and zeal for the law entails "a commitment to struggle for the purity of Israel's monotheistic worship and obedience, construed in terms of the Law of Moses, against threats from opponents."[262] Evidently, then, Saul's self-conscious zeal is one of the things that gave him "confidence in the flesh," an acute assurance of his superlative status in Jewish measures; and it led him to be a "persecutor" of a Jewish sect that allegedly mounted a major challenge to the Pharisaic vision of Israel's holiness, worship, and obedience.[263] Just as some of the Pharisees had challenged and plotted against Jesus, so too Saul the Pharisee attacked the followers of Jesus

[262] Windsor, *Paul and the Vocation of Israel*, 91.
[263] There is no doubt that Paul's account of "zeal" refers to an attitude that aggressively agitates and acts for Israel's purity and set-apartness against foreigners and idolatry (rightly, J. D. G. Dunn, *Theology of Paul the Apostle* [Grand Rapids, MI: Eerdmans, 1998], 529–532; N. T. Wright, *What Saint Paul Really Said* [Grand Rapids, MI: Eerdmans, 1997], 25–37, 92–94). Some have tried to mute this ethnic dimension and argue instead that zeal is more about "activism" than "separation" (e.g., V. M. Smiles, "The Concept of 'Zeal' in Second-Temple Judaism and Paul's critique of It in Romans 10.2," *CBQ* 64 [2002]: 282–299). However, the fact is that Jewish discourse about "zeal" operates in a horizon characterized by vigorously opposing social contamination by foreigners combined with avoiding religious defilement caused by idolatry. That said, the zeal to stop such violations by means of violence itself is an expression of religious

because they offered a different view of Torah and the Jewish way of life that was not only deficient but was considered to be an affront to Israel's set-apart-holiness (see Gal 1:13–14; Acts 22:3–4).[264] Lightfoot's paraphrase is apt: "I was zealous above them all; I asserted my principles with fire and sword; I persecuted, imprisoned, slew these infatuated Christians; this was my great claim to God's favour."[265] Paul's ferocious obedience and zealous violence for Israel's holiness was an example of what Reinhold Niebuhr called "the fury of self-righteousness."[266]

## Closer Look: Why Did Saul of Tarsus Persecute Christians?

Why did Saul of Tarsus, the pre-Christian Paul, persecute the Church (see 1 Cor 15:9; Gal 1:13, 23; 1 Tim 1:13)?[267] According to Luke, persecutions included pursuing Christians as far as adjacent territories, seeking their extradition, making murderous threats against them, voting for their execution, inflicting imprisonment and punishment, and vicious attempts to force them to commit blasphemies against Jesus (see Acts 8:1–3; 9:1–2; 22:4–5; 26:9–11). Saul of Tarsus probably persecuted Christians for the same reason that Saul, in his persona as the Apostle Paul, was himself persecuted by the Jews: Jewish Christ-believers were considered "a rogue cult" that was leading Israel astray.[268] In the end, there probably were many reasons why Saul persecuted Christians: their devotion to a crucified man as Israel's Messiah was abhorrent as it seemed absurd, veneration of same crucified man on par or parallel

devotion and relies on a moral vision of Judean society, hence too, the "zeal" of the righteous to bring justice for the poor in 4Q424 frag. 3 8–11. Zeal to protect Israel's holiness is a robust demonstration of one's devotion to God (see D. C. Ortlund, *Zeal without Knowledge: The Concept of Zeal in Romans 10, Galatians 1, and Philippians 3* [LNTS 472; London: T&T Clark, 2012], esp. 150–176, even though the ethnic aspects are slightly more subdued than I [Bird] would prefer).

[264] A. J. Saldarini, *Pharisees, Scribes, Sadducees in Palestinian Society: A Sociological Approach* (Wilmington, DE: Michael Glazier, 1988), 136.

[265] Lightfoot, *Philippians*, 148.

[266] R. Niebuhr, *An Interpretation of Christian Ethics* (New York: Harper & Brothers, 1935), 230.

[267] A. J. Hultgren, "Paul's Pre-Christian Persecutions of the Church: Their Purpose, Locale and Nature," *JBL* 95 (1976): 97–111; J. Taylor, "Why Did Paul Persecute the Church?" in *Tolerance and Intolerance in Early Judaism and Christianity* (eds. G. Stanton and G. Strouma; Cambridge: Cambridge University Press, 1998), 99–120; L. W. Hurtado, "Pre-70 C.E. Jewish Opposition to Christ-Devotion," *JTS* 50 (1999): 35–58; T. Seland, "Saul of Tarsus and Early Zealotism: Reading Gal 1,13–14 in Light of Philo's Writings," *Bib* 83 (2002): 449–471; Dunn, *Beginning from Jerusalem*, 335–346; *PFG*, 1155.

[268] E. P. Sanders, *Paul: The Apostle's Life, Letters, and Thought* (Minneapolis: Fortress, 2013), 194–195, 191.

to worship of YHWH was injurious to monotheism and therefore blasphemous, their Torah-observance was perceived as lax in some regards, some members of the Church were fraternizing with Gentiles and accepting them as equals in communal gatherings, they perhaps rehearsed Jesus' own critique of the temple, and their growing numbers caused concern among both the official leaders of Judea connected to the temple and to the more popular yet unofficial leaders among the Pharisees who perceived them as potential rivals. The Christ-believers, whether called "followers of the way" (Acts 9:2; 22:4) or "Nazarenes" (Acts 24:5), were vigorously and violently opposed by the young zealous Pharisee from Tarsus because they were a threat to Israel's holiness, worship, and covenant obedience. In the tradition of Phinehas and Mattathias, the zealous Saul strove with all of his strength to destroy them.

Yet it was his Christophany, the encounter with Christ on the road to Damascus, that left Saul's world in a state of theological upheaval, cosmic reconfiguration, and a dramatic reversal of convictions, not the least in relation to Torah and Christ.[269] Consequently, Jesus was not only the Messiah and Son of God, but it was Jesus, not the Torah, who was at the center of God's purposes; it was Jesus not Torah who was now to be identified with God's glory; allegiance to Jesus not Torah determined one's position before God; Jesus' crucifixion was Israel's cursedness laid upon him just as Jesus's resurrection was Israel's vindication embodied in him; it was Jesus in whom the nations would hope; and the Church was not an apostate sect, but the visible presence of the risen Jesus's body on earth. According to Martin Hengel:

For him [Paul], the encounter with the Resurrected One near Damascus set before him the question of the *law or Christ* in the form of a *soteriological* alternative. For Judaism of that time the *Torah* was in manifold expression the essence of salvation, and could be identified with the fundamental religious metaphor, 'life.' Since the opposition between Torah and Jesus of Nazareth had made him into a persecutor, now the relationship between Christ and Torah had to become a fundamental issue, in which the inversion of the opposition immediately became apparent: he, the Resurrected One is *zōē* for those who believe.[270]

---

[269] On which, see T. L. Donaldson (*Paul and the Gentiles: Remapping the Apostle's Convictional World* [Minneapolis: Fortress, 1997], 286): "His persecuting zeal was fuelled by a perception that the Christ proclaimed in the gospel represented a rival boundary marker for the people of God."

[270] M. Hengel, "The Stance of the Apostle Paul toward the Law in the Unknown Years between Damascus and Antioch," in *Justification and Variegated Nomism: Volumes 2 – The Paradoxes of Paul* (eds. D. A. Carson, P. T. O'Brien, and M. Seifrid; Grand Rapids, MI: Baker, 2001–2004), 2 vols., 2.84.

Fourth, v. 6 rounds out with Paul claiming that his Torah obedience and zealous exploits to the point of holy violence meant that he was, "as to righteousness under the law, blameless." By "righteousness" (*dikaiosynē*) he means a status of being-in-the-right with respect to God and by "blameless" (*amemptos*) he probably means not an absolute forensic state of sinless perfection but a general character that was acceptable to God.[271] Paul formerly relied on his conscientious observance of Torah, which included within it a provision for atonement and appeasement under the terms of the covenant.[272] Paul had, then, a "palpable satisfaction" with his behavior before God and before his compatriots.[273] As Christ's apostle, Paul aspires for his Macedonian congregations to be "blameless" at the day of Christ Jesus, not sinless perfectionism, but faithful to the Lord Jesus to very end (see Phil 1:10; 2:15; 1 Thess 2:10; 3:13; 5:23). Paul's pre-conversion account of himself was that his energies and exemplarity in Judaism was such that he was self-assured of his position before God and his superiority over other Judeans. Paul's next move was to say that while many would consider that to be an achievement, an advantage, a cause for boasting, even a "gain," now, instead, by knowing Christ, believing in Christ, and participating in Christ, he considers the whole righteousness-by-Torah project to be "loss."

---

### Bridging the Horizons: Paul and the White Privileged Church

The discussion of privilege, especially, "white privilege" is a hot button subject that gets routinely discussed in news commentary, social media, in sociology classes, or anywhere where race is a presenting issue. For me (Bird) as white male to address such a subject could be judged as potentially unwise since it is so easy to court offence on such an emotive topic. Yet, I think Phil 2 and 3 offers us some resources to address such a sensitive topic as racial relations and white privilege and what it means for the Christian churches, who see in Paul's letter to the Philippians God's word for them to read, mark, digest, and live out in community with others.

---

[271] Similarly E. P. Sanders, *Paul and Palestinian Judaism* (Minneapolis: Fortress, 1977), 203; Dunn, *New Perspective on Paul*, 479–480; *PFG*, 989.

[272] M. A. Seifrid, *Justification by Faith: The Origin and Development of a Central Pauline Theme* (Leiden: Brill, 1992), 174; F. A. Thielman, *Paul and the Law: A Contextual Approach* (Downers Grove, IL; InterVarsity Press, 1994), 155.

[273] Donaldson, *Paul and the Gentiles*, 138–139.

To begin with, I think it is exceedingly difficult to deny that being white does present itself with distinct privileges in most Western environs. The way one is screened at an airport or treated by police in a roadside stop is generally different for whites and blacks. Added to that, in the United States, UK, and Australia, whites are more likely to go to college than blacks and blacks are more likely to experience incarceration than whites. Then one could compare life-expectancy rates or average incomes to see further disparities. It is demonstrably true then that white people enjoy certain privileges based on their skin color and blacks experience certain disadvantages and discrimination because of theirs.

Of course, less we think that is all to say in the matter, there are three caveats we should make: (1) Privilege in the end is still relative. Irrespective of what *general* advantages or disadvantages accrue because of one's ethnicity, they are still *relative* to the socioeconomic status, family stability, educational setting, vocational opportunities, and place of origin that one is born into. One can be black and still experience relative advantages of prosperity and family stability just as one can be born into white rural poverty characterized by dysfunction and disadvantages. (2) Merely acknowledging white privilege does not end its negative effects on minorities. More often than not, acknowledging white privilege merely becomes a pretense to wield privilege in a paternalistic patronage over minorities. In other words, the solution to white privileges should not be a white savior complex. (3) My experience of listening to students of diverse backgrounds has taught me that racial, ethnic, and tribal prejudices are not limited to white cultures and they exist also among Asian, Arab, Latin American, and African peoples too. Cultures characterized by matrices of prejudice and power are sadly ubiquitous across the globe. White privilege is merely one version of the type of racial and ethnic inequalities that can be found in other parts of the world.

What does any of this have to do with Paul's letter to the Philippians? Well, given Paul's narrative of Christ divesting himself of the privilege of divine equality to become a servant, and given Paul's own biographical description of how he divested himself of his Jewish privileges in order to know and gain Christ, what should our response be? What privileges are we called to set aside so that we can imitate Christ and Paul? For those of us who live in a multicultural and multiracial context, we have an inevitable question that we must confront, namely, how does one live out the Spirit-created reality that in Christ there is neither black nor white, neither Asian nor Arab, but all one in Christ Jesus (Gal 3:28)? To be more specific, if Paul was among us now, and we gave him a crash course on the history of the British Empire and the United States, how might he react to the racial, cultural, and economic privileges that we often discuss?

As a modest proposal for an enormous topic, I would suggest that this requires, in the first instance, recognizing the historical factors that have shaped the present moment including the heritage of slavery, segregation, patterns of immigration, the systematic exploitation of indigenous populations, and the history of civil rights and discrimination protections. Knowing the ugliness and the triumphs of our legacies pertaining to colonization, race-relations, immigration, and legislation will help us to face the future. In the second instance, it entails discerning within the precincts of one's own conscience how one can move beyond privilege to inclusion and equality, in both the Church and within wider society.

A white majority church can divest itself of the privilege of race by: (1) empowering and listening to the voices of minorities who speak in the pulpit and public square so that their perspectives are acknowledged and acted upon; (2) recognizing that minorities have lived experience of alienation and disempowerment from which they can lead our churches when they feel alienated and disempowered from the majority culture; (3) moving beyond toleration and tokenism to apprehend an equality within churches pertaining to the opportunities for Christians of all kinds to exercise their spiritual gifts; (4) training and calling indigenous and ethnic leaders to lead white majority churches; and (5) ending all caste systems that create hierarchies of power and privilege based on ethnicity, nationality, tribe, or language in favor of an equality principle moored in the gospel of Jesus Christ.

In the end, however, the best thing white majority churches can do to divest themselves of their privileges is to implement the ecclesial corollaries that follow on from Paul's remarks ruling out *diastolē* ("distinction") between believers (Rom 3:22; 10:12) and *prosōpolēmpsia* ("favoritism") before God and within the Church (Rom 2:11; Gal 2:6; Eph 6:9; Col 3:25; 1 Tim 5:21). Paul's gospel calls us to imitate Christ in his divestment of privilege with a view to serving others rather than consciously or unconsciously merely absorbing and baptizing the resident prejudices that we live among. That is at least part of what it means to have the mind of Christ Jesus (Phil 2:5).

3:7–11: PAUL AND THE SURPASSING KNOWLEDGE OF CHRIST

[7] Yet whatever gains I had, these I have come to regard as loss because of Christ.

[8] More than that, I regard everything as loss because of the surpassing value of knowing Christ Jesus my Lord. For his sake I have suffered the loss of all things, and I regard them as rubbish, in order that I may gain Christ

[9] and be found in him, not having a righteousness of my own that comes from the law, but one that comes through faith in Christ, the righteousness from God based on faith.

[10] I want to know Christ and the power of his resurrection and the sharing of his sufferings by becoming like him in his death,

[11] if somehow I may attain the resurrection from the dead.

Paul claimed in vv. 4–6 that he can outdo and out-Jew any of his Jewish Christ-believing rivals in the normal Jewish indices of measuring one's position before God. But Paul will now say in vv. 7–9 that a metaphorical gold medal in the Maccabean Games for Torah-interpretation, religious zeal, separation from sinners, and national righteousness is worthless, less than worthless, it is loss or disadvantage in the epoch of the new covenant wrought by Christ. In the Roman idiom Paul is saying that his own *Res Gestae* ("Things Accomplished") and his own ascent across the *Cursus Honorum* ("course of [prestigious] offices")[274] matters for naught. Paul asserts that he can win in any game of competition for status, but he now turns to ridicule the entire program of attaining status in the flesh, that is, in human accomplishment.[275] For Paul, the only currency that counts is Christ, the only status that avails is in Christ, and the only boast that matters is of Christ. Everything else is nothing, less than nothing, it is rubbish in comparison.[276]

In something of a volte-face,[277] Paul declares that his inherited Jewish privileges (Israelite ancestry, Hebrew parents, and circumcision) and his Jewish achievements (Pharisaism, zeal, persecution of the Church, righteousness from the law, and blamelessness before God) are not "gain" (*kerdos*), something earned or for one's advantage.[278] To the contrary, "these I have come to regard as loss because of Christ," and by "loss" (*zēmia*) this pertains to "damage, disadvantage, loss, forfeit" (v. 7).[279] This is financial imagery to the effect that all of his former gains, all of his assets so to speak, have been transferred to the liability column in order to gain

---

[274] On the significance of the *cursus honorum*, see J. Hellerman, Reconstructing Honor in Roman Philippi: *Carmen Christi* as *Cursus Pudorum* (SNTSMS; Cambridge: Cambridge University Press, 2008), chap. 2.

[275] L. G. Bloomquist, *The Function of Suffering in Philippians* (JSNTSup 78; Sheffield: JSOT Press, 1993), 178.

[276] Lightfoot (*Philippians*, 149) rightly points to the "earnest repetition" of language across vv. 7–9: gain, consider, loss, Christ, all things, faith, righteousness.

[277] Dunn, *New Perspective on Paul*, 481.

[278] BDAG, 541; LN 57.192.

[279] BDAG, 428; LN 57.69.

Christ.[280] Paul is saying that he once regarded his Jewish identity, his Pharisaism, his Torah observance, and his persecution as his advantage and achievement in the Jewish tradition, a grounds to assert his covenantal righteousness. Let me add too, this is not just Paul recounting his impressive CV in religious fanaticism, the Judean equivalent of Jihadism; this was the stuff that supposedly marked out those who were going to be vindicated in the great assize, the coming age, the great reversal, YHWH's decisive liberation of the nation, and prove one's worthiness at the final judgment. Paul thought all those things gave him the inside track toward God's favor and God's ultimate reversal for faithful Jews. But the impact of Jesus the Messiah was so immense for Paul that even revered traditions and values were relativized by the revelation of the Messiah.[281] Such things that Paul once had confidence in are now considered loss on account of the Messiah. For the Messiah, Paul has died to such things, especially to the Torah (see Gal 2:19; Rom 7:4). Paul presents himself as a Christ figure who has stripped himself of his privilege and given up prestige in order to be found in Christ and to embrace the faithfulness of Christ.[282]

Paul then intensifies this line of reasoning: "More than that, I regard everything as loss because of the surpassing value of knowing Christ Jesus my Lord" (v. 8a). The conjunction and particle *alla menounge* are an emphatic rehearsal of the same thought, "More than that" (NRSV, CSB, NET), "What is more" (NIV), or "Indeed" (ESV).[283] The loss accumulates, not because Torah or Jewish identity are inherently bad, rather, they accrue loss only in a comparative sense, "because of the surpassing value of knowing Christ Jesus my Lord." Knowing Jesus as Lord, "my Lord" no less, an echo of Phil 2:11, is something that pervades, empowers, and inspires all that Paul values and aims for. This knowledge yields a series

---

[280]  The language of *kerdos* ("gain") and *zēmia* ("loss") is commercial, so Bockmuehl, *The Epistle to the Philippians*, 204–205; Thurston, *Philippians and Philemon*, 123; Reumann, *Philippians*, 488; Hansen, *Philippians*, 237; N. T. Wright, *Paul for Everyone: The Prison Letters* (London: SPCK, 2002), 118–119; Keown, *Philippians*, 2.145–146; Hellerman, *Philippians*, 180; more cautious is Silva, *Philippians*, 167.

[281]  Dunn, *New Perspective on Paul*, 481.

[282]  Witherington, *Philippians*, 182; cf. Hellerman, *Reconstructing Honor*, 129; Hansen, *Philippians*, 231–232. See Park (*Submission*, 61–62): "Paul intentionally patterns himself on the image of Christ in 2.6–8 ... soteriology requires, indeed enables, *imitation* of Christ" (italics original).

[283]  See Porter, *Idioms*, 206.

of benefits that Paul will soon describe in v. 9. Suffice to say, his immediate point is that knowing Messiah Jesus as Lord renders his previous way of life as redundant and rubbish in comparison. Knowledge of the Messiah is superior to advancement in Judaism and it relegates the things that marked achievement and status in his former way of life as superfluous. Just as Christ did not consider his equality with God as something he could exploit, and which he abandoned during his time of humiliation, so too Paul now abandons the privileges that once set him apart and over other Jews, he abandons them in order to know Christ.[284] Paul invites his readers to abandon all claims to worth, status, and superiority based on heritage or heroics, being circumcised or taking on the toga, public accomplishment, or election to priestly orders. In addition, although one might not notice this at first glance, Paul's claim for the surpassing value[285] of knowing Christ indicates the surpassing value of Christ himself. As Veronica Koperski puts it: "The confession is so strong that though Paul does not literally use the words 'Christ is God,' his depiction of the utter incomparability of Christ can lead to no other conclusion."[286]

Paul clarifies further, "For his sake I have suffered the loss of all things, and I regard them as rubbish, in order that I may gain Christ" (v. 8b). In obtaining knowledge of the Messiah, Paul has indeed borne a cost and incurred a loss. Paul has lost standing and status in Jewish communities, perhaps been ostracized by family, lost family inheritance, given up a promising rabbinic career, lost potential financial rewards as part of the patron-client relationships in Jerusalem under high priestly sponsorship, and suffered various hardships as a direct result of his faith in Christ.[287]

---

[284] Hooker, "Philippians," 527. Hansen (*Philippians*, 231) maps the connections between Phil 2:5-11 and 3:5-11: (1) Christ *considered* equality with God as not something to be exploited, just as Paul *considers* his previous privileges a loss; (2) Christ was *found* in appearance as a human being, just as Paul is *found* in Christ; (3) Christ took on the *form* of a servant, just as Paul seeks to be *conformed* to Christ's death; and (4) Christ is exalted as Lord, just as Paul acknowledges Christ as Lord. See also P. Wick, *Der Philipperbrief* (Stuttgart: W. Kohlhammer, 1994), 70-73; W. S. Kurz, "Kenotic Imitation of Paul and of Christ in Philippians 2 and 3," in *Discipleship in the New Testament* (ed. F. F. Segovia; Philadelphia: Fortress, 1985), 103-126; Park, *Submission*, 57-62.

[285] The substantive participle *to hyperchon* connotes authoritative and qualitative superiority, Christ is above all things and better than all things; that is, "Christ is supreme over all things" (Keown, *Philippians*, 2.142).

[286] Koperski, *The Knowledge of Christ*, 323.

[287] Reumann (*Philippians*, 519) says: "[The] losses were not just for a moment on [the] Damascus Road; the bill kept coming in for years thereafter."

The irony is that Paul has only lost the things that he now doesn't consider loss in light of knowing the Messiah. Paul considers them to be *skybalon*, which pertains to "dung, refuse, garbage,"[288] and, despite common misconception, this is not a vulgarity for "crap" or "shit,"[289] it is a bland term for "useless or undesirable material that is subject to disposal."[290] Yet such loss was necessary in order to gain the Messiah, which is better by far. The sharpness of Paul's contrast is not so much a denigration of the Jewish way of life that he once considered gain, as much as to enhance to a superlative degree the value he now places on Christ, the knowledge of Christ, gaining Christ, being righteous in Christ, and the prospect of being raised with Christ.[291]

In sum, Paul "considers" (*hēgeomai*) all things in the Messiah and that is no fleeting thought but refers to an acute intellectual process. Paul was forced by his encounter with Christ to engage in a comprehensive rearranging of the cerebral furniture in his mind and a radical reevaluation of his accomplishments and aspirations. As a result, Paul realized that the Messiah's faithfulness, his achievement in his sacrificial death, was the only grounds for his righteousness and the only thing worth gaining. Paul has only lost what can be considered loss because he has gained something that has surpassing value, namely, knowing the Messiah and his benefits. Everything else is redundant and refuse. Or, we might say, in knowing Jesus as Lord everything else in comparison is about as important as knowing the reproductive habits of plankton.

The benefits of knowing Christ are then laid out beginning in v. 9 with emphasis given to how Paul himself is the example of someone receiving a righteous standing before God based upon entrusting oneself to the faithfulness of the Messiah (more on that in a minute!). Paul reasons that to know Christ is to gain Christ, and to gain Christ is to "be found in him," that is, to participate in his person, to enter into the eschatological event of the Messiah's cross and resurrection, and to make the messianic story one's own story. This language, "in him" or "in Christ" is a condensed way of referring to one's participation in the Messiah that entails being part of the

---

[288]  LN 6.225.
[289]  J. F. Hultin, *The Ethics of Obscene Speech in Early Christianity and Its Environment* (Leiden: Boston, 2008), 150–154; Lightfoot, *Philippians*, 149.
[290]  BDAG, 932.
[291]  Dunn, *New Perspective on Paul*, 481.

renewed Israel as defined and delivered by the Messiah.[292] In this participation the main salvific dividend is righteousness.[293] It is "in him," in
Christ, that one receives the gift of a "righteousness from God."[294] This
righteousness is the outworking of union with Christ.[295] According to
Dunn: "His righteousness from God and his being in Christ were two
sides of the same coin, fully integrated in his own understanding of God's
saving righteousness."[296]

In Paul's letters, the phrase "righteousness of God" (*dikaiosynē theou*)
operates in different ways:[297] (1) It can refer to a divine attribute and divine
saving action, that is, God's uprightness as the God who promises to rescue
creation and to rectify those who have wandered from the covenant (Rom
1:17, 3:21–22); (2) It can represent a metonym for the totality of God's saving
action (2 Cor 5:21); and (3) It can designate the gift of a righteous status that
God bestows on believers (Rom 10:3–4). Paul's usage here in Phil 3:9 is
closest to this third sense since the preposition *ek* ("from") indicates that
there is a status that derives from God and is granted to the persons in
Christ. This "righteousness" is not an actual righteousness produced in
cooperation with divine enablement (à la Phil 1:11; 2:12–13),[298] nor the
imputation of Jesus's active obedience to fulfill a "covenant of works,"[299]
but the gift of a righteous status graciously bestowed on the undeserving

---

[292] See esp., *PFG*, 989.
[293] Hooker ("Philippians," 527) calls this "a right relationship with Christ," for Keown
(*Philippians*, 2.162) "righteousness as right standing before God."
[294] Understood this way, the participle clause ("not having my own righteousness")
explains the mode by which one is to "be found in him" (Bockmuehl, *The Epistle to
the Philippians*, 209; Hellerman, *Philippians*, 185; Keown, *Philippians*, 2.150) or perhaps
elaborates on what it means to gain Christ (Fee, *Philippians*, 320).
[295] Campbell, *Paul and Union with Christ*, 187–188.
[296] Dunn, *New Perspective on Paul*, 490.
[297] Barclay (*Paul and the Gift*, 474 n. 65) notes how Pauline scholars can use the phrase in
relation to diverse conceptual frames related to gift, power, promise, covenant, and
apocalypse. In his mind, it is a "polyvalent phrase" that cannot be "given a single
meaning or fitting into any one conceptual matrix."
[298] Contra Holloway, *Philippians*, 164.
[299] Contra J. Piper, *Counted Righteous in Christ* (Wheaton, IL: Crossway, 2002), 83–85;
Silva, *Philippians*, 160. The problems are: (1) Strictly speaking the righteousness here is
God's not Jesus's (yes, Jesus is God, but that's not the point); (2) If anything, the
righteousness that comes from/through Jesus mentioned in the letter is ethical as in
Phil 1:11; (3) This righteousness is no more imputed directly from God than it is directly
from the Torah; and (4) It is better to say that "righteousness" is a gift given by God to
those "in Christ" and imputation is perhaps at most a corollary of a forensic status
married to union with Christ.

(see Rom 4:4–5; 5:8, 15–17).[300] I (Bird) have argued – for nearly two decades now – that this "righteousness," or what we more broadly call "justification," is forensic, eschatological, covenantal, and participatory. In other words, God creates in the Messiah a new people, with a new status, in a new covenant, as an anticipation of the ultimate putting-things-to-right in the age to come.[301] Paul assures the Philippians that there is no greater righteousness other than that *from* God and this righteousness accessed *in* Christ is worth having.[302] Chrysostom elegantly declares: "This is the righteousness of God; this is altogether a gift. And the gifts of God far exceed those worthless good deeds, which are due to our own diligence."[303]

A further question is what is the instrument for receiving this righteousness from God? In one sense it is very clear that faith (*pistis*) is the instrument for receiving righteousness since the prepositional phrase *epi tē pistei* at the end of the sentence means "based on/depends upon faith" (e.g., RSV, NRSV, ESV). However, Paul mentions faith twice, and there is considerable debate as to who is precisely the subject exercising faith(fulness) in both instances. Compare the following translations (see Table 3).

It seems very clear that Paul ends the sentence by accenting human faith when he writes "based upon faith" (*epi tē pistei*). But what is less certain is whether *dia pisteōs Christou* in the middle of the sentence means: (1) "through faith in Christ" (objective genitive), thereby creating a double emphasis on righteousness by faith rather than by Torah-observance; or (2) "through the faithfulness of Christ" (subjective genitive), so that Christ's faithfulness rather than Torah is identified as the determinative cause of righteousness, which in turn is appropriated by human faith. This genitive construction *pisteōs Christou* is not unique to Phil 3:9 and similar constructions with the same ambiguity can be found in Rom 3:22, Gal 2:16, 19, 3:22, and Eph 3:12 and this has spawned a whole industry of debate in monographs and articles about Paul's view of Christ, faith, and

---

[300] Bird, *Saving Righteousness*, 81; Wright, *Justification*, 150–151; Keown, *Philippians*, 2.162.
[301] Bird, *Saving Righteousness*, 3–4; idem, *An Anomalous Jew*, 140; idem, *Evangelical Theology*, 566–568; idem, "Justification: A Progressive Reformed View," in *Justification: Five Views* (eds. P. Eddy and J. Beilby; Downers Grove, IL: InterVarsity Press, 2011), 131–157.
[302] A. H. Snyman, "A Rhetorical Analysis of Philippians 3:1–11," *NeoT* 40 (2006): 259–283.
[303] Chrysostom, *Hom. Phil.* 11. Migliore (*Philippians and Philemon*, 124) is similar: "True righteousness is not something we inherit or achieve but a gift from God, something that God gracious does on our behalf to make right what is awry."

Table 3 *Interpreting* Pistis *in Phil 3.9*

| Objective genitive – faith in Christ | Subjective genitive – faithfulness of Christ |
|---|---|
| And be found in him, not having a righteousness of my own that comes from the law, but one that comes through <u>faith in Christ</u>, the righteousness from God based on <u>faith.</u> (NRSV) | And be found in him. In Christ I have a righteousness that is not my own and that does not come from the Law but rather from <u>the faithfulness of Christ.</u> It is the righteousness of God that is based on <u>faith.</u> (CEB) |
| And be found in him, not having a righteousness of my own that comes from the law, but that which is through faith in Christ – the righteousness that comes from God on the basis of faith. (NIV) | And be found in him, not because I have my own righteousness derived from the law, but because I have the righteousness that comes by way of <u>Christ's faithfulness</u>– a righteousness from God that is in fact based on <u>Christ's faithfulness.</u> (NET) |
| And be found in Him, not having a righteousness of my own from the law, but one that is through <u>faith in Christ</u> – the righteousness from God based on <u>faith.</u> (CSB) | *When it counts*, I want to be found belonging to Him, not clinging to my own righteousness based on law, but actively relying on the <u>faithfulness of the Anointed One</u>. *This is true* righteousness, supplied by God, acquired by <u>faith.</u> (VOICE) |

justification.[304] The objective genitive English translation of Phil 3:9 is certainly as old as William Tyndale's rendering "that which spryngeth of the faith which is in Christ," while the subjective genitive has attracted a lot of scholarly support in the last forty years for a mixture of exegetical and theological reasons. The fact of the matter is that the construction is ambiguous, which is why older English translations (Geneva, Douay-Rheims, and KJV) deliberately retained the ambiguity and rendered the genitive phrase as "through the faith of Christ."[305]

---

[304] See M. F. Bird and P. M. Sprinkle, eds., *The Faith of Jesus Christ: Exegetical, Biblical, and Theological Studies* (Milton Keynes: Paternoster, 2009); M. C. Easter, "The Pistis Christou Debate: Main Arguments and Responses in Summary," *CBR* 9 (2010): 33–47.

[305] Cohick (*Philippians*, 172) suggests: "Perhaps we do not need to make a hard distinction among these options, for Paul may be deliberately ambiguous, reinforcing that all life in God – the knowing, the doing, the gaining, the suffering – all is through faith." Similar is F. Watson (*Paul and the Hermeneutics of Faith* [London: Bloomsbury, 2016], 68): "Faith, then, is 'faith of Jesus' in the dual sense that Jesus Christ, the embodiment of God's

The case for the objective genitive reading is as follow:[306] (1) Paul's prior reference to "believing in him [Christ]" (Phil 1:29, *to eis auton pisteuein*) and the double mention of "the knowledge of Christ Jesus" (Phil 3:8, *tēs gnōseōs Christou Iēsou*) and "to know him [Christ]" (Phil 3:10, *tou gnōnai auton*) clearly demonstrates Paul making Christ the object of both faith and knowledge and further inclines us toward regarding *pistis* as tantamount to faith, trust, and assent; (2) A natural reading of Phil 3:8–9 suggests that Paul is contrasting a righteousness gained by Torah-observance with a righteousness gained by putting faith in Christ; (3) The double mention of *pistis* is not a redundancy requiring different subjects of faith(fulness) but more of an "earnest reiteration" that faith alone saves;[307] (4) Paul consistently employs in his letters *dia* ("through") and *ek* ("by/from") to indicate that human faith in Jesus Christ is the instrument by which believers are justified or declared to be in the right with God (Rom 3:22, 25; 5:1; Gal 2:16); (5) Ancient commentators universally understood *dia pisteōs Christou* in Phil 3:9 to be referring to "faith in Christ,"[308] Chrysostom, a native Greek-speaker, wrote: "He means the faith 'of knowing him and the power of his resurrection and the sharing in his sufferings."[309]

saving action, is as such both the origin and the object of faith. In this way, the ambiguous genitive formulations . . . may be clarified, not by grammar but by context."

[306]   R. B. Matlock, "The Rhetoric of *pistis* in Paul: Galatians 2.16, 3.22, Romans 3.22, Philippians 3.9," *JSNT* 30 (2007): 173–203; idem, "Saving Faith: The Rhetoric and Semantics of pistis in Paul," in *The Faith of Jesus Christ*, 75–78; R. H. Bell, "Faith in Christ: Some Exegetical and Theological Reflections on Philippians 3:9 and Ephesians 3:12," in *The Faith of Jesus Christ*, 111–120; F. Watson, "By Faith (of Christ): An Exegetical Dilemma and Its Scriptural Solution," in *The Faith of Jesus Christ*, 147–163; V. Koperski, "The Meaning of *Pistis Christou* in Philippians 3:9," *Louvain Studies* 18 (1993): 198–216; Hawthorne and Martin, *Philippians*, 195; Fee, *Philippians*, 325–326; Garland, "Philippians," 242; Silva, *Philippians*, 161; Hansen, *Philippians*, 241–242; Reumann, *Philippians*, 495–496; Barclay, *Paul and the Gift*, 378–384; Hellerman, *Philippians*, 186–187; Keown, *Philippians*, 2.155–161.

[307]   Lightfoot, *Philippians*, 150. Further, *epi tē pistei* refers to human faith and the article *tē* is anaphoric and points back to Paul's own faith (*dia pisteōs*) in the preceding clause (Fee, *Philippians*, 325 n. 45; Hansen, *Philippians*, 242).

[308]   The only explicit reference to a subjective rendering of *pistis Christou* comes from Hippolytus's *Christ and Anti-Christ* in the early third century, see M. F. Bird and M. R. Whitenton, "The Faithfulness of Jesus Christ in Hippolytus' *De Christo et Antichristo*: Overlooked Patristic Evidence in the *Pistis Christou* Debate," *NTS* 55 (2009): 552–562.

[309]   Chrysostom, *Hom. Phil.* 11.

The case for the subjective reading trades in the following arguments:[310] (1) *pisteōs Christou* rehearses the earlier emphasis on Jesus's obedience in Phil 2:8 and corresponds with the wider motif of Jesus's obedience/faithfulness in Pauline theology (see, e.g., Rom 5:19); (2) The double mention of *pistis* is neither repetition nor redundancy, but more properly Paul's argument and its grammatical construction conceives of Christ's faithfulness as the means by which divine righteousness is distributed to or bestowed upon those who respond with faith in Christ Jesus; (3) Paul explicitly associates faith in Phil 3:9 with a wider array of christological convictions that involves attaining Christ's resurrection, fellowshipping in Christ's sufferings, and being conformed to the likeness of Christ's death in Phil 3:10. Thus, faith is simultaneously something one has toward Christ and something one experiences in him, a participation in Christ's faithfulness who is also the source of one's own faith, righteousness, life, and hope.[311]

I (Bird) must confess that after studying this debate for some time, even editing a book on the topic by the best exponents of each view in English-speaking scholarship, that I still feel somewhat torn as the arguments are fairly balanced in my mind. When pushed to take a position, I generally lean toward the objective genitive view since it works better at the level of Greek grammar and syntax and better accounts for the reception of the *pistis Christou* texts in the history of interpretation.[312] That said, here in

---

[310]  R. B. Hays, *The Faith of Jesus Christ: An Investigation of the Narrative Substructure of Galatians 3:1–4:11* (Grand Rapids, MI: Eerdmans, 2002), 2nd ed.; *PFG*, 836–851; Wright, *Paul for Everyone*, 120; P. Foster, "Pistis Christou Terminology in Philippians and Ephesians," in *The Faith of Jesus Christ*, 91–100; Barth, *Philippians*, 101–102; Bockmuehl, *The Epistle to the Philippians*, 210–211; Hooker, "Philippians," 528; J. L. Sumney, *Philippians: A Greek Student's Intermediate Reader* (Peabody, MA: Hendrickson, 2007), 80; Cousar, *Philippians*, 73–74; Witherington, *Philippians*, 204–205; Thurston, *Philippians and Philemon*, 124; Migliore, *Philippians*, 125–126.

[311]  See M. A. Seifrid, "The Faith of Christ," in *The Faith of Jesus Christ*, 145. Interestingly, Jesus is both source of faith and object of faith in Peter's speech in Acts 3:16, "And *by faith in his name*, his name itself has made this man strong, whom you see and know; and *the faith that is through Jesus* has given him this perfect health in the presence of all of you," and there is a similar expression in Ignatius, *Phild.* 8.3: "But to me Jesus Christ is the place of all that is ancient: His cross and death, and resurrection, and *the faith which is through him*, are undefiled monuments of antiquity; by which I desire through your prayers, to be justified."

[312]  See S. E. Porter and A. W. Pitts, "Pistis with a Preposition and Genitive Modifier," in *The Faith of Jesus Christ*, 33–53; plus my own summary concerning Rom 3:22 in M. F. Bird, *Romans* (SGBC; Grand Rapids, MI: Zondervan, 2016), 112–115.

Phil 3:9, this is the one instance where I think the subjective genitive reading of the "faithfulness of Christ" might have the better of it and what tips me over the edge is the chiastic structure proposed by Wolfgang Schenk (see Table 4).[313] In Schenk's arrangement, Paul sets out *pisteōs Christou* as the causal agency of salvation within the matrix of gaining Christ and in the mode of being found in Christ.[314] This *pistis* is not merely repeating the motif of human faith as instrument, nor a simple contrast of believing in Christ as opposed to the doing of Torah. More pointedly, just like Phil 2:8, Paul makes Jesus's faithfulness/obedience the *efficacious cause* of salvation, even while human faith is affirmed as the *instrumental cause* of this salvation.

Furthermore, we can break the horns of the subjective versus objective dichotomy when we realize that Paul's conception of faith is consistently christological and thoroughly participatory. Consider this: (1) Paul speaks of faith not as a human effort but as a gift given by God (Phil 1:29); (2) The Philippians are exhorted to apprehend a mind-set/manner that is "in Christ Jesus" (Phil 2:5), so the knowledge of Christ (Phil 3:8, 10) transcends the subject-object divide, because it is an experiential knowledge "in him," a knowledge from within union with Christ. The same no doubt applies to faith, it is not something outside of Christ, but comes from God through Christ and is apprehended in union with Christ; (3) Consequently, however we render the "faith of Christ" (*pisteōs Christou*), clearly in this letter

Table 4 *Diagramming Phil 3.9*

| | |
|---|---|
| *mē echōn emēn* | not having my own |
| *dikaiosynēn* | righteousness |
| *tēn ek nomou* | from the Torah |
| *alla tēn dia pisteōs Christou* | but through the Messiah's faithfulness |
| *tēn ek Theou* | from God |
| *dikaiosynēn* | righteousness |
| *epi tē pistei* | based upon faith |

[313] W. Schenk, *Die Philipperbriefe des Paulus* (Stuttgart: Kohlhammer, 1984), 250–251; affirmed by Silva, *Philippians*, 160 and Keown, *Philippians*, 2.87; the next best alternative is probably Fee, *Philippians*, 321–322.

[314] Schenk (*Philipperbriefe*, 312) doesn't interpret *pisteōs Christou* as Christ's faithfulness, but instead sees it as an epexegetical genitive; that is, the message of faith in Christ, the gospel, and its contents.

Paul does not conceive of *pistis* as reducible to something cognitive, something one puts into Christ or projects toward Christ – yes, it includes that, but it cannot be only that. Paul conceives of *pistis* in relation to a wider constellation of motifs associated with believing in Christ, boasting in Christ, knowing Christ, gaining Christ, fellowshipping in the sufferings of Christ, conforming to the death of Christ, and attaining the resurrection of Christ. The believer's faith can only be a faith from God, fixed on Christ, and participating in Christ's own faithfulness.

What I think Paul is hinting at is that Jesus was faithful to his messianic vocation, he was the obedient son and servant, faithful unto death upon a cross, which proves that Jesus was the Davidic deliverer, the true Israel, the new Adam, and faithful where all others failed before him. Stanley K. Stowers synergizes Phil 2:8 with 3:9 to the effect: "'Christ's faithfulness' serves as shorthand for 'Christ's obedience unto death, Christ's servanthood and self-giving in obedience to God.'"[315] It is, then, within the matrix of Jesus's messianic fidelity that he reconstitutes a new people within himself, Jew and Greek, slave and free, who participate in his death and resurrection, from whence those called receive faith, righteousness, and resurrection. In sum, *pistis Christou* is God's deliverance wrought in the Messiah's faithfulness, bringing people to faith, marking them out as his people, and declaring them righteous. This righteousness from God is received by entrusting oneself to the Messiah's faithfulness – that, I submit, is Paul's point.

This scheme of receiving a righteous status from God by believing and participating in the Messiah's faithfulness is set in contrast with trying to establish one's own righteousness acquired from Torah-observance. Paul elsewhere states that Israel has pursued a "Torah of righteousness," or Torah as a means to righteousness (Rom 9:31 [trans. MFB]); and Paul contrasts "the righteousness that comes from the Torah" with "the right-eousness that comes by faith" (Rom 10:5–6 [trans. MFB]). Paul clearly has in mind those who think they are righteous on account of mere possession of the Torah (Rom 2:17–24) or by mistakenly supposing that they have properly performed the Torah (Rom 3:19–20; Gal 3:10–11; 6:13). Such a contrast maps perfectly onto Phil 3:7–8. Instead of Torah as the source of

---

[315] Stowers, "Friends and Enemies in the Politics of Heaven," 121.

righteousness, righteousness comes from God. Instead of works of Torah as that which determines righteousness, we find the faithful Messiah. Instead of Torah as the identity-marker for those who will be declared righteous on the last day, we find human faith.[316] If Pauline Christianity has one key thread it is this: God's righteousness comes through Christ not through Torah.

Paul is not giving a caricatured image of the Torah in Judaism; the reality is that some Jews believed that God's covenantal grace and God's election of Israel had made it possible to attain life through Torah. This yielded a "Torah of life," with Torah as both a way of life and a way unto life before God (Sir 17:11; 45:5). In the apocalypse known to us as 2 Baruch (post-70 CE), the city of Zion was laid waste by the Babylonians with the result that "the flavor of the smoke of the incense of the righteousness of the Law has been extinguished everywhere in the region of Zion," suggesting that the Jerusalem cultus, when dutifully carried out in accordance with the Torah's regulations, was a source of national righteousness for Israel (2 Bar 67.6 [OTP]). In the Testament of the Twelve Patriarchs (composed in stages of redaction ca. 100 BCE–200 CE), Gad urges his children not to run into evil and hatred, instead, "And now, my children, hearken to the words of truth to work of righteousness, and all the law of the Most High (T. Gad 3.1 [ANF]). In the third book of the Sibylline Oracles (ca. 1–200 CE), the Jews are described as the "sacred race of pious men who attend to the counsels and intention of the Most High," who avoid idolatry, adultery, and pederasty, but also honor God with acceptable sacrifices and offerings, with the result that they are "sharing in the righteousness of the law of the Most High" (Sib. Or. 3.573–580 [OTP]). In the Qumran scrolls, a letter written to the priestly leadership claims that adopting the halakah of Qumranites, that is, performing the "works of the Torah," means "it shall be reckoned to you as righteousness" (4QMMT 113, 117). All this is to say that Torah, whether taking pride in its givenness to Israel, making it a palisade to separate Jews from the pagans, or performing it with pharisaic exactness, this is not a path to righteousness according to Paul.

To give a notoriously short precis of Paul's view of the Torah vis-à-vis Christ, I would surmise that Paul rejects Torah as a means to righteousness

---

[316] Wright, Justification, 151.

and life because the Torah was temporary rather than terminal, it was the platform for the future people of God, not a permanent palisade to be erected around God's people. Torah did not bring the glory of Adam back, nor did Torah transform Israel into that kingdom of priests it was supposed to be. Torah at its best prophetically points to Christ and pedagogically leads Israel to Christ; but Torah at its worst brings covenantal curses and condemnation and is conscripted into the service of Sin and Death. Torah did not fix Adam's fallen progeny, it only served to make him/them transgressors. There is no righteousness in the Torah, if there was then Christ's death was pointless, rather, Christ brings the Torah to its intended climax, Israel redeemed and Gentiles made obedient to God, so that there might be righteousness for everyone who believes. Thus, Torah is not a bad thing now done away with, but a good thing, whose *telos* is Christ and whose requirements are fulfilled through life in the Spirit.[317]

What some Jews considered to be grounds for perceived worth before both God and the badge marking out the elect, such as lineage and law-observance, Paul now considers worthless in light Christ's death and resurrection and his participation in him by faith. For Paul, God's action in Messiah Jesus renders the markers of inherited Jewish privileges (circumcision, Jewish parentage), recognized achievements in pharisaic halakah (adhering to the Pharisee's practice of the Torah), and fanaticism to the point of violence (zeal manifested in persecuting Christ-followers), not as the grounds for superiority over others, nor for claiming worth before God, but something to be treated with a mixture of regret and indifference.

Moreover, Paul is not contrasting two systems of salvation separated by abstract notions of "trusting" versus "doing," that dichotomy is dispelled by Paul's own urgent exhortations: "live ... in a manner worthy of the gospel" (Phil 1:27) and "work out your salvation with fear and trembling" (Phil 2:12). The contrast is instead about nodes of salvation, Torah versus Christ, and its sociological corollaries. On the one hand, Paul urges that Torah, neither its possession nor performance avails before God, nor for that matter does the Jewish measure of estimating one's worth before God based on Torah's categories. Instead, it is faith in the Messiah and participating in the Messiah's faithfulness that avails before God, and it is God's

---

[317] See the excellent treatment of this topic by B. S. Rosner, *Paul and the Law: Keeping the Commandments of God* (NSBT; Downers Grove, IL: InterVarsity Press, 2013).

verdict in the Messiah that provides worth despite the unworthiness of the recipient. On the other hand, the result is that Paul sets up a divide between two types of communities, those that are defined and marked by allegiance to Torah and the tokens of Jewish belonging, and those that are marked out by the Messiah with accompanying signs like faith and Spirit as emblems of belonging to him.[318] Paul here makes a preemptive strike against Jewish Christ-believing proselytizers who might come to Macedonia to agitate and torment the Philippians over Torah and circumcision. Paul thus flaunts his Jewish credentials and supererogatory Torah zeal, precisely what any intruders might do themselves, and he says that it counts for nothing, it's not a gain, but a loss in comparison to Christ.[319] Paul says this so that if such intruders do arrive, the Philippians will remain steadfast in their faith in Christ and continue to be the community of faith that he is urging them to be.

Paul continues to narrate the "surpassing" benefits of knowing Christ: "I want to know Christ and the power of his resurrection and the sharing of his sufferings by becoming like him in his death, if somehow I may attain the resurrection from the dead" (vv. 10–11). Paul reiterates from v. 8 the value of knowledge of Christ in v. 10. The infinitive *gnōnai* is purposive and explains the goal of gaining Christ, from the comparative state of lostness, in terms of the benefits that are immediately described thereafter.

First, this knowledge has Christ as its object, yet it is far from nakedly factual, it is a relational knowing. This knowledge is that of the experience of Christ. It is to know Christ and to be known by Christ from within union with Christ. Proof of that is that such knowledge pertains to knowing Christ's love for believers in whom they experience the profound depths of God's love (see Rom 8:35; 2 Cor 5:14; Gal 2:20; Eph 3:19; 5:2, 25). This knowledge also marks a transformation that is noetic, ontic, and telic (i.e., this knowledge shapes the mind, existence, and one's destiny).[320]

Second, it is knowledge of the power of Christ's resurrection. This could be a genitive of source, that is, the power that comes from Christ's resurrection, the authority of the risen Lord Jesus over the Church, the

---

[318] Watson, *Paul, Judaism, and the Gentiles*, 147.

[319] G. P. Anderson, *Paul's New Perspective: Charting a Soteriological Journey* (Downers Grove, IL: InterVarsity Press, 2016), 65.

[320] Keown (*Philippians*, 2.166) describes this knowledge as intimate, relational, experiential, and participative.

reign of the "Son of God-in-power" through believers (Rom 1:4). More likely, this refers to God's power exerted in Christ's resurrection, something Paul refers to frequently (Rom 6:4; 8:11; 1 Cor 6:14; 2 Cor 13:4; Eph 1:20; Col 2:12). As such, by knowing Christ, Paul wants to know too the life-giving, death-crushing, and new world-creating power of God.

Third, it is knowledge of fellowship in Christ's sufferings and being conformed to Christ's death. Paul conveys here the sentiment of having "fellowship" (*koinōnia*) with Christ in his sufferings. This *koinōnia* is a participation in Christ's cross (Phil 3:10), which is remembered and rehearsed in the Lord's Supper (1 Cor 10:16) and embodied existentially in cruciform love for others (Phil 2:1-4).[321] Then, mirroring the same thought, there is a sharing and assimilation (*symmorphizō*) into Christ's death, and the present participle conveys an ongoing process of "being moulded to the pattern of his death" (NJB). Thus, to know Christ, to gain Christ, to be in Christ, all this means to participate in his sufferings and being conformed to the pattern of his death. This reflects an important motif in Pauline theology that believers have died with Christ (Rom 6:4-6; Gal 2:19-20; Col 2:20). The meaning of this is that they have entered the story of Christ's crucifixion, where sin is dealt with, atonement is achieved, victory over the powers of the age is won, and redemption from sin's power has begun. Paul can show from his own example that the Christian life is an ongoing process of being conformed to Christ's death (2 Cor 4:10-12).[322] The aim is not suffering, but to become Christ-like in suffering.[323] Of course, what Paul usually mentions too, and is affirmed in vv. 10-11 with the mention of resurrection, is that believers have also been raised with Christ in the newness of life and will share in his resurrection (Rom 6:4-5, 8; 8:11; Eph 2:6; Col 3:1). Or, as Paul reasons in Romans, believers are, "heirs of God and joint heirs with Christ – if, in fact, we suffer with him so that we may also be glorified with him" (Rom 8:17).

Fourth, it is knowledge of attaining a place in the resurrection of the dead: "if somehow I may attain the resurrection from the dead" (v. 11). While Paul wants to know the power of the resurrection in the present, he

---

[321] M. J. Gorman, *Inhabiting the Cruciform God: Kenosis, Justification, and Theosis in Paul's Narrative Christology* (Grand Rapids, MI: Eerdmans, 2009), 113.
[322] Hooker, "Philippians," 529.
[323] Garland, "Philippians," 243.

Table 5 *Parallels of Phil 3 with Romans and Galatians*

| | | |
|---|---|---|
| Circumcision and belonging | Phil 3:3 | Rom 2:29 |
| Membership in Israel | Phil 3:5 | Gal 2:15; Rom 11:1 |
| Righteousness by faith of Christ | Phil 3:9 | Gal 2:16; Rom 3:22, 26; 9:30 |
| Righteousness is not by Torah | Phil 3:9 | Gal 2:16, 21; 3:11; Rom 3:20–21; 10:3 |
| Paul's example of himself | Phil 3:4b–16 | Gal 1:13–14; 2:19 |
| Participation in Christ | Phil 3:9–11 | Gal 2:15–20; 3:22–29; Rom 6:5; 8:29 |
| Final judgment and salvation | Phil 3:21 | Gal 5:21; Rom 6:21; 14:10; 16:18 |

hopes to partake of the actual resurrection from the dead in the future. This "resurrection" is the general resurrection, hence the plural *ek nekrōn* (lit. "from the dead corpses"), and refers to the raising up of the righteous and the wicked at the end of history (see Dan 12:2; Mk 12:18, 28; Matt 22:30–31; Luke 14:14; John 5:29–30; 11:24; Acts 23:6; 24:15; Rom 1:4; 1 Cor 15:42; *m.Sanh.* 10.1). The grammatical construction, "If somehow I may attain" (*ei pōs katantēsō*) suggests a certain degree of contingency, or at least "an unusual element of hesitation."[324] Perhaps this is purely a humble switch from the heights of triumph to a "modest hope."[325] But it would be wrong to see here an element of doubt,[326] since Paul has confidence in God completing his purposes (Phil 1:6; 2:13), he looks forward to receiving the prize ahead of him in the upward call (Phil 3:14), and Christ has already apprehended him (Phil 3:12). So, while Paul has assurance of his salvation (Phil 1:20–23), he does not presume upon God's final judgment that all believers must face (see 1 Cor 3:13–15; 2 Cor 5:10; Rom 14:10), because in between is the necessity of cruciformity (Phil 3:10; Table 5).[327]

3:12–16: PRESSING TOWARD THE GOAL

[12] Not that I have already obtained this or have already reached the goal; but I press on to make it my own, because Christ Jesus has made me his own.

[13] Beloved, I do not consider that I have made it my own; but this one thing I do: forgetting what lies behind and straining forward to what lies ahead,

---

[324] Bockmuehl, *The Epistle to the Philippians*, 217.
[325] Lightfoot, *Philippians*, 151.
[326] Rightly, Hawthorne and Martin, *Philippians*, 200.
[327] See esp. the evenhanded discussion in Hellerman, *Philippians*, 192.

<sup>14</sup> I press on toward the goal for the prize of the heavenly call of God in Christ Jesus.

<sup>15</sup> Let those of us then who are mature be of the same mind; and if you think differently about anything, this too God will reveal to you.

<sup>16</sup> Only let us hold fast to what we have attained.

After Paul's rhetorically charged assertions about his former way of life vis-à-vis Judaism, the superlative value of knowing Christ, his conformity to Christ's death, and hope for attaining resurrection in 3:1–11, he next adopts a more subdued disposition in vv. 12–16 where he views his current life as a struggle that he is engaged in. The apostle wants to make sure that his confidence in Christ and sense of jubilant hope does not get mistaken for an over-realized eschatology. As if Paul is now already enjoying all of these things: resurrection power and resurrected body! Paul, using an array of athletic imagery, stresses that he has not arrived at some blissful destination ahead of the Philippians. To the contrary, he himself continues to struggle in the race, striving toward the goal to which Christ has called him, and the Philippians must do the same.

Paul drops gears from resurrection hope to present reality: "Not that I have already obtained this<sup>328</sup> or<sup>329</sup> have already reached the goal; but I press on to make it my own, because<sup>330</sup> Christ Jesus has made me his own" (v. 12). While Paul has seen the risen Lord (1 Cor 9:1), was called by God and had the Son revealed in him (Gal 1:14–16), has experienced heavenly visions (2 Cor 12:1–4), and knows Christ in the present time (Phil 3:7–11), nonetheless, he also knows that he still lives in the not-yet period of apocalyptic anticipation (Phil 3:20–21; 1 Thess 1:10; 4:16; 2 Thess 1:7; 1 Cor 15:20–26). Such a hope cannot be collapsed into an interiorized and de-eschatologized spiritual

---

[328] The clause *ouch hoti ēdē elabon ē teteleiōmai* (lit. "Not that already I received or already have been completed") has no object, so translations add "it" (NASB, NJB) or "this" (NRSV, NIV), which probably hints toward the "prize" or "goal" of v. 14. In effect: "It's not that I have already reached this goal" (CEB).

[329] In our earliest copy of Philippians ($\mathfrak{P}^{46}$) and several Western witnesses (e.g., D* Irenaeus<sup>Lat</sup> Ambrosiaster) a scribe has added "or am already completely justified" (*ē ēdē dedikaiōmai*) to reinforce the notion of the not-yet.

[330] The Greek *eph ho* appears in Rom 5:12, 2 Cor 5:4 and here in Phil 3:12. The preposition and pronoun are best understood as having a causal sense of "because." See Hellerman, *Philippians*, 202; J. A. Fitzmyer, "The Consecutive Meaning of ἐφ'ᾧ in Romans 5:12," *NTS* 39 (1995): 330.

plane of claiming to enjoy things that are still impending in the arc of redemptive history. Paul admits that he has not reached (*lambanō*) nor finished (*teleioō*) the final stage of the journey.[331] Instead, like an athlete, he persists in the contest, for the purpose of *apprehending* that which Christ first *apprehended* him (double of use of *katalambanō*).

Paul expands upon the point in vv. 13–14 that he is on an ongoing journey or part of a struggle of which the goal pertains to God's call in Christ Jesus.

Launching from familial language in v. 13, "Brothers and sisters" (see Phil 1:12; 3:1), Paul confesses that, "I do not consider that I have made it[332] my own." Paul's measured estimation of himself is that while he might be something like a coheir with Christ (Rom 8:17) he does not yet have his victor's crown (1 Thess 2:19; 2 Tim 4:8). Even so, Paul's sober evaluation of his current state leads him to an earnest resolution to pursue his desired end-state: "but this one thing I do: forgetting what lies behind and straining forward to what lies ahead" (v. 13). This is the imagery of an athlete with a single-minded pursuit of a goal, blocking out what is behind, and focusing intently on what lies ahead. The word *epekteinoma* means "to exert oneself to the uttermost, *stretch out, strain.*"[333] Paul thus imagines his Christian life as a race where he heeds no peripheral distractions nor concerns himself as to who is catching up: just struggling, straining, striving, and stretching-out toward the finish line.

Paul goes on to say: "I press on toward the goal for the prize of the heavenly call of God in Christ Jesus" (v. 14). Paul's pursuit is for the *skopos*, the goal, or perhaps target for which an athlete strives toward, that is, the finish line. Then, as per most athletic contests, the victor receives the "prize" (*brebeion*) for his labors. Paul defines that prize in relation to,

---

[331] While many commentators think that Paul's usage of *teleios/teleioō* means he is echoing and reversing the terminology of some opponents in 3:12, 15 (Gnostics, Jewish perfectionists, mystery cults, libertines, etc.), these words can be taken "without an explicit polemical edge" and the overall tone is "not polemical, but inviting and inclusive" (Keown, *Philippians*, 2.196, 212). In v. 12, Paul is saying no more than the eschatological goal of knowing Christ (v. 10) and resurrection (v. 11) still lays ahead of him. See too Sumney, *Philippians*, 84; Hellerman, *Philippians*, 200–201, 206–207.

[332] The clause *adelphoi egō emauton ou logizomai kateilēphnai* (lit. "Brothers, not that I consider myself to have attained") has no object, so translations provide "it" (NRSV, NIV, CEB) or "this" (NET).

[333] BDAG, 361.

literally, the "upward call of God" (*anō klēseōs tou theou*) – rightly CEB, ESV, NASB, NET; not "heavenly call of God," contra NIV, NRSV, NJB, CSB – given "in Christ Jesus." The prize in relation to the upward call of God could be a genitive apposition so that the prize consists of the "call" (*klēsis*) and this "upward call" can be understood as the "high calling" of Christian service (KJV) or the call to one day enter God's "kingdom and glory" (1 Thess 2:12). The problem is that given the athletic metaphor it would be odd to say that the prize is the calling into God's kingdom. More likely, the goal is the prize that *pertains* to the upward calling of God in Christ Jesus.[334] In other words, the prize is the reward one receives *within the calling*, the calling itself is not the prize itself. Several scholars suggest, in keeping with the athletic imagery, that the call is a summons given to the athlete to approach the judge's stand to receive the prize (see 2 Tim 4:7–8). In this scenario, God calls up the victorious athlete to give him (or her) the prize that is contained in Christ Jesus.[335]

What we find in vv. 15–16 is either Paul rounding off the previous argument in 3:12–14 (ESV, CEB, NET, NRSV, NASB) or else Paul presaging the subsequent exhortations in 3:17–4:1 (NIV). I favor the former because the demonstrative pronoun *touto* ("same/this" in most English versions) in v. 15 relates to the preceding exhortations, not just in vv. 12–14, but probably encompassing the whole of vv. 1b–14. Also, v. 1b and v. 16 bookend the section on the note of the Philippians' continued well-being in the faith. In sum, Paul invites those who are mature to adopt his perspective, and, to those who are hesitant, hopefully God will give them special insight to approve what Paul has instructed them. This is a path not merely to maturity, but to security, so they will resiliently retain what they have so far attained in Christ Jesus.

Paul urges them: "Let those of us then who are mature be of the same mind" (v. 15). A link to the preceding section is signaled by *oun* for "then" (NRSV, NIV) or "therefore" (CSB, NET). Those who participate in Christ like athletes in a race should align their minds to a certain way of thinking. Paul assumes that those who are "mature" (*teleios*, which, in Jewish

---

[334] Bockmuehl, *The Epistle to the Philippians*, 222–223.
[335] I. Hussey, *The Soteriological Use of Call by Paul and Luke* (ACTMS; Eugene, OR: Wipf & Stock, 2018), 84–85; D. J. Williams, *Paul's Metaphors: Their Context and Character* (Peabody, MA: Hendrickson, 1999), 262.

contexts, signifies a sincere and wholehearted devotion to God, see, e.g., Gen 6:9; Deut 18:13; 2 Sam 22:6; 1 Kgs 8:61; 11:4; Sir 44:17 [LXX])[336] will adopt a particular mind-set, the very one spoken about in a previous section (Phil 2:1–11), and for which Euodia and Synteche will receive earnest reminding (Phil 4:2). Whereas Paul and his audience are not *teleioō* ("completed") in terms of the eschatological hope (v. 12), Paul considers as *teleios* ("mature") those who have their thinking shaped by that eschatological hope (v. 15). In other words, in a quaint irony, "maturity consists in knowing that you have not yet reached maturity!"[337] Ultimately Paul wishes their minds to be formed by the story of Christ's humiliation and exaltation, their own striving in salvation, Christ's faithfulness, their knowledge of Christ, knowing their place in a metaphorical race, yielding moral qualities like humility, joyfulness, thanksgiving, and love, and shining like stars. Paul then adds: "and if you think differently[338] about anything, this too God will reveal to you" (v. 15). Paul acknowledges a possible difference of opinion on these matters, yet he regards potential dissent in strikingly irenic terms. This is Paul himself modeling fellowship in Christ, not seeking partisans or trying to score points, but a genuine desire for unity and mutuality, which requires the ability to live with differences, to embrace certain diversities, and permits gentle disagreement within an overall sense of oneness and accord. And if Paul cannot convince them, hopefully God will, whether by reflection or by revelation, through the Spirit's prophetic activity within the ongoing life of the Philippian house-churches.[339]

Paul rounds off the section with a short but penetrating exhortation: "Only let us hold fast to what we have attained" (v. 16). The coordinating conjunction *plēn* is concessive and should be translated as "Nevertheless" (KJV, NET) or "However" (NASB) because Paul introduces circumstances that might arrest his objective, but in the end do not. Paul, speaking

---

[336] Bockmuehl, *The Epistle to the Philippians*, 225.

[337] *PFG*, 551.

[338] The *heterōs* can refer to something merely "different" (BDAG, 400), but it can also pertain to something negative as in "amiss" or "bad" (Lightfoot, *Philippians*, 153), perhaps "badly" or "wrongly" (LSJ, 702); Silva (*Philippians*, 187) offers a paraphrase of the "wrong frame of mind." Fee (*Philippians*, 357 n. 25) is not convinced that it has a negative connotation in this context; all the more likely since the irenic tone shows that Paul is not flustered or bothered by these differences (Keown, *Philippians*, 2.214).

[339] Bockmuehl, *The Epistle to the Philippians*, 227–228.

inclusively of himself with the Philippians ("us"), exhorts[340] them to "keep in step" (*stoicheō* for "to live in conformity with some presumed standard or set of customs")[341] with what they have attained in Christ (*phthanō* for "to attain or arrive at a particular state").[342] The accent falls upon their steadfastness in the faith; they need to keep walking in that path that God has set them upon in Christ.

### 3:17–4:1: PAUL'S EXAMPLE APPLIED TO THE PHILIPPIANS

[17] Brothers and sisters, join in imitating me, and observe those who live according to the example you have in us.

[18] For many live as enemies of the cross of Christ; I have often told you of them, and now I tell you even with tears.

[19] Their end is destruction; their god is the belly; and their glory is in their shame; their minds are set on earthly things.

[20] But our citizenship is in heaven, and it is from there that we are expecting a Savior, the Lord Jesus Christ.

[21] He will transform the body of our humiliation that it may be conformed to the body of his glory, by the power that also enables him to make all things subject to himself.

Philippians 4:1 Therefore, my brothers and sisters, whom I love and long for, my joy and crown, stand firm in the Lord in this way, my beloved.

The mention of "keeping in step" (v. 16) segues into a further exhortation to imitate Paul in his walk (v. 17) and an admonition about those who walk as enemies of the cross (v. 18). About such enemies Paul deploys sectarian language to portray them as debauched and doomed (v. 19). Paul urges the Philippians to see their citizenship as oriented toward the heavenly *politeuma* from whence shall come their Savior to transform their bodies in the resurrection of the dead (vv. 20–21). Which in turn yields a further exhortation to remain steadfast (v. 1 of Phil 4).

---

[340]   See Porter, *Idioms*, 202 and Hellerman, *Philippians*, 209 on how infinitives like *stoichein* can exhibit an imperatival function.

[341]   LN 41.12.

[342]   LN 13.16.

Once more, Paul uses the familial address of "Brothers and sisters" this time to ask the Philippians to "join together in imitating me" (*symmimētēs* is a Pauline neologism).[343] What that requires is for them to "observe those who live according to the example you have in us" (v. 17). The word used here is *peripateō*, ordinarily translated as "live" but more literally means "walk." This is rooted in the Jewish idiom of *halakah* as one's walk or way of life (e.g., Ps 1:1; Prov 8:20; Sir 13:13). Paul is instructing the Philippians to find role models, including himself, but not restricted to himself – probably Timothy, Ephaphroditus, Clement, Euodia, Synteche, and Lydia – who provide a pattern of faith and fidelity that is worthy of imitation.[344] Paul will rehearse the same point again later: "Keep on doing the things that you have learned and received and heard and seen in me" (Phil 4:9). Just as the imitation of Christ is an inoculation against the cutthroat culture of competition, the insatiable hunger for honor, and the rhetoric of rivalry, so too the imitation of Paul is an inoculation against the dogs-evil workers-mutilators (v. 3) and enemies of the cross (v. 18).

By this point one should notice that Phil 3:2–21 is intensely autobiographical and sets forth Paul's example of one who renounces his inherited privileges, forfeits losses to gain Christ, suffers with Christ, pursues the upward calling, hopes to attain resurrection, and aims for maturity in Christ, something the Philippians should themselves aspire to emulate.[345] As Paul narrates the story of how he came to be "in Christ" in Phil 3:2–21, he claims to embody the normativity of the Christ-story for others to imitate. Paul's own conception of being "in Christ" fuses a messianic *mimesis* with Greco-Roman notions of civic partnership, and combines cruciformity with an athletic struggle toward hope, to yield a distinctive account of the self in relation to others: self-emptying, self-giving, and striving together.[346] Thus, the *imitatio Christi* and *imitatio Pauli* become

---

[343] The prepositional prefix *syn* means the Philippians are to join Paul in his pattern of life (Fee, *Philippians*, 364–365; Sumney, *Philippians*, 92; Silva, *Philippians*, 188; Hansen, *Philippians*, 261; Reumann, *Philippians*, 567).

[344] See P. S. Cable, "*Imitatio Christianorum*: The Function of Believers as Examples in Philippians," *TynBul* 67 (2016): 87–103.

[345] See too Thompson and Longenecker, *Philippians and Philemon*, 94–96.

[346] Wright (N. T. Wright, "Philippians: Lecture 8." Lectures Delivered at Regent College [1990]) nuances the point well: "So it's not just a matter of, 'I happen to belong to one particular race, I gave up all that stuff, why don't you do so as well?' There's something more profound and theological going on. This is the true story of Israel, a story of

the basis for ecclesial authority and communal life. Paul is not trying to manufacture his own personality cult; rather, Paul's exhortation trades in mutuality and friendship, an invitation to follow him in the journey of knowing Christ and attaining the resurrection.[347]

It must be stressed that the practice of imitation is vitally important for Christian ethics more generally and for Paul in particular. For a start, there is Christ's own example of service and self-giving love (Mk 10:41–45; John 13:15). The apostle Peter appealed to the example of Christ when it came to suffering under adversity (1 Pet 2:21), John the Elder likewise urged believers to live in the world like Jesus (1 John 4:17), and the author of Hebrews too exhorted his audience to, "Consider him who endured such hostility against himself from sinners, so that you may not grow weary or lose heart" (Heb 12:3).

Paul himself makes clear references to Christ's example of humility when writing to the Philippians (2:5–11) and to the Corinthians when he presents Jesus as an exemplar of the one who becomes poor to make others rich (2 Cor 8:9). What is unique to Paul is that he does not merely urge the imitation of Christ, but the imitation of himself as one who follows Christ. Hence, his plea to the Corinthians: "Be imitators of me, as I am of Christ" (1 Cor 11:1). What is even more astounding is that Paul can go so far as to say that his own pattern of life in Christ is the one thing, the *one thing*, yes, the ONE THING that he has taught in all the churches:

For though you might have ten thousand guardians in Christ, you do not have many fathers. Indeed, in Christ Jesus I became your father through the gospel. I appeal to you, then, be imitators of me. For this reason, I sent you Timothy, who is my beloved and faithful child in the Lord, to remind you of my ways in Christ Jesus, as I teach them everywhere in every church. (1 Cor 4:15–17)

There is an abundance of mimetic motifs in the Thessalonian correspondence. Paul praises the Thessalonians for becoming "imitators of us and of the Lord" (1 Thess 1:6), becoming "imitators of God's churches in Christ that are in Judea" by enduring attacks from their own people (1 Thess 2:14), and so becoming themselves "a model to all the believers in Macedonia and Achaia" (1 Thess 1:7). Paul and his coworkers set them

privilege renounced. And if that is so, then the story of the world must be a story of privilege renounced."

[347] Hansen, *Philippians*, 261.

an example by working with their own hands (2 Thess 3:7, 9). Finally, in 1 Timothy, Paul urges Timothy to "set the believers an example in speech and conduct, in love, in faith, in purity" (1 Tim 4:12).

The point is powerful because humans are mimetic creatures, we imitate what we admire, thus the challenge is to admire the right type of people, for the right reasons, and to reproduce what is exemplary in their attitudes and behaviors. According to Richard Hays,

> The distinctive shape of obedience to God is disclosed in Jesus Christ's faithful death on the cross for the sake of God's people. That death becomes metaphorically paradigmatic for the obedience of the community: to obey God means to offer our lives unqualifiedly for the sake of others. The fundamental norm of Pauline ethics is the christomorphic life. To imitate Christ is also to follow the apostolic example of surrendering one's own prerogatives and interests.[348]

The need for imitation is all the more pressing because of the adversarial context and the likelihood of discovering bad examples, those who walk according to a different rule. Hence Paul adds: "For many live as enemies of the cross of Christ." The gravity of such a warning is that Paul interjects his solemn plea on that matter with emotive force: "For, as I have often told you before and now tell you again even with tears" (v. 18). As Paul did before (see v. 1), Paul admits that he is repeating himself, not because the Philippians are forgetful, but because of the weightiness of the topic.

Of course, we need to ask, who are these enemies of the cross? One could nominate Roman civil authorities, the Jews of Judea and the diaspora, or any people invested in pagan religion as enemies of the cross of Christ. Paul could have any or all of these people in mind (see, e.g., 1 Cor 1:18–2:5, where the cross is a stumbling block to Jews and foolishness to Greeks). However, as stated in the earlier excursus, it is more likely that Paul is referring to Jewish Christ-believers given the context of Phil 3 as a whole and the resonance of avoiding persecution for the sake of the cross in Gal 5:11 and 6:12. Paul's message, summed up as the "cross of Christ," is a message that provokes opposition, and such opposition should not

---

[348] R. B. Hays, *The Moral Vision of the New Testament: A Contemporary Introduction to New Testament Ethics* (San Francisco: HarperCollins, 1996), 46; see also J. B. Hood, *Imitating God in Christ: Recapturing a Biblical Pattern* (Downers Grove, IL: InterVarsity Press, 2013), esp. 117–133.

produce any attraction for which the Philippians can be drawn toward (see 1 Cor 1:17, 23; 2:2; Gal 3:1; 6:12–14; Col 1:20; 2:14–15).

Then, much like v. 3, Paul invokes some Jewish sectarian polemics to disparage those who would be enemies of the cross in v. 19. Paul levels four charges against them.[349]

First, "Their end is destruction." Earlier Paul declared that the Philippians' faith is a sign to their pagan adversaries that they themselves will be destroyed (Phil 1:28). Here Paul says that the final end-state of any sectarian rivals will be one of *apōleia* for "destruction" or "annihilation."[350] Paul does not explicitly identify God as the destroyer, but such a notion is congruent with Paul's view of God who incorporates judgment into his plan and purposes (e.g., Rom 2:16; Rom 9:22/Isa 54:16 [LXX]; Rom 14:10). John Coulson surveys the various judgment passages in Philippians (1:6, 10; 28; 2:16; 3:19) and concludes: "Philippians presents God's judgment in the context of the ministry of the gospel ... There is no mention of [a] temporal judgment of unbelievers. The emphasis in the present is on the opportunity to receive the grace of God. But if people reject the gospel and inflict suffering on the church, there can be only one end for them: 'destruction' on the day of Christ."[351] When such warnings are coupled with the walking metaphor, Paul is saying that these persons have a *halakah* that puts them on the path to *hell*.

Second, "their god is the belly."[352] To begin with, this is the language for condemning overindulgent and hedonistic behaviors (e.g., Sir 23:6). Paul can censure a kind of carnality in Corinth that entailed treating the body with moral indifference: "'Food is meant for the stomach and the stomach for food,' and God will destroy both one and the other" (1 Cor 6:13). Philo's

---

[349] On the similarities between Isa 45:15–25 (LXX), see Gnilka, *Philippians*, 202; Hansen, *Philippians*, 271; Keown, *Philippians*, 2.225–226.

[350] LN 20.31; BDAG, 127.

[351] J. R. Coulson, *The Righteous Judgment of God: Aspects of Judgment in Paul's Letters* (Eugene, OR: Wipf & Stock, 2016), 48.

[352] Mearns, "The Identity of Paul's Opponents," 198–200, cf. Watson, *Paul, Judaism, and the Gentiles*, 145; Müller, *Philipper*, 178. J. Moiser ("The Meaning of Koilia in Philippians 3:19," *ExpTimes* 108 [1997]: 365–366) points out that *koilia* can be a euphemism for genitals (see, e.g., 1 Chron 17:11/2 Kgs 7:12 [LXX], "I will raise up your seed after you, which shall be of your *koilia*"), and *aischynē* might refers to shameful appendages, whereby Paul would refer to his Jewish Christian opponents as not only penis worshippers, but, because of their focus on circumcision, comparing them to phallic cults such as that of Priapus.

list of things contrary to the worship of God includes people who are "willing to barter their freedom for indulgent foods, strong wine, of sweetmeats, of beauty, the pleasures of the belly and of the private parts below the belly; the wretched end of such gratification is destruction of both body and soul" (*Vir.* 182 [trans. MFB]). Further, the ancient rhetorician Athanaeus addressed the glutton "whose god is your belly" (*Deipn.* 97c). In Euripides, Cyclops says, "I offer sacrifice . . . to this belly of mine, the greatest of deities."[353] At the same time, this language also pertains to censuring apostasy in intra-Jewish polemics. Third Maccabees refers to Hellenizing Jews "who for the belly's sake had transgressed the divine commandments" (3 Macc 7:11). Paul himself adds a kind of warning note at the end of Romans about Jewish Christ-believing proselytizers who may also turn up on the scene: "I urge you, brothers and sisters, to keep an eye on those who cause dissensions and offenses, in opposition to the teaching that you have learned; avoid them [NRSV]. For they that are such serve not our Lord Jesus Christ, but their own belly [KJV]" (Rom 16:17–18). If Paul is taking an equally sectarian and polemical approach, then perhaps he is making a swipe at fellow Jewish Christ-believers who insist on pushing the Jewish dietary regulations from the Torah onto Gentiles. So these persons prioritize and even idolize food so much that they are worshipping their very own stomachs.[354] Interestingly, and more likely for our mind, Karl Olav Sandnes suggests a figurative explanation of the belly (*koilia*) whereby this metaphorical belly-worship refers to a manner of life characterized by love of self that is placed in juxtaposition to Jesus' sacrificial self-giving love that defines the mode of life for his followers according to Phil 2:5–11.[355] Sandnes points to the example of Demosthenes, who characterized certain persons as belly-devotees on account of their bad citizenship. Those who seek their own pleasure and are not willing to give themselves for their country are belly-devotees rather than good citizens. This example fits well with the context of Phil 3:19–20, which also juxtaposes belly-worship with a

---

[353] Cited from Reumann, *Philippians*, 571; Keown, *Philippians*, 2.258.

[354] Mearns, "The Identity of Paul's Opponents," 198–200; Wright, "Philippians: Lecture 8"; Lincoln, *Paradise Now and Not Yet*, 95–97; Hawthorne and Martin, *Philippians*, 224; Müller, *Philipper*, 176–181; rejected by Bockmuehl, *The Epistle to the Philippians*, 231, Garland, "Philippians," 247, and Keown, *Philippians*, 2.228–229.

[355] K. O. Sandnes, *Belly and Body in the Pauline Epistles* (SNTSMS; Cambridge: Cambridge University Press, 2002).

proper exercise of citizenship. Sandnes comments, "There is a hidden agenda in Paul's use of the belly-topos here. Believers who seek only their own ends, and who are unprepared to undertake a self-abnegating life according to the pattern set by Christ, have neglected their heavenly citizenship."[356] However, unlike Sandnes, we do not think this passage refers to self-absorbed libertines,[357] rather, by using such freighted language, Paul characterizes his Jewish Christ-believing rivals as greedy, indulgent, unfaithful to God's commands, and citizens of earth not heaven.[358]

Third, "their glory is in their shame." On the surface Paul may simply be referring to those who are boastful about behaviors that they should be ashamed of (see, e.g., Rom 1:32). However, Paul might also have in mind "shame" as a form of judgment, something experienced by those who are unfaithful or hostile to God (e.g., Isa 23:4; 41:11; Mic 7:16). Paul arguably conceives of a reversal from glory to shame with scriptural allusions to Hab 2:16, "You will be sated with contempt instead of glory. Drink, you yourself, and stagger! The cup in the LORD's right hand will come around to you, and shame will come upon your glory!" and Hos 4:7, "The more they increased, the more they sinned against me; they changed their glory into shame." That Paul imagines an eschatological form of shame being cast upon his opponents and also reflects his earlier comment that he hopes Christ will be exalted in his body rather than himself be put to shame (Phil 1:20).

Fourth, "their minds are set on earthly things." Instead of having a mind shaped by Christ (Phil 2:1–5) and the upward call (Phil 3:14), the opponents are focused on earthly matters (see Col 3:5). While not so heavenly minded to be of no earthly good, the adversaries are so terrestrial that they show active disregard for the perspectives and prerogatives of Jesus the exalted Lord of heaven (Phil 2:9–11). For Paul, to put one's trust in Torah rather than embrace the faithfulness of Christ is to set oneself on earthly things.[359]

---

[356] Sandnes, *Belly and Body*, 151; and others, for example, Hooker, "Philippians," 534–535.
[357] Lightfoot (*Philippians*, 155) likewise thinks this group to be "antinomian reactionists." See similarly, e.g., Jewett, "Conflicting Movements," 382; Bockmuehl, *The Epistle to the Philippians*, 231–232; Thielman, *Philippians*, 198; Hellerman, *Philippians*, 218–220.
[358] Silva (*Philippians*, 180) puts it well: "If the reference is to libertines, they appear to come from nowhere and go nowhere."
[359] Witherington, *Philippians*, 215.

To put it succinctly, Paul considers these people to be debauched, destined for disgrace, and ultimately they will be utterly destroyed. Paul then, in vv. 20–21, contrasts the skewed perspectives and sinister practices of the enemies of the cross with another perspective, an eschatological perspective, more fitting for those who choose to imitate the example of Christ and his apostle to the Gentiles.[360] What we find in vv. 20–21 is a compressed summary of Paul's eschatology, more elaborate than 1 Thess 1:10 yet more condensed than 1 Cor 15:23–27, 51–54, and based on the two poles of Christ's return and believers' resurrection. Paul conceives of the saints in Philippi as like a heavenly colony, earnestly awaiting the return of their Lord, in this case not to enjoy some pageantry and to talk politics, but to transform their earthly bodies to be like his own glorious and immortal body. "This little statement contains in a nutshell," says N. T. Wright, "more or less all Paul's thoughts on the subject. The risen Jesus is both the *model* for the Christian's future body and the *means* by which it comes about."[361]

Paul moves his argument along with an explanatory statement that is meant as a contrast to the perspective of the enemies of the cross.[362] In contrast to the tawdry and terrestrial orientation of such opponents, Paul declares, "But our citizenship is in heaven, and it is from there that we are expecting a Savior, the Lord Jesus Christ" (v. 20). Paul says that "we" – speaking inclusively of himself, his coworkers, and the Philippians – possess a *politeuma*, a citizenship that is "in heaven." The word *politeuma* "denotes a colony of foreigners or relocated veterans."[363] The citizenship imagery would resonate closely with the Philippians since Philippi was a Roman colony where Roman veterans had been settled after the civil wars of 42 BCE and 31 BCE. The city enjoyed the privileges of Roman citizenship and was considered an extension of Roman culture.

---

[360] Some think vv. 20–21 represent a fragment of hymnic or traditional material, see J. Reumann, "Philippians 3.20–21 – A Hymnic Fragment?" *NTS* 30 (1984): 593–609, rejected by R. H. Gundry, *SŌMA in Biblical Theology: With Emphasis on Pauline Anthropology* (SNTS 9; Cambridge: Cambridge University Press, 1976), 177–181.

[361] N. T. Wright, *Surprised by Hope* (London: SPCK, 2014), 161 (italics original).

[362] Thus, while *gar* means literally "for," the NRSV, NIV, CSB, ESV, and NET are contextually correct to translate it as "But."

[363] BDAG, 845; see Keown, *Philippians*, 2.269–271 for problems with translating this word as colony, commonwealth, empire, or republic.

We should note too, as N. T. Wright points out,[364] that Roman citizenship was bestowed on subjects for specific reasons.

First, Roman citizenship did not mean that Rome was a person's true home, it was about allegiance to Rome itself. The city of Philippi was an important outpost toward Thrace along the Via Egnatia with access to a vital port into the Aegean Sea. It was then imperative to keep Philippi secure as a Roman client-city and to give it good reason to support Roman interests. Citizenship was granted to cities like Philippi to spread Roman culture, to enlarge networks of people loyal to both emperor and empire, and to create interlocking webs of patronage and dependence that converged across the empire. Granting citizenship provided a populace with legal benefits and tax incentives that ensured the *Romanitas* or Romanness of the city, embedding it within the echelons of imperial power, and secured its allegiance to Roman interests and the Roman way of life.

Second, granting Roman citizenship and establishing colonies in conquered territories dealt with the problem of overcrowding in Rome. It was better to have citizens out in the provinces enjoying a taste of "Rome away from Rome" than to have even more people in the already overcrowded metropolis of the empire. Much better to reward veterans with farms to tend and businesses to run in the provinces than to have them back in Italy vying for the limited plots of land and potentially stewing over grievances that could be easily weaponized and then mobilized by treacherous leaders looking to usurp power for themselves.

It is vital to remember that "heaven" here is not meant as a transcendent refuge from one's mortal coil, the habitat of an immortal soul, or a place of serenity characterized by a dreary eternity of endless hymns. Further, heaven is most definitely not "the place or location in which one has the right to be a citizen"[365] since the Philippians enjoy their heavenly citizenship in the present moment and in their present location. Rather, heaven here signifies the God-dimension of reality, the seat of divine power, where God's future purposes are stored up, so that at the appropriate moment God can execute those plans, a plan that involves the return of Christ, the

---

[364]  Wright, *Surprised by Hope*, 111–112, 143–145; idem, *The Resurrection of the Son of God* (Minneapolis: Fortress Press, 2003), 229–232; *PFG*, 1292–1295; see too Fee, *Philippians*, 379; Hooker, "Philippians," 535; Garland, "Philippians," 248–249.
[365]  Contra LN 11.71.

resurrection of believers, and the transformation of the earth. Heaven is the mysterious dimension from whence Christ shall come as Savior to put an answer to his disciples' prayer that things be on earth as they are in heaven.[366] To repeat Wright's apt illustration, one might have a beer stored up in the fridge for a friend, but one does not make the friend climb into the fridge in order to drink it.[367] Just as the Philippians enjoyed Roman citizenship without ever going to Rome, similarly, the Philippians enjoy a heavenly citizenship without first entering heaven and purely on account of their allegiance to the one who shall come from heaven to save them. The point is not salvation upon reaching heaven, but the Savior coming from heaven to earth to bring victory, vindication, and vivification to his people – perhaps parodying the image of Caesar coming from Rome with legions to rescue a city that has been put to siege by an enemy. According to J. Richard Middleton (himself channeling N. T. Wright), "The text is talking not about going to heaven, but rather about the source of our confidence to live on earth in a manner different from (and in tension with) the present fallen world, until Christ's return."[368]

Viewed this way, Paul portrays the Philippian Christ-believers as perhaps fellow soldiers of Christ, just like Epaphroditus (Phil 2:25), settled in Philippi and called to actively promote the interests of their heavenly master and savior upon the domain of earth. They are citizens of heaven, not in the sense of passively waiting to go there when they die, but are called "to colonize earth with the life of heaven."[369] Believers possess what Judith Lieu calls a "transfigured citizenship,"[370] where the categories of colonial polity and civic duty are reinterpreted through the lens of belonging to God's purposes; purposes, although laid up in heaven for now, that are nonetheless destined to be realized on earth. The point is not so much the hope of returning to the place of one's citizenship in the

---

[366] Wright, "Philippians: Lecture 8."

[367] Wright, *Surprised by Hope*, 164.

[368] J. R. Middleton, *A New Heaven and a New Earth: Reclaiming Biblical Eschatology* (Grand Rapids, MI: Baker, 2014), 218.

[369] Wright, *Surprised by Hope*, 293; *PFG*, 1292.

[370] J. Lieu, "Identity Games in Early Christian Texts: The *Letter to Diognetus*," in *Ethnicity, Race, Religion: Identities and Ideologies in Early Jewish and Christian texts, and in Modern Biblical Interpretation* (eds. K. M. Hockey and D. G. Horrell; London: Bloomsbury, 2018), /1.

future, but how heavenly citizenship shapes life in the present. Allegiance to the God of heaven and faith in the Son who shall come from heaven gives direction to their earthly enterprises and ethics. A view wonderfully expounded in the *Epistle to Diognetus* where the author says of Christians:

> But while living in both Greek and barbarian cities, as each have obtained by lot, and while following the local customs both in clothing and in diet and in the rest of life, they demonstrate the wonderful and most certainly strange character of their own citizenship. They live in their own countries, but as aliens. They share in everything as citizens and endure everything as foreigners. Every foreign country is their country, and every country is foreign. They marry like everyone, they bear children, but they do not expose their offspring. They set a common table, but not a common bed. They happen to be in the flesh but do not live according to the flesh. They spend time upon the earth, but have their citizenship in heaven.[371]

The mention of Jesus as "Savior" (*sōtēr*) presents him as the deliverer and rescuer of Christians. The title "Savior" is used only in Phil 3:20 in the undisputed Pauline letters, although it is found more commonly in the disputed Pauline letters (Eph 5:23; 2 Tim 1:10; Tit 1:4; 2:13; 3:6), and is ubiquitous in later expressions of Christianity (e.g., Acts 5:21; 13:23; Ignatius, *Eph.* 1.1; Polycarp, *Phil.* 1.1; *Mart. Pol.* 9.3; 19.2; *Diogn.* 9.6; 2 Pet 1:1; 3:2; *P. Oxy* 840; 2 *Clem.* 20.5). Plutarch (*De Coriolanus*, 11) said that the Greeks ascribe the title *sōtēr* to their rulers because of their great accomplishments. Ancient inscriptions and papyri make references to the emperors of the 50s, both Claudius and Nero, as "Savior" of Rome and all her peoples.[372] That is because salvation from civil war, raiding parties, famine, and lawlessness is what Caesar offered the people in exchange for their fealty and allegiance. In fact, it was during the reign of Claudius some ten years earlier (44–45 CE) that Roman legions annexed nearby Thrace due to civil unrest that threatened to spill over into Macedonia.[373] "In the first century AD," declares Peter Oakes, "the one whom most people would see as saving in accordance with his power to subject all things to himself was the Emperor."[374]

[371]  *Diogn.* 5.5–9 (trans. R. Brannan).
[372]  See *LANE*, 363–365; *NDIEC* 9.4–5.
[373]  Oakes, *Philippians*, 139; Verhoef, *Philippi*, 15–16.
[374]  Oakes, *Philippians*, 140.

The subversive element of what Paul is saying need not be overplayed, as if every affirmation of Jesus is an automatic denunciation of Caesar.[375] Nonetheless, Jesus is at least an alternative Savior to Caesar and something of a definitive rival to Caesar in the final eschatological saga that will unfold at the end history. Caesar with his legions is one of the powers that Jesus delivers his people from (note the allusion to Isa 11:10 [LXX] about the root of Jesse rising to rule over the Gentiles in Rom 15:12, Rev 12:4, 19:15). Wright offers a good insight on this point:

> The Philippians, believing that Jesus was the only one at whose name every knee should bow, were faced with the task of working out, in the practical details of everyday life within Caesar's world, what it would mean, what it would look like and feel like, to explore the *sōtēria* which Jesus offered instead. Paul gives them some pointers, but in a short letter he can hardly do more than provide suggestions. He is, however, confident that the one true God is at work among them, so that they will be able to understand their own variety of 'salvation', just as they must learn the meaning of their own variety of *politeuma*, 'citizenship'.[376]

Paul next spells out, if rather briefly, what the Savior will do upon his return: "He will transform the body of our humiliation that it may be conformed to the body of his glory, by the power that also enables him to make all things subject to himself" (v. 21). Paul envisages, much like 1 Cor 15:20–28, 51–52 and 1 Thess 1:10, 4:15–18, 5:23, Christ's return met with the instantaneous resurrection of deceased and living believers. Here "the body" is a metonym for the entire person and this "body" is to be transformed[377] from a state of humiliation and mortality to be conformed to the likeness of Christ's glorified risen body. The body is not discarded like a butterfly's chrysalis nor does it evolve into some kind of pneumatic material, rather, it is transformed and christoformed! As Paul wrote to the

---

[375] Lynn H. Cohick ("Citizenship and Empire: Paul's Letter to the Philippians and Eric Liddell's Work in China," *JSPL* 1 [2011]: 145) offers a wise word of warning: "Paul's primary focus in Philippians is not a coded attack on the imperial cult but a spirited defense, public and bold, of the gospel, which relegated to secondary status any pagan claims, be they part of the imperial cult or aspects of paganism and imperial government generally. All are part of the present evil age, which is passing away." See similarly Hawthorne and Martin, *Philippians*, lxx–lxxi; Barclay, *Paul and the Gift*, 456 n. 15.

[376] *PFG*, 1295.

[377] Paul refers to being "transformed" (*metaschēmatizō*) and "conformity" (*symmorphos*) in Phil 3:21, being "changed" (*allassō*) in 1 Cor 15:51, and being "transformed" (*metamorphoo*) in 2 Cor 3:18.

Romans, "If the Spirit of him who raised Jesus from the dead dwells in you, he who raised Christ from the dead will give life to your mortal bodies also through his Spirit that dwells in you" (Rom 8:11) and being "predestined to be conformed to the image of his Son" (Rom 8:29). Paul expects the glorious transformation of the current lowly body to be like Jesus's glorious body as a direct result of God's all-conquering and life-infusing power over death, evil, and the powers of this age.

The result, first, is a new body that is incorruptible, immortal, animated-by-the-spirit, infused with divine power, and glorious (1 Cor 15:35–44). Then, second, the body is conformed to the glorious nature of Christ's own body, with a transformation that is ontological in that it participates in Christ's resplendence but also vocational in that the body is now fit to reign with Christ.[378] What lies behind all this might be a christological, ecclesiological, and eschatological reading of Ps 8:5–6: "Yet you have made them a little lower than God, and crowned them with glory and honor. You have given them dominion over the works of your hands; you have put all things under their feet." Jesus is resurrected and exalted to a position of divine-regency in the Father's kingdom, then, when he returns to rescue his people, he brings them into his exalted glory and into his adamic and messianic vocation to be God's human ruler over creation.

This transformation of the body and the christoformity of the person takes place "by" (*kata*) the "power that also enables him to make all things subject to himself." Paul affirms that at the return of Christ the mortal bodies of believers are to be transfigured into a heavenly body like that of their exalted Lord. The power that effects this bodily transformation and its accompanying christification is the same power by which the exalted *human* Jesus is able to subject "all things" (*ta panta*) under his supremacy. Of course, this harks back to Phil 2:6–11, where Jesus moves from being in the form of God/equality with God, to humiliation and subjection, and then is exalted to divine honor and glory. So too, if only analogically, believers move from bodily humiliation (mortality) and social shame (ostracism and persecution) to divine honor and sharing in Christ's vocation.[379] Andrew Lincoln has identified the following links between Phil 2:6–11 and 3:20–21 (Table 6).

---

[378] On this see H. G. Jacob, *Conformed to the Image of His Son: Reconsidering Paul's Theology of Glory in Romans* (Downers Grove, IL: InterVarsity Press, 2018).
[379] See Lincoln, *Paradise Now and Not Yet*, 87–89.

Table 6 *Comparing Phil 2:6–11 and Phil 3:20–21*

| Phil 2:6–11 | Phil 3:20–21 |
|---|---|
| *morphē* ("form") 2:6 *morphēn* ("form") 2:7 | *symmorphē* ("conformed") 3:21 |
| *hyparchōn* ("being") 2:6 | *hyparchei* ("to be, is") 3:20 |
| *schēnati* ("appearance") 2:7 | *metaschēmatisei* ("transform") 3:21 |
| *etapeinōsen* ("humbled") 2:8 | *tapeivōseōs* ("humiliation") 3:21 |
| *epouraniōn* ("heavenly") 2:10 | *ouranois* ("heaven") 3:20 |
| *pan gonu kampsē . . . kai pasa glōssa exomolgēsetai* ("every knee bow . . . and every tongue confess") 2:10, 11 | *tou dunasthai auton kai hypotaxai autō ta panta* ("the power [that enables] him to subject to him[self] all things") 3:21 |
| *kurios Iēsous Christos* ("Jesus Christ [is] Lord") 2:11 | *kurion Iēsoun Christon* ("Lord Jesus Christ") 3:20 |
| *doxan* ("glory") 2:11 | *doxēs* ("glory") 3:21 |

What is quite striking is that in most Christian interpretations of Ps 8:5–7 (LXX), God is the one who subjects all things under the dominion of the "son of man" (see, e.g., 1 Cor 15:27; Eph 1:22; Heb 2:6–9; Polycarp, *Phil.* 2.1), while here it is the exalted Jesus who himself subjugates "all things" under the aegis of his own authority.[380]

Zooming out to the big picture for a moment, I would be prepared to argue that God's plan was always for humans to rule over his creation; a plan that, in light of the fall, requires the rescue of humanity and the renewal of the created order. Thus, as the redemptive saga unfolds, God ordains Abraham's family (Gen 18:18; 22:18; Gal 3:8), Israel (Exod 19:5–6; Isa 42:6; 49:6), Israel's king (Isa 9:7; 32:1; Ps 72:17; 1 Cor 15:25; Rev 11:15), a restored Israel (Dan 7:14, 27), and a redeemed humanity (John 3:3, 72 Cor 5:17; Eph 2:15; 4:24; Col 3:10; 1 Pet 1:3) to project his salvation into the world and to reign with him and for him (Matt 19:28/Luke 22:19–20; 2 Tim 2:12; Rev 5:10; 20:6; 22:5). This plan of God-reigning-through-this-new-humanity is realized in the first stage in the exaltation of the human Jesus – who is the new Adam, Abraham's seed, Israel's embodiment, Israel's king, the firstborn from among the dead – to cosmic regency (Mark 14:62; Eph 1:20–23; Col 1:18; 2:10; 1 Cor 15:25; Heb 2:9; Rev 1:5, 18; 11:15; 12:10; 20:4). Then, in the second stage, humanity is rescued from sin and death, exalted with Jesus, and then incorporated into Jesus's adamic and messianic vocation to reign with God the Father over creation. In

---

[380] See similarly, Bockmuehl, *The Epistle to the Philippians*, 236; Reumann, *Philippians*, 600.

other words, God's plan is "to bring unity to all things in heaven and on earth under Christ" (Eph 1:10) so that a transformed Israel would transform the world,[381] to create a multiethnic worldwide family conformed to the image of the Son (Rom 8:29), and, in the new creation, a rescued and resurrected humanity would reign with the Messiah (2 Tim 2:12).

The chapter division that separates chapters three and four unconsciously prejudices readers to think that Phil 4:1–9 is a discreet section, however, 4:1 is better regarded as the conclusion to a section began at 3:17.[382] Paul's exhortation to apostolic imitation and eschatological anticipation in the face of opposition comes to a close with the words: "Therefore, my brothers and sisters, whom I love and long for, my joy and crown, stand firm in the Lord in this way, my beloved" (4:1).

The language here is familial ("brothers and sisters") and affectionate ("whom I love and long for" and "beloved"), and it aptly sums up the friendly texture of the letter and the warm tenor of Paul's relationship with the Philippians. All this while concurrently exercising a stern call for resilience in the face of multiple causes of coercion including possible apostacizing, judaizing, and returning to pagan indices of estimating honor and worth. Paul calls them – as he also does of the Thessalonians – his "joy and crown" (see 1 Thess 2:19). Put in the coordinates of the now/not-yet of Paul's eschatology, we might say that the Philippian congregations *presently* are a source of joy for him in their fellowshipping with him and *they will be* his crown,[383] or the cause of his jubilation, triumph, and reward as he offers them to the Lord and boasts about them on the "day of Christ" (Phil 2:16; cf. 1 Cor 15:31). To them he offers a relatively short and simple charge: "stand firm in the Lord in this way."[384] This rehearses earlier exhortations toward faithfulness (Phil 1:27; 2:12–16; 3:12–16) and mirrors

---

[381] T.W. Manson, *Only to the House of Israel?: Jesus and the Non-Jews* (Philadelphia: Fortress, 1964), 18.

[382] So too Hooker, "Philippians," 531; Witherington, *Philippians*,181, 184; Osiek, *Philippians*,107; Silva, *Philippians*,143; Thompson and Longenecker, *Philippians and Philemon*, 90; Wright, *Prison Letters*, 124; Thurston, *Philippians and Philemon*, 130; Holloway, *Philippians*, 178; Hellerman, *Philippians*, 212.

[383] As Lightfoot (*Philippians*, 157) points out, "crown" (*stephanos*) here is not about regality, but associated with victory and merriment, a wreathe worn by the military victor and the holiday-maker!

[384] Wright (*Prison Letters*, 127) takes this to mean: "giving allegiance to Jesus, rather than to Caesar, as the true Lord."

similar encouragements to steadfastness found in Paul's other letters (1 Cor 15:58; 16:13; 2 Cor 1:24; Gal 5:1; 1 Thess 3:8; 2 Thess 2:15; Eph. 6:13–14; cf. Exod 14:13; Dan 11:32). Therefore, given the language in 3:17–21 of imitation and anticipation, citizenship and consummation, transformation and destruction, Paul calls his beloved Philippians to exhibit the same (*houtōs*, lit. "in this manner") steadfast devotion to God and Christ that he himself exemplifies as their apostle.

## 4:2–9: EXHORTATION TO UNITY, GENTLENESS, AND EXCELLENCE

² I urge Euodia and I urge Syntyche to be of the same mind in the Lord.

³ Yes, and I ask you also, my loyal companion, help these women, for they have struggled beside me in the work of the gospel, together with Clement and the rest of my co-workers, whose names are in the book of life.

⁴ Rejoice in the Lord always; again I will say, Rejoice.

⁵ Let your gentleness be known to everyone. The Lord is near.

⁶ Do not worry about anything, but in everything by prayer and supplication with thanksgiving let your requests be made known to God.

⁷ And the peace of God, which surpasses all understanding, will guard your hearts and your minds in Christ Jesus.

⁸ Finally, beloved, whatever is true, whatever is honorable, whatever is just, whatever is pure, whatever is pleasing, whatever is commendable, if there is any excellence and if there is anything worthy of praise, think about these things.

⁹ Keep on doing the things that you have learned and received and heard and seen in me, and the God of peace will be with you.

Phil 4:2–9 has long been treated as a concluding hortatory section of the letter; that is, Paul moves away from the central theological content of the letter to offer some counsel about how to live.[385] In a very basic way, this is indeed somewhat common in Paul's letters (see 1 Thess 5:12–28; Gal

---

[385]  See Hawthorne and Martin, *Philippians*, 238

5:1–6:18), but two clarifying points should be made. First of all, Paul tends to give exhortations and commands *throughout* his epistles (e.g., Rom 5–8), not just at the close.[386] Second, there are some peculiar elements included in this section in Philippians that prevent it from serving as "general exhortation" *per se*. Here, for example, Paul addresses directly the situation involving Euodia and Syntyche (4:2–3). Therefore, we will link the material in 4:2–9 as closely to the previous content of the letter as seems contextually and rhetorically beneficial.

One of the initial challenges with reading and interpreting Phil 4:2–9 is discerning the structure of this passage.[387] A rough outline would look as follows:

Calling Euodia and Syntyche to Gospel Unity (4:2–3)
Call to Celebrate in the Lord (4:4)
Call to Gentleness and Peace (4:5–7)
Call to Pauline Virtue in Thought and Action (4:8–9)

All of these calls and commands go back to 4:1 (and the wider section of 3:18–4:1) where Paul exhorts the Philippians to stand firm in the faith. But he does not say this as a drill sergeant or taskmaster, but as someone who loves and cherishes them, wanting what's best for them, as they are his "joy and crown" (cf. 1 Thess 2:19). In no other Pauline letter, nor in any other New Testament book or text, do we find such a pervasive infusion of celebration, joy, and hope in the issuing of commands and exhortations. We will return to this theme with more earnest when we examine 4:4 in detail.

But we will begin our examination of this passage with 4:2–3 and the most obvious question: who were these two women? Unfortunately, we know nothing about Euodia and Syntyche apart from what Paul writes here.[388] We know they are Greek names, the former name meaning "good journey," the latter "good luck." A few scholars have surmised that one or

---

[386]  See C. Roetzel, *Paul: The Man and the Myth* (Minneapolis: Fortress, 1999), 86; Horrell, *Solidarity and Difference*, 97–98.

[387]  So Hawthrone and Martin comment on "how difficult a task it is to outline any logical flow of the apostle's thoughts from first to last"; *Philippians*, 238.

[388]  R. F. Hull, Jr. has written a reliable history and summary of scholarship on the figures of Euodia and Syntyche in Phil 4:2–3; see "Constructing Euodia and Syntyche," *Priscilla Papers* 30 (2, 2016): 3–7.

both of these women may have been *liberta*, slaves who became free.[389] Whatever their background and history, what we *can* confidently infer from Paul's letter is that these two women were leaders in the Philippian church.

Closer Look: The Status and Power of Women in Philippi

There is a popular assumption that women in antiquity operated with little agency or power in society due to patriarchy. While patriarchy was pervasive in the Greco-Roman world, historians have developed a more complex and nuanced understanding of the roles played by women in places like Philippi. Elizabeth Carney explains that in ancient Macedonia we do have evidence that women were not confined to household and domestic duties. Thanks to material such as inscriptions and papyri (e.g., correspondence) we observe them "conducting business, practicing some trades, selling and buying slaves and other goods, getting honorific statues."[390] We also know Macedonian women participated in fundraising and efforts to improve civic services, they held civic offices, and were sometimes recipients of honorary statues and inscriptions. Often these women were honored alongside husbands and sons, but sometimes they alone were praised.[391] Carney and others have identified that it was especially in the sphere of religion and religious rituals that we see a strong presence of female activity and leadership.[392] With this context in mind, we have every reason to believe that Euodia and Syntyche held prominent positions of leadership in the church, perhaps as *episkopoi*.[393]

[389] See Oakes, *From People to Letter*, 64; C. S. de Vos, *Church and Community Conflicts: The Relationship of the Thessalonian, Corinthian, and Philippian Churches with Their Wider Civic Communities* (Atlanta, GA: Scholars Press, 1999), 252–256. De Vos notes only four extant occurrences of the Greek name Euodia; two refer to *liberta*.

[390] E. Carney, "Macedonian Women," in *Brill's Companion to Ancient Macedonia* (eds. J. Roisman et al.; Oxford: Wiley-Blackwell, 2010), 409–247, here 424.

[391] Carney, "Macedonian Women," 424–425; cf. C. Osiek and M. Y. MacDonald, *A Woman's Place: House Churches in Earliest Christianity* (Minneapolis: Fortress, 2006), 5.

[392] Carney, "Macedonian Women," 425; U. Kron, "Priesthoods, Dedications and Euergetism: What Part Did Religion Play in the Political and Social Status of Greek Women?" in *Religion and Power in the Ancient Greek World* (eds. P. Hellström and B. Alroth; Upsalla: University of Upsalla, 1996), 139–182; T. Calpino, *Women, Work, and Leadership in Acts* (WUNT 2.361; Tübingen: Mohr Siebeck, 2014), 184; J. Lamoreaux, *Ritual, Women, and Philippi: Reimagining the Early Philippian Community* (Eugene, OR: Cascade, 2013), 43–100.

[393] See Reumann, *Philippians*, 632.

One is struck by Paul's seemingly abrupt public "naming" of Euodia and Syntyche. A few elements of Paul's wording are notable. First, he exhorts them somewhat indirectly. Instead of writing, "I urge *you*, Euodia . . . and *you*, Syntyche," he addresses them obliquely. I take this as a call for the whole church to take notice, and take responsibility for this call to gospel unity. Their disagreement is clearly not just a petty personal matter, but something that affected the whole community. Second, Paul goes out of his way to exhort each one, repeating the imperative "urge" (*parakaleō*). This small addition reflects Paul's unwillingness to "take sides." His goal is cooperation, and he holds each one accountable to active participation in reconciliation and partnership. Third, he urges them to be "of the same mind in the Lord." This is not about one person *caving in* and it is not even about "agreeing" (*pace* RSV); rather, Paul repeats a notion he introduced earlier in 2:2, that the church has the capacity to come to together *as if with one mind* to serve the Lord. To be "of the same mind" is to share a singular passion and mission for the sake of the gospel.[394]

What was the nature of these women's disagreement? Unfortunately, we can only guess. The most plausible theory that I have encountered is the notion that Euodia and Syntyche disagreed specifically about whether or not to support Paul's ministry and mission. Mark Jennings writes,

As leaders of the church, they were possibly part of the initial decision to withhold aid to Paul (4:10), as well as the more recent decision to resume it. Though this is speculative, one can easily imagine Epaphroditus reporting that the cessation and resumption of support was connected to the dispute between Euodia and Syntyche.[395]

The attractiveness of this theory is that it would make sense for Paul to mention this explicitly in the letter, and it does shed some light on the awkward "thank you" in 4:10–20 (see later). In 4:3, Paul brings into the conversation a few more mediators to help restore gospel unity. Paul invites help from one of the church people whom he calls "my loyal companion" (literally "my true yokefellow"), giving here the image of a reliable coworker, someone that could act in Paul's stead. There are a number of possible identities for this unnamed person – Silas, Luke,

---

[394]   D. M. Allen, "Philippians 4:2–3: 'To Agree or Not to Agree? Unity Is the Question.'" *ExpTimes* 121.11 (2010): 535–538.
[395]   Jennings, *The Price of Partnership*, 154.

Timothy, or a local leader. Again, there is no foolproof evidence, but I find most convincing the argument that the "yokefellow" is Epaphroditus, the bearer of the letter. As Hooker argues, since Epaphroditus was commended extensively in chapter two, he would not have to be named explicitly here, and, moreover, if he brought the letter to the Philippians, it would make good sense for him to serve as Paul's proxy.[396] Furthermore, calling him a "true yokefellow" would add another touch of Paul's admiration and praise for Epaphroditus who has the apostle's leadership "stamp of approval," as it were.

This compatriot of Paul's is enjoined to help or assist these women. At this point Paul offers an extended word of praise for these women, underscoring their importance in the community. They have "struggled" alongside Paul in the work of the gospel. Paul used the same verb in Phil 1:27 in reference to how the Philippians as a whole were to live as good citizens of the gospel commonwealth "striving side by side with one mind."[397] The purpose of Paul's commendation of Euodia in Syntyche appears to be to treat them as equally significant in the work of the church, people whom all should honor and respect even though they stand on opposite sides of some unnamed disagreement. Again, we have no concrete information about the leadership roles Euodia and Syntyche played in the Philippian church, but many surmise that they were important figures.[398]

In addition, Paul mentions a man named Clement and offers a general reference to other coworkers (4:3c). Again, we know nothing about Clement, but it could be that he and these others were caught up in whatever disagreement was transpiring between Euodia and Syntyche, or perhaps he was another church leader who could step in to help resolve the issue. Why does Paul mention their status as those whose names are written in the

---

[396] Hooker, "Philippians," 540.

[397] Scholars debate whether this is an athletic or military metaphor; outside of Philippians, there is only one occurrence of this verb (*synathleō*), and its meaning in that context is unusual (*Diodorus Siculus* 3.2). My inclination is to see this broadly speaking as nodding toward a military metaphor given Paul's affinity for such (Phil 2:25), but here it may simply just be generic language for struggling together in a context of difficulty or resistance. For a recent argument in favor of athletic imagery, see D. Kurek-Chomycz, "Fellow Athletes or Fellow Soldiers? *Synathleō* in Philippians 1.27 and 4.3," *JSNT* 39.3 (2017): 279–303.

[398] Some propose that they were house-church hosts; see C. Osiek, "What We Do and Don't Know about Early Christian Families," in *A Companion to Families in the Greek and Roman Worlds* (ed. B. Rawson; Oxford: Wiley-Blackwell, 2010), 198–213, here 203.

book of life? It may be as simple an idea as that all such persons mentioned and included among Paul's coworkers are fellow-believers, comembers of the covenant. Each person has their rightful place in the community and, despite their current differences, they have all been faithful contributors to the community. Sometimes in disagreements it is easy to forget the commonalities and shared values, and to exaggerate the differences. Paul reminds them that they all share one life and one hope.

Paul pauses from his flow of thought to call the Philippians to rejoice (or to celebrate) – twice (4:4). Put another way, if the text went from 4:3 to 4:5, nothing would seem amiss. But this intrusion of joy is all the more noticeable and would have undoubtedly jarred the first readers (and hearers). Here was Paul, prisoner, cut off from his civic freedom, with every reason to be despondent and cynical, and yet calling for the Philippians to rejoice just as he is able to rejoice (again, see Phil 2:17–18; 3:1; 4:10; cf. 4:12).

---

Bridging the Horizons: Augustine on Joy

Augustine does well to ponder Paul's appeal to joy in his *Confessions*. First, he observes that some only feel "fed" and well when life circumstances are salutary. But Augustine treats such people as those whose "god is their belly" (*Conf.* 13.26; cf. Phil 3:19). Paul indeed did rejoice when the Philippians sent him material gifts, but the provisions themselves were not Paul's *real* source of joy – the renewed fellowship and loving care that was communicated by this gift was his cause to celebrate, Augustine argues (13.26). So in Phil 4:4 Paul commands (twice) these believers to see a cause for celebration in their fellowship with each other and with God, *what a gift!* In his letters, Augustine models Paul's attitude and perspective. In a correspondence with his friend Jerome, Augustine mentions that he has heard rumors that people say he criticizes Jerome openly in his works. Augustine wrote to Jerome to set the record straight, first, that he never wrote any *ad hominem* work against his friend, and, second, wherever he has mentioned a difference of opinion, it was done respectfully. In this short letter (no. 20), Augustine invites Jerome to correct him in any way ("I even demand and claim it as a right"), and ends his epistle by reminding Jerome of how fond he is of their friendship.

O that it were possible to enjoy sweet and frequent converse in the Lord with you; if not by living with you, at least by living near you! But since that is denied us, I beg you to do your best to maintain and increase and perfect this one object, that we should be together, as far as we can, in Christ, and not to disdain replying to me, even if it be only occasionally. (20.3)

I find Augustine's attitude and words to be a practical reflection of what Paul himself was modeling and cultivating with the Philippians, joy in the Lord, especially in sweet fellowship with other believing friends.

We have already commented more extensively on Paul's thematic emphasis on joy in Philippians (see the Introduction), but it bears repeating in brief here that the Apostle calls the Philippians to celebration and hope even in the midst of difficulty and disagreement; so David Garland writes about Phil 4:4, "This is the sanctifying vision of a strong, victorious man resolved not to succumb to despair in the face of persecution and discouragement."[399] English translations regularly render the repeated verb as "rejoice," which of course is technically accurate. But we might do better to translate it as "celebrate" (finding a more familiar English word that resonates with how people talk about joy and happiness today). Keep in mind that the imperative form of this verb is often used in greetings ("salutations!"). It is not unfathomable, then, that Paul was telling the Philippians; *yes, you have this disagreement, it may be major, it may have troubled your community, but first things first – throw a party! Celebrate! What are we celebrating? God! We should celebrate what the Lord has done, is doing, and will do.* No doubt when this letter was read aloud, at this statement everyone's ears perked up, and they leaned in closer, eager to know more about what this celebration talk was all about.

Paul does indeed continue his line of reasoning by calling the community to peace and corporate harmony. In 4:5 he points the whole community toward *epiekēs* (NRSV "gentleness"). Perhaps a better translation is "forbearance" (see RSV; cf. 1 Pet 2:18; Josephus, *Vita* 176; *Aristeas* 188). Based on its usage elsewhere, it carries the sense of yielding thoughtfulness with respect to the other. It does not deny the rights or justice for oneself, but assumes that I am looking out for the best interests of other(s) as of special concern. George Caird has offered the gloss "sweet reasonableness."[400] Perhaps my favorite translation is "magnanimity" (also suggested by Caird).[401] Not only should the Philippian believers aspire to represent

---

[399] See Garland, "Philippians," 329–331.
[400] Caird, *Paul's Letters from Prison*, 150.
[401] Caird, *Paul's Letters from Prison*, 150.

this virtue, but their reasonable and magnanimous disposition should be known to all mortals.[402]

Without a connecting conjunction like "and" (*kai* or *de*), Paul bluntly states "the Lord is near" (4:5b). What does he mean by this? This terse statement could be taken in either of two ways, depending on how one reads the language of "near." It could be *temporal*, as in, *the Lord is coming soon* (cf. Rom 13:12; Jas 5:8; 1 Pet 4:7; Rev 3:11).[403] This would potentially fit within a Jewish perspective of the imminent Day of the Lord (Ezek 7:7; Joel 1:15; Zeph 1:14). However, appeal to the imminent coming of the Lord tends to focus on *judgment* (Matt 24:45–51), to instill a sense of holy fear and reverence in preparation, watchfulness, and anticipation of judgment. But here in Philippians, Paul has the opposite intention of comforting these believers and mollifying their anxieties by appeal to the nearness of the Lord. His purpose in mentioning that "the Lord is near," therefore, fits better with the sentiment of (for example) Ps 145:18 (LXX 144:18): "The Lord is near to all who call on him" (cf. Ps 34:18). Also, in Ps 119 we read

In your steadfast love hear my voice; O Lord, in your justice preserve my life. Those who persecute me with evil purpose draw near; they are far from your law. Yet you are near, O Lord, and all your commandments are true. (119:149–151)

While I lean in favor of the spatial interpretation, it may be artificial to sharply divide the two views; it may be a case of both-and: *the Lord is close to his people – so don't fret – and he is coming soon to make all things right*.[404]

Paul transitions, then, to a word of comfort in 4:6–7. He first consoles the Philippians by telling them not to worry or be anxious (*merimnaō*). In some ways, to be human is to be anxious and feel unease. After all, humans can't control all circumstances and cannot predict the future. But we can also say that a certain kind of uneasiness is beneficial. For example, Paul already used this verb earlier in his letter in relation to Timothy's *concern* (*merimnaō*) for the Philippians' well-being. So, the core idea of *merimnaō*

---

[402] Paul plays here on the language of "making known" – *make known your reasonableness to mortals* (4:5a), *make known your prayer requests to God* (4:6).

[403] Hansen advocates for this view, see *Philippians*, 289. To support this interpretation in view of Paul's message in Philippians, he points to Phil 3:20–21, where Paul appeals to the coming of the savior who will "*bring everything under his control*" (italics original).

[404] See R. Bauckham, *Jesus and the God of Israel* (Grand Rapids, MI: Eerdmans, 2008), 187–189.

involves a preoccupation with something. But it *can* easily turn into stress, anxiety, and misery. Paul's counsel is not to just "let go," but ultimately to trust God and to entrust one's cares and concerns to God.

Probably the most resonant passage in the New Testament that relates to Phil 4:6–7 is the portion of the Sermon on the Mount where Jesus teaches about releasing worries and recognizing God's gracious provision (6:25–34). In fact, Matthew uses this same verb (*merimnaō*) when he relays Jesus' words "do not *worry* about your life" (6:25; cf. 6:31, 34). Interestingly, Jesus here even mentions the tendencies of Gentiles/pagans to chase desperately after resolving their problems of money and other needs of life; but what Jesus urges is simple faith in the God who gives his people daily bread (cf. Matt 6:9–13). The priority of God's people, Jesus teaches, is seeking the "kingdom of God" (6:33). Similarly, Paul exhorts the Philippians not to operate out of panic, fear, or anxiety, but to turn to God in prayer. Perhaps as a counterexample, we can reference the widely known story of when the people of Tyre faced an attack by Alexander the Great. Fearing that their patron deity Apollo would abandon them, they proceeded to chain Apollo's public status to the ground to secure his presence and goodwill.[405] This is perhaps an extreme case, but it is remarkable the closeness and intimacy that Paul's understanding of prayer reflects in contrast. Believers need not fear getting the prayer words exactly correct; rather, like a child talking to a parent, there is such good will on the side of the caregiver, the child can approach with ease, confidence, and simple trust.

In 4:7 Paul calls the Philippians to pray "with thanksgiving." Here we have a context where the Philippians were experiencing deep distress and trouble over problems outside and inside the church – and Paul himself was enduring prison conditions – and yet Paul calls for *thanksgiving* alongside his earlier invitation to joy. On what basis? How could this be anything more than wishful thinking (at best) and delusional (at worst)? It is important to keep in mind that this is a standard teaching for Paul: "Give thanks in all circumstances; for this is the will of God in Christ Jesus for

---

[405] *Diodorus Siculus* 17.41.7–8; Plutarch, *Alex.* 24.5–8; *Quintus Curtius Rufus* 4.13.21–22; cf. N. K. Gupta, "They Are Not God!" *CBQ* 74 (2014): 704–419; G. Petridou, *Divine Epiphany in Greek Literature and Culture* (Oxford: Oxford University Press, 2015), 49–50.

you" (1 Thess 5:18). God's people, the people in Messiah Jesus, are to live in trust knowing the lavish provision of God in the past, the present, and the future. While present circumstances may be distressing, believers are meant to live out of their hope in divine rescue, redemption, and restoration, what Paul tells the Corinthians is "an eternal glory that far outweights [present troubles]" (2 Cor 4:17). Furthermore, Paul reminds the Corinthians that often the troubles in front of their eyes are temporary, but the promised divine glory is eternal (2 Cor 4:18).

With respect to the plight and anxieties of the Philippians, Paul enjoins them to expect the "peace of God" that will guard their hearts and minds in Christ Jesus (Phil 4:7). Perhaps it may come as a surprise to know that it is uncommon for Paul to refer to the "peace of God" (*hē eirēnē tou theou*). In fact, this is the only place in Paul's letters where this specific wording is found. However, on a couple of other occasions he refers to the "God of peace" (Rom 15:33; 16:20). In the context of Philippians, there is more than one way to interpret Paul's reference to God's peace. One option is to see it as the peace-making rule of God that has the power to heal communities and establish social peace. Given the incident with Euodia and Syntyche (4:2–3) and the overall concern with unity in this epistle, such a reading has some merit. But a more favored reading would interpret "peace of God" in a more personal or more emotion-centered way, since Paul explicitly mentions comforting the heart and mind, and this statement comes directly on the heels of his desire to pacify their anxieties.[406] But, either way, this is not disconnected from Paul's hopes for communal peace and unity in the Philippian church. It does not take much imagination to see how unanxious hearts and minds are better able to come together in decision and discussion.[407]

Phil 4:8 marks another (minor) transition in the letter (*to loipon*; cf. 3:1). Many interpreters in the past have separated 4:8 from the rest of the letter, because it does have the quality of a generic teaching on truth, goodness, and aesthetics. However, Paul immediately follows this virtue list with a

---

[406] We might read this on par with the Johannine Jesus' teaching on peace for his troubled disciples: "Peace I leave with you; my peace I give to you. I do not give to you as the world gives. Do not let your hearts be troubled, and do not let them be afraid." (John 14:27).

[407] So note: "Now may the Lord of peace himself give you peace at all times in all ways. The Lord be with all of you" (2 Thess 3:16).

call to imitate him (4:9a; cf. Phil 3:17) and another appeal to the God who gives peace ("And the God of peace will be with you"; 4:9b). It is sensible to read 4:8–9, then, as Paul taking a deep breath and a big step back with the Philippians to help refresh their thinking about peace and hope in the community.

Paul lists a string of inspiring terms, not quite a "virtue list" (even though the word "virtue," *arete*, does appear here). Most of these words are reflections of what is good, pleasing, perfect, and beautiful in the world. This word-set is unlike anything else in Paul or in the New Testament. Some of these terms are found in inspirational or virtue sayings or lists in Greek and Roman authors.[408] For example, Dio Chrysostom (40–115 CE) reflects on the problem of hypocrisy in society. Many people talk about the importance of moral formation and noble aspirations, but then focus all their attention on money, business, sports, and hobbies, and end up miserable. In the many admirable things Dio lists, he includes valor, righteousness, wisdom, virtue, prudence, wisdom, goodness, that is, many such things reflecting what is "divine" and "august" (*Disc.* 69.1–3).[409] As with Dio, so Paul, these lists are not meant to be exhaustive, but suggestive.

### Closer Look: Roman Civic Virtues

The Roman Empire and emperors tried to broadcast civic virtues in various ways. Augustus received an honorary shield from the senate (27 BCE) in view of his courage (*virtus*), mercy (*clementia*), justice (*iustitia*), and respect for gods and mortals (*pietas*) (*Res Gestae* 34). Historian Jed W. Atkins points out that imperial coins often promoted civic virtues, especially *aequitas* (fairness), *pietas* (devotion/

---

[408] See S. E. Porter, "Paul, Virtues, Vices, and Household Codes," in *Paul in the Greco-Roman World* (London: T&T Clark, 2016), 2.369–390; J. W. Thompson, *Moral Formation according to Paul* (Grand Rapids, MI: Baker, 2011), 87–109. But scholars are quick to note that virtue lists or appeals to noble thought can also be found in Jewish texts. For instance, in the *Testament of the Twelve Patriarchs* the father Zebulun passes extended wisdom teachings onto his progeny, calling them to love, goodness, and righteousness (8.5–9).

[409] Fee and Holloway point to Cicero's statement: "What is there in man better than a mind that is sagacious and good? The good of the mind is virtue; therefore happy life is necessarily bound up with virtue. Consequently all that is lovely, honourable, of good report ... is full of joys" (*Tusc. Disp.* 5.23.67, LCL, 493); see Fee, *Philippians*, 416; Holloway, *Philippians*, 418.

respect), *virtus* (courage), *liberalitas* (generosity), *providentia* (foresight), *pudicitia* (chastity), and *fortitudo* (fortitude).[410]

Paul prompts the Philippians to contemplate such things, and so set (and reset) their minds and hearts on what is good, beautiful, and true in the world. Again, Paul does not mention these things as some kind of aside. Rather, this is wise advice to a troubled and splintering church.[411] Garland keenly contextualizes 4:8 in this way

> One way to fight anxiety is for Christians to focus their minds on virtues – 'the real goods of virtue' as opposed to the 'false goods of pleasure'. This exhortation for them to consider whatever is true, honorable, and just is without analogy in Paul's other letters and arises from his desire to restore harmony to the community.[412]

The reality of struggling with messy relationships is that humans can get stuck in cycles of negativity – psychologist John Gottman refers to this as "negative sentiment override" (NSO).[413] NSO happens when someone begins to only see the other person through a negative filter. Counteracting NSO requires consciously building a more positive outlook. Of course we cannot pretend Paul knew anything about modern psychology, but he does seem to be advocating for a similar idea; *climb out of the ditch of anxiety and rejection and move towards positive thought.*[414]

In 4:9, Paul turns a somewhat abstract reflection into a commitment to practices. Again, Paul calls for imitation of himself, a steady discipleship

---

[410]   See J. W. Atkins, *Roman Political Thought* (Cambridge: Cambridge University Press, 2018), 79–80; cf. E. Forbis, *Municipal Virtues in the Roman Empire* (Berlin: de Gruyter, 1996), 93, 258–259.

[411]   See Bockmuehl, *The Epistle to the Philippians*, 250.

[412]   Garland, "Philippians," 253.

[413]   J. Gottman, *Principia Amoris*: The New Science of Love (New York: Routledge, 2015), 207.

[414]   It is worth noting that Paul does not use a more expected word for "thinking" here, such as *mimneskomai* (remember), *proneō* (think), or *dianoeomai* (reflect on). Rather, he employs *logizomai*. One guess as to why this verb was chosen may be that in the Greek Bible it is not uncommon to see *logizomai* paired with *kakos* in reference to "scheming evil plans" (LXX Ps. 34:4; 40:8; Mic 2:1; Zech 8:17; Jer 18:11; 31:2; 36:11; cf. Prov 16:30; Jer 18:8; 1 Cor 13:5). Paul, then, would be prompting the Philippians to turn their thoughts away from revenge or malice, and toward the noblest and highest thoughts we can imagine.

that attempts to live out these ideals of truth, righteousness, and virtue. So Sevenster explains

[W]hat may be gathered from the fact that [these virtues are] followed immediately by verse 9 is that obedience to "what you have learned and received and heard and seen in me" is what is ultimately of most importance for the church . . . Life and fellowship, as it is here formulated with the aid of terms taken from Greek moral philosophy, entails obedience to God's commandments, an obedience which . . . proceeds from belonging to Christ and from the possession of the Spirit which is at work in the church. And so it is that there is something rather provisional about verse 8: in appealing to the Philippians Paul takes into account their environment in order to obtain every possible support and understanding for what he wishes to say in verse 9.[415]

And, of course, in this particular situation, there would be no better "practice" of what is worthy of praise than forgiveness and reconciliation with a brother or sister. Paul caps off this passage with a statement of divine presence and divine peace. The God of peace has demonstrated his investment in his "peace program," as it were, by sending his Son and giving up his Son to model the kind of love and sacrifice that is healing (Phil 2:1–4, 5–11).

### 4:10–20: PAUL'S THANKSGIVING FOR FELLOWSHIP WITH THE PHILIPPIANS

[10] I rejoice in the Lord greatly that now at last you have revived your concern for me; indeed, you were concerned for me, but had no opportunity to show it.

[11] Not that I am referring to being in need; for I have learned to be content with whatever I have.

[12] I know what it is to have little, and I know what it is to have plenty. In any and all circumstances I have learned the secret of being well-fed and of going hungry, of having plenty and of being in need.

[13] I can do all things through him who strengthens me.

[14] In any case, it was kind of you to share my distress.

---

[415] J. N. Sevenster, *Paul and Seneca* (NovTSup 4; Leiden; Brill, 1961), 155–156.

<sup>15</sup> You Philippians indeed know that in the early days of the gospel, when I left Macedonia, no church shared with me in the matter of giving and receiving, except you alone.

<sup>16</sup> For even when I was in Thessalonica, you sent me help for my needs more than once.

<sup>17</sup> Not that I seek the gift, but I seek the profit that accumulates to your account.

<sup>18</sup> I have been paid in full and have more than enough; I am fully satisfied, now that I have received from Epaphroditus the gifts you sent, a fragrant offering, a sacrifice acceptable and pleasing to God.

<sup>19</sup> And my God will fully satisfy every need of yours according to his riches in glory in Christ Jesus.

<sup>20</sup> To our God and Father be glory forever and ever. Amen.

The last section of Paul's letter to the Philippians serves as a kind of bookend to his first section (1:3–11). That is, he enters again into a posture of thanksgiving to God for his special relationship and partnership with this believing community. Many scholars have noted that Paul was following cultural expectations that he address the gift that was sent to him via Epaphroditus, and he chose to make this his final word. Paul seems to have already alluded to this gift in 1:5, and certainly the gift is in view in 4:10–20 (explicitly 4:18), but what Paul is up to far exceeds gift-response conventions. The *real* subject of this passage is not Paul's receipt of their gift, nor even his thankfulness or joy in view of the gift; rather, Paul's focus is on what the gift indicated, namely a continuing and renewed bond and partnership between them and him in the work of the gospel. This is well demonstrated in a simple outline of this text:

Partnership Appreciated (4:10)
Paul's Resilience in Need (4:11–13)
The Philippian Partnership (4:14–16)
Divine Blessing for Ministry Partnership (4:17–20)

It is important to keep this main concern in mind, because this remains one of the most exegetically controversial passages in Paul. There are two main questions or concerns about which interpreters wonder in relation to Paul's language and mind-set in 4:10–20: what is the nature of his "fellowship" language? And if this is an acknowledgement of his receipt of their gifts, why does Paul seem to avoid saying "thank you"? On the second matter, it is often observed that Paul does not use the explicit language of "thanks" in this text. In a relationship of mutuality, it is expected that a receiving party would express gratitude to the giver(s). Often cited in this discussion is the model of thanks presented by Pseudo-Demetrius that represents what one might find in a Greco-Roman "thankful letter":

> I hasten to show in my own actions how grateful I am to you for the kindness you showed me in your words. For I know that what I am doing for you is less than I should, for even if I gave my life for you, I should not be giving adequate thanks for the benefits I have received. If you wish anything that is mine, do not write and request it, but demand a return. For I am in your debt.[416]

If this indicates a natural response to gift-giving, no wonder some scholars have referred to Phil 4:10–20 as a "thankless thanks."[417] What can account for this absence of "thank you" here for Paul? Some have chalked this up to ambivalence over money matters; that is, Paul did not want to be beholden to any financial supporters. As Hooker puts it, "he regarded them as his partners in the gospel, and not as his paymasters."[418]

The second issue considers how Paul viewed his relationship to the Philippians with the hopes this would shed light on why he brings this matter up, and the *way* he brings it up, at the close of the epistle. Throughout Philippians, Paul frequently used "fellowship" language: *koinōnia* (1:5; 2:1; 3:10); *syngkoinos* (1:7); *syngkoinōneō* (4:14); *koineō* (4:15). This appears to indicate a special relationship. In terms of the social framework for Paul's association with the Philippians, interpreters appear to fall into two major categories: "friendship" or "formal partnership."

## Fellowship as Friendship

In the early 1990s, Gerald Peterman argued that Paul was following a social convention whereby those considered to be "friends" need not express

---

[416] Letter Type 21; as cited in A. Malherbe, *Ancient Epistolary Theorists* (Atlanta, GA: Scholars Press, 1988), 41.

[417] This language goes back to Martin Dibelius, *An die Thessalonicher I–II; An die Philipper* (HNT 2.11; Tübingen: Mohr Siebeck, 1925), 95: "dankloser Dank."

[418] Hooker "Philippians," 543; cf. Hawthorne and Martin, *Philippians*, 259, 276; Fee, *Philippians*, 431.

explicit thanks.[419] Peterman's interpretation dovetailed with other biblical scholarship that took an interest in the subject of friendship in the Greco-Roman world and how Philippians might even be read as a "letter of friendship."[420] Luke Timothy Johnson has posited in regards to Philippians that "For Greek readers, 'fellowship' [koinōnia] automatically connoted 'friendship' (philia)."[421] He goes on to explain, "If friendship in the Greek world is proverbially 'life together' (symbios), Paul could hardly find a more effective way to communicate to the Philippians that they were to be a community of friends."[422] Fee refers to the type of koinōnia that they had established as "contractual friendship," a relationship of reciprocal obligation and benefit, but one that still can be viewed under the wider umbrella of friendship.[423] When Philippians 4:10–20 is read from this perspective, Paul's response to the Philippians' gift is one of warmth and appreciation, but as a "friend" and equal to them, he did not want to "thank" them formally in such a way that would turn the matter into business or quid pro quo.

Despite the overall popularity of this "friendship" approach to Paul's letter to the Philippians, there are a number of dissenting voices. The first problem with this friendship approach is the fact that Paul never uses the key terms "friendship" (philia) or "friend" (philos) in Philippians, nor in any of his other letters. And other connections to a friendship topos, then, could be coincidental. When it comes to "fellowship/partnership" (koinōnia and its cognates), it is often mentioned that this language is certainly not exclusive to friendships. It is a basic word that refers to some social connection, and only context determines the exact nature of that relationship.

---

[419]  G. W. Peterman, "'Thankless Thanks': The Epistolary Social Conventions in Philippians 4:10–20," *TynBul* 42.2 (1991): 261–270.

[420]  Interpreters who designate Philippians as a letter of friendship include S. Stowers, *Letter Writing in Greco-Roman Antiquity* (Philadelphia: Fortress, 1986), 50–70; J. T. Fitzgerald, "Philippians," ABD 5.320; Fee, *Philippians*, 1–10. Hansen cautiously classifies it as friendship (and more), in part because he reads Paul's fellowship language as a friendship-partnership (see *Philippians*, 7–10). For a helpful history of the development of interest in ancient friendship, see Still, "More than Friends?," 53–55.

[421]  Johnson, "Making Connections," 163; see similarly, J. T. Fitzgerald, "Christian Friendship: John, Paul, and the Philippians," *Interpretation* 63.3 (2007): 284–296, here 293–294; Lyons and Malas, "Paul and His friends within the Greco-Roman Context," 55–56.

[422]  Johnson, "Making Connections," 163.

[423]  Fee, *Philippians*, 27, 445; cf. also pp. 6, 73, 446.

## Fellowship as Alliance

Among those scholars who do *not* use "friendship" as the grid through which *koinōnia* language should be understood in this letter, there are some who imagine that what Paul had established with the Philippians was some form of formal partnership. P. J. Sampley put forth this idea in 1977, reading Paul's fellowship language as reflective of a Roman *societas*, a legally binding partnership.[424] Sampley believed that this could account for the more business-like tone of Phil 4:10–20, where Paul uses business and commercial language, referring to a formal relationship of "giving and receiving" (4:15). In recent years, J. Ogereau has attempted to strengthen Sampley's proposal, especially by examining more closely how *koinōnia* language was used in extant papyri (letters) and inscriptions. He concludes that such language "often denoted an economic partnership of some kind which . . . would have been assimilated with the Roman economic and legal concept of *societas*."[425] Ogereau urges that any sense of associating *koinōnia* with spiritual fellowship or community would be anachronistic; this terminology is better understood in terms of the English word "alliance," often bound up with legal and economic assumptions. The giving of gifts, then, was not tokens of friendship, but rather obligatory contributions as part of an agreement of partnership.

M. Jennings is sympathetic to this "alliance"-type approach to Paul's *koinōnia* with the Philippians. He stops short of imagining this as some sort of legally binding contract, but interprets it as much more than friends giving "gifts." Paul and the Philippians entered into some kind of purposeful, goal-directed partnership, and Jennings argues in his monograph that his letter has a primary intent of reinforcing and securing that partnership.[426] So, Jennings writes, their renewed aid-gift represents "a sanctified, righteous fruit that authenticates the church's faith because it demonstrates their fidelity to him and his gospel mission."[427]

---

[424] J. P. Sampley, "Societas Christi: Roman Law and Paul's Conception of the Christian Community," in *God's Christ and His People* (eds. J. Jervell and W. Meeks; Oslo: Universitetsforlaget, 1977), 158–174.

[425] J. Ogereau, *Paul's Koinonia with the Philippians* (WUNT 2.377; Tübingen: Mohr Siebeck, 2014), 348; see summary also on p. 216. In an appendix (over one hundred pages long), Ogereau details *koin\** language in Greek inscriptions and papyri; see pp. 354–499.

[426] Jennings, *The Price of Partnership*.

[427] Jennings, *The Price of Partnership*, 181.

## Other Proposals

Aside from the major views that 4:10–20 should be interpreted from the perspective of friendship conventions, or alliance expectations, there are a couple of other frameworks proposed. David Briones, for example, argues that Paul had a deeper theological rationale for his statements in 4:10–20, inspired by the Roman concept of brokerage. Paul wanted the Philippians to see themselves as brokers or mediators of gifts that actually originate from God, and *through* the Philippians they are passed on to Paul. This explains for Briones why Paul does not directly state his thanks. "As a client of the divine patron, Paul rightly gives thanks to God in 1.3, before inviting the community, in 4.10–20, to express their gratitude to the primary giver in the economy of [*charis,* grace]."[428] Similarly, Nathan Eubank argues that Paul intentionally avoids a horizontal "thank you" for their gifts because he wants to bring God more fully into the equation, as it were. Eubank portrays Paul as promoting a Jewish-style alms piety where he "consistently makes God the unseen recipient and reciprocator of the gifts."[429] As a suggestive parallel, Eubank points to Prov 19:17: "Whoever is kind to the poor lends to the LORD, and will be paid in full" (NRSV). In the LXX version of this verse, we find the word *doma* (gift), just as in Phil 4:17. From this perspective, Eubank reasons that Paul imagined the Philippians' gift as a "loan or offering that will lead God to attend to the Philippians' own needs in the future."[430]

## Summary on Interpretive Frameworks for 4:10–20

When it comes to detecting a friendship theme or topos in Philippians overall, I remain skeptical. I see no clear or convincing reason why Paul would position the Philippians as spiritual "friends," and then avoid using the most expected and common terminology of friendship (*philia, philos*). When it comes to the language of fellowship or partnership (*koinōnia*), scholars like Ogereau have more than proven that this language fits many kinds of relationships, not just friendship. I find *more* likely the proposal

---

[428]  D. Briones, "Paul's Intentional 'Thankless Thanks' in Philippians 4.10–20," *JSNT* 34.1 (2011): 47–69, here 62.
[429]  N. Eubank, "Justice Endures Forever: Paul's Grammar of Generosity," *JSPL* 5 (2015): 169–187, here 175.
[430]  Eubank, "Justice Endures Forever," 186.

that Paul had worked out some kind of alliance with the Philippians. Like Jennings, I hesitate to label this as a formal business or legal arrangement. Rather, I view it as a kind of good-faith bond of partnership in the promotion of the gospel of Jesus Christ. In this passage, 4:10–20, then, Paul expresses joy at this renewal of the partnership, but ultimately points beyond the gift or the people involved toward the God who saves and who is to be praised. Now we turn to a closer exegetical analysis of these verses.

Paul begins in 4:10 by mentioning his great joy in view not only of their gift but especially their *concern* for him. He mentions here that there was a delay or interruption in their ongoing support, but finally it bloomed again (*anathelō*). Again here we find the verb *phroneō* (translated as "concern" in the NRSV), which represents a holistic way of thinking that leads to action.[431] Ultimately, Paul was not desperate for money or aid (4:11–13), but more concerned with his churches coming together with him to invest in and support his ministry. I assume they had established some kind of support agreement with Paul, and had failed to keep up their end.[432] This troubled Paul, so it was all the more encouraging to receive their latest gift.

The next few verses (4:11–13) serve as a kind of digression from his reflection on their partnership. But this digression has proven to be one of the most insightful and inspiring sections of Paul's letters, as he talks openly about his theology or philosophy of contentment and personal happiness. To begin with, Paul makes clear that his great joy is not about the gift *per se*. That is, his focus in prison has not been on measuring his vitality and peace based on his material satisfaction. The same word Paul uses here for "need" (*hysterēsis*) is found in Mark's mention of the widow giving generously out of her "poverty" (*hysterēsis*; Mk 12:44). Indeed, Paul was struggling with a major crisis (Phil 4:14) and undoubtedly their aid helped. But, again, his purpose in mentioning their gift is especially focused on their faithfulness in commitment to their gospel partnership with Paul.

In the second part of Phil 4:11, Paul divulges how he has learned to be "content." The Greek word *autarkēs* more plainly means "self-sufficient" or what we might think of as financially independent. The fact that Paul

---

[431] See Hawthorne and Martin, *Philippians*, 261.
[432] We can only speculate about the *reasons* for their lack of/delay in support; Bockmuehl reasons that it could be circumstantial, such as lack of money or inability to get the aid to Paul; see Bockmuehl, *The Epistle to the Philippians*, 260.

talks about *learning* this means that his self-sufficiency is not primarily about having or making a certain amount of money; rather, it is about learning to live simply and humbly such that occasional abundance is a nice blessing, but days of austerity and poverty are not distressing. The Stoic philosopher Seneca offers a similar sentiment on contentment. He writes that the "wise man" does not live by the hopes of fair external circumstances (*Ep.* 2.39, LCL). He must be so focused on his goal of attaining virtue that he is not affected in "poverty, nor pain, nor anything else that deflects the inexperienced and drives them headlong, restrains him from his course." He remains steady and unflinching "in the midst of wealth, or, if not, in poverty; if possible, in his own country – if not, in exile; in sound health – if not, enfeebled. Whatever fortune he finds, he will accomplish therefrom something noteworthy" (*Ep.* 2.39, LCL). So such a mind-set was present among some philosophers in Paul's time. But Paul did not learn this from Stoics.[433] Within the Jewish tradition itself we see much interest in a philosophy of contentment. Ben Sira says "Good things and bad, life and death, poverty and wealth, come from the Lord" (11:14; cf. 10:22); and also "In the time of plenty think of the time of hunger; in days of wealth think of poverty and need" (18:25); and "The poor are honored for their knowledge, while the rich are honored for their wealth" (10:30). In 2 Corinthians, Paul promotes a spirit of generosity as the believer knows the provision of God. In 9:8 he tells them that God is looking out for their needs so they will be "self-sufficient" (*autarkeia*), such that then they might focus their attention on giving to others graciously (cf. 2 Cor 6:10). Paul was inspired by the manna-feeding narrative from Exod 16:1–36. When the manna fell, each person was meant to have just enough, not too much or too little (Exod 16:8; cf. 2 Cor 8:15). Because the believer trusts God, their attention should be on serving God and blessing others, not on safeguarding their own necessities (cf. 2 Cor 9:10–11).

In Phil 4:12, Paul goes into more detail about his up-and-down experiences of life. First he mentions those times when he has had little. We might look to 2 Cor 11:27 for elaboration: "toil and hardship, through many

---

[433] Fee refers to Paul's use of the word *auterkēs* (self-sufficient) as a philosophical technical term, "like a meteor fallen from the Stoic sky into his epistle" (*Philippians*, 431). Hellerman argues that, despite the term's popularity among Stoics, Paul's emphasis on divine empowerment (Phil 4:12) undermines any connection to a philosophy of "self-sufficiency." See Hellerman, *Philippians*, 259.

a sleepless night, hungry and thirsty, often without food, cold and naked." But Paul also confesses to having a bounty on occasion. This surely applies to the receipt of the Philippi's gift, because he seems to say this in 4:18: "I am fully satisfied" (*perriseuō*). Presumably this includes provisions like food, clothing, perhaps also balms and ointments – and we cannot forget the warm friendship of Epaphroditus.

The big picture for Paul is that circumstances will inevitably change; the only thing a person can *always* control is their mind-set and personal sense of peace and happiness. In 4:12b, Paul talks about learning this "secret." The verb he uses here is peculiar. It was a technical term for initiation into a mystery religion (*mueomai*). However, in Paul's time it seems to have taken on a more general meaning as transcendent insight into spiritual realities revealed by God (see Philo, *Cher.* 48–49). Why does Paul choose to express his lesson in contentment using such a rare and unusual verb? Paul believed that only *God* could put the kind of peace in Paul's heart that leads to this kind of contentment – keep in mind he writes "in chains" to them about this. *But what exactly is the "secret" he has learned?* The NIV adds "of being content," which is not in the Greek text itself. Closer to Paul's exact phrasing is the NRSV: "of being well-fed and of going hungry." But no one really needs to be taught fullness or hunger. Conceptually, it makes sense to fill in the gap; Paul has been taught by God *how* to live with hunger and need, and *how* to live in fullness and plenty. I think the RSV does well, then, to phrase it as "the secret of facing plenty and hunger."

Paul is quick to point to his inspiration as divine empowerment (Phil 4:13). This verse in popular American culture is often taken out of context to apply to dreaming big and pursuing challenging accomplishments. This is not helped out by the fact that most translations opt for a translation about "doing": "I can do all things through him who strengthens me" (NRSV). The main verb Paul chooses here (which he only uses once elsewhere in his letters, Gal 5:6), *ischyō*, is about strength and endurance in relation to the contentment and self-sufficiency he addressed earlier. Therefore, the NAB and CEB render it much better:

I have the strength for everything through him who empowers me. (NAB)
I can endure all these things through the power of the one who gives me
  strength. (CEB)

Paul's point here is that facing hardship and living the kind of content and balanced life he has suggested is not *simply* a matter of "positive thinking." Rather, he firmly believed he was protected and empowered by God (cf. Eph 6:10). As Hawthorne and Martin put it, "The secret of Paul's independence was his dependence upon Christ. His self-sufficiency came from being in vital union with the One who is all-sufficient."[434] Given, again, that Philippians is full of case studies in a lived theology of faith, resilience, courage, and hope (e.g., Paul, Christ, Epaphroditus, Timothy, Euodia, Syntyche), Paul no doubt intended for this statement to inspire the Philippians to also know and be sure of their strength in the Lord. And this strength should lead to a unified and focused partnership with Paul in the ministry of the gospel.

Paul then returns to the continued Philippian alliance demonstrated by their recent gift: "it was kind of you to share my distress" (4:14). One can see how Paul viewed their aid. It was considered to be sharing in his suffering, a practical form of empathy. Ben Sira commends just this sort of mutuality and community in this exhortation: "Gain the trust of your neighbor in his poverty, so that you may rejoice with him in his prosperity. Stand by him in time of distress, so that you may share with him in his inheritance" (Sir 22:23).

Paul further reminds them of their history of commitment to Paul's mission (Phil 4:15). They were the only church that entered into a relationship of "giving and receiving" (*eis logon doseōs kai lēmpseōs*). Some scholars argue that this is semiformal terminology, indicating a business-like agreement.[435] Others observe that it is also found in the context of the friendship relationship.[436] But I have found that a study of the extant Greco-Roman literature demonstrates a wide variety of use. At the most general level, Cicero comments that "giving and receiving" is a normal and necessary part of civilized society, where humans work together and help each other for the common good (*Off.* 2.4). In Roman society, this, then, is a core value present in group treaties and alliances and political benefaction (Valerius Maximus 5; Appian *Hist. rom.* 6.8; Xenophon *Anab.* 5.9–12). Paul, then, in reference to

---

434 Hawthorne and Martin, *Philippians*, 266.
435 Commercial terminology: "They invariably refer to financial transactions" (Hawthorne and Martin, *Philippians*, 270); cf. Bockmuehl, *The Epistle to the Philippians*, 263.
436 See K. L. Berry, "The Function of Friendship Language in Philippians 4:10–20," in *Friendship, Flattery, and Frankness of Speech* (ed. J. T. Fitzgerald; Leiden: Brill, 1996), 107–124, here 118. Berry points to Cicero, *Amic.* 16.26–29, 58.

the partnership of giving and receiving with the Philippians, reminds them of their cooperation in the activity of a new commonwealth of the gospel; as Reumann aptly puts it, "Paul appeals to Christians, with their *politeuma* in heaven, not to invest in fountains or festivals but Paul and mission."[437] Paul reminds them that, at one time, they were far more committed to partnership with Paul than anyone else (Phil 4:15–16). They had complete trust and investment in Paul, not just financially of course, but material support would have been instrumental and indicative of their "buy in," as it were.

Again, in 4:17, Paul takes a step back to put the matter in wider theological perspective. He was not desperately waiting for their gift, as if the gospel or his ministry solely depended on their contributions. Put another way, Paul was *not* viewing the Philippians primarily as *givers*; rather, God was at work through their gifts to support Paul, *and* Paul was concerned with their support so that they would be blessed by the Giver ("I seek the profit that accumulates to your account").[438]

Paul uses recognizable transaction terminology when he wrote "I have been paid in full" (*apexō . . . panta*; 4:18a) – as Hawthorne and Martin put it "here, then, is my receipt for everything you have given me."[439] He lacks in no way; they had given graciously and he was blessed abundantly. They had done all they could to share in his suffering, ministry, and mission. But more important than Paul's material relief was the way this gift served as an offering to God. He refers to it as "a fragrant offering, a sacrifice acceptable and pleasing to God" (4:18d–e). Earlier Paul had employed a cultic metaphor in relation to his ministry and the potential he might have his life poured out (in death) as a drink offering spilled onto the sacrificial service of their faith (Phil 2:17). This highlights their missional union, colaborers for the gospel, fellow sufferers in Christ. In the Greco-Roman world, partners could get caught up in expectations of reciprocity and the feeling that one's financial or material investment would "pay off" in personal benefits. Paul's purposes here were to direct their attention to God as the true recipient of their gift.

---

[437]  Reumann, *Philippians*, 663.

[438]  Bruce perhaps overspiritualizes this, but his overall interpretation is correct: "He [Paul] emphasizes that he is grateful not simply because they sent it to him but also because their sending it is a token of heavenly grace in their lives and, so to speak, a deposit in the bank of heaven that will multiply at compound interest to their advantage. They meant Paul to be the gainer from their generosity, and so indeed he is; but on the spiritual plane the permanent gain will be theirs" (*Philippians*, 154).

[439]  Hawthorne and Martin, *Philippians*, 271.

Their concerns, efforts, and material sacrifices had done their good work of pleasing God. Finally, Paul addresses the matter of reciprocal benefit for the Philippians. But instead of focusing on what *he* (Paul) is going to do, he calls to attention to the benevolence and attentiveness of *God*: "And my God will fully satisfy every need of yours according to his riches in glory in Christ Jesus" (4:19). What are these Philippian "needs" to which Paul refers here? Theodoret of Cyrus presumes that this Philippian gift was a hardship for them, even pushing them into poverty (he even says "extreme poverty").[440] They can count, Theodoret says, on the one who gives "daily bread" to his children.[441] While not neglecting a reference to divine provision for physical needs, Bockmuehl is right to add these blessings to Paul's statement: "joy and steadfastness in Christ, humility and concord amongst each other."[442] But we must also recognize that when Paul refers to divine aid for the Philippians in their need, surely he imagines this might come through *another* church or friend. Just as the Philippians gave generously to Paul, and Paul felt blessed by God, so too God will meet the needs of the Philippians, and it just might come from an unexpected person or place. This statement, then, may have contributed to Paul's message in this letter that, even if Paul himself departed from this world and went to Christ (Phil 1:23), all hope is not lost. The gospel and its ministry is unstoppable, and not dependent on any one servant, not even Paul. If their partnership should end, God's work and provision never ends. That is surely why Paul was inspired to end this passage with a word of worship and praise: "To our God and Father be glory forever and ever. Amen" (4:20).[443]

### 4:21–23: FINAL GREETINGS

[21] Greet every saint in Christ Jesus. The friends who are with me greet you.

[22] All the saints greet you, especially those of the emperor's household.

[23] The grace of the Lord Jesus Christ be with your spirit.

---

[440]  R. C. Hill, trans., *Theodoret of Cyrus: Commentary on the Letters of St. Paul* (Brookline, MA: Holy Cross Orthodox Press, 2001), 79–80.
[441]  Hill, *Theodoret of Cyrus*, 80.
[442]  Bockmuehl, *The Epistle to the Philippians*, 266.
[443]  See G. D. Fee, "To What End Exegesis? Reflections and Exegesis and Spirituality in Philippians 4:10–20, *BBR* 8 (1998): 75–88, here 85–86.

Paul's letters typically end with a short final message of grace and greetings. These moments offer a window into the community of the letter recipients. Throughout the letter, the church was largely treated as an undifferentiated whole ("you all"). Occasionally Paul did mention individuals like Euodia, Syntyche, and Clement. In these closing words, he focuses again on the *individual* believer in Christ. "Greet *every saint (or holy person)*" (Phil 4.21). Greeting (*aspazomai*) is not just a simple "hello." If we think more theologically about this – keeping in mind that Paul tends to deepen and spiritualize epistolary conventions – a "greeting" is about acknowledgment, respect, and blessing. Given that this church was experiencing internal relational troubles, no doubt Paul was reminding them to love and respect and to wish all God's best for each and every person. This is not a suggestion, but an expectation for all those who are "in Christ Jesus." He refers to the believer here as "saint" (NRSV), or "holy person." In Philippians, Paul had virtually nothing to say on the subject of holiness (cf. 1 Thess 4:3–8; 1 Cor 6:1–20). In fact, the only reference prior to this was in the prescript ("To all the saints who are in Christ Jesus in Philippi"; 1:1). This is a Pauline habit, where he naturally referred to fellow believers as "saints." We ought to keep in mind that this indicated their connection to the holy God, perhaps especially the Holy Spirit (1 Cor 6:11). Throughout his letters, Paul regularly attempted to reshape and establish his readers' identity in God, Christ, and the Spirit, over and against the world. Holiness, for Paul, was about being with God and like God, and not like the world. In the context of Philippians, then, being holy would entail living as a good citizen of Christ's kingdom (1:27–30), and bearing the fruit of righteousness (1:11), and living purely and blamelessly with a life that shines like a resurrection star in a dark world (2:15).

Paul also sends greetings and salutations from those with him. The NRSV refers to these as "friends." This is an unfortunate translation. The Greek word here is *adelphoi*, "brothers and sisters." Given how important kinship theology is for Paul, it makes little sense to disregard this image (Table 7).

Here in 4:21b, Paul seems to be reminding the Philippians that not only are they family in Christ with one another (and with Paul), but that there is this worldwide family of God where believers are likewise experiencing persecution and joy, shame and honor, suffering and hope. That is to say, these discouraged Philippians ought not to feel alone, but are in the thoughts, prayers, and respect of other brothers and sisters in Christ.

Table 7 *Family Metaphors in Philippians*

| Family metaphor | Philippians |
| --- | --- |
| God as Father | 1:2, 2:11; 4:20 |
| Philippians as brothers and sisters | 1:12; 3:1, 13, 17; 4:1, 8; 4:21 |
| Believers with Paul as brothers and sisters | 1:14 |
| Philippians as children of God | 2:15 |
| Timothy like a son to Paul | 2:22 |
| Epaphroditus as "brother" to Paul | 2:25 |

Offering further "greetings," Paul mentions the salutations from "the emperor's household."

### Closer Look: The Emperor's Household

When we read about "Caesar's household" we might get the wrong impression and assume this refers to the emperor's biological family. But in the Greco-Roman world, the "household" (*oikia*) includes a much wider enterprise. For a wealthy elite, his "household" would include all persons whom he owned (i.e., slaves) and other dependents like those that work permanently on his properties. When we translate that to the emperor, we must imagine thousands of slaves and freedmen. And, geographically, this "household" spread across the whole Roman Empire, not just the emperor's "main" residence. The emperor controlled many estates and properties where servants and slaves filled numerous roles (e.g., management, maintenance, clerical work, groundskeeping). Michael Flexsenhar hypothesizes that Paul may have been referring to believing slaves who worked in "Caesar's Household" in Ephesus and who knew believing slaves in Philippi through interactions with imperial couriers.[444]

Why does Paul point to this group "especially" (*malista*)? Perhaps they know the challenges that believers face in a Roman colony where the expectations are high that the people take divine honors for the emperor seriously. Perhaps Paul had been sharing with this group in particular his admiration and respect for the Philippian believers who found joy in the midst of difficulty.

---

[444] See M. A. Flexsenhar III, *Christians in Caesar's Household: The Emperor's Slaves in the Makings of Christianity* (University Park: Pennsylvania State University Press, 2019).

The final words of this letter resemble closely, but are not identical to, his other letters, except for Philm 25.

The grace of the Lord Jesus Christ be with your spirit. (Phil 4:23)

The grace of the Lord Jesus Christ be with your spirit. (Philm 25)

The grace of our Lord Jesus Christ be with you. (Rom 16:20b; 1 Thess 5:28)

May the grace of our Lord Jesus Christ be with your spirit, brothers and sisters. Amen. (Gal 6:18)

Just because this grace-wish is a Pauline epistolary convention does not mean it didn't have deep meaning for Paul. Quite the opposite. This was a signature theme for the Apostle. Many of his letters he wrote to churches in crisis, often communities opposed from the outside and showing tension within. Throughout most of his letters, in response to such challenges, he is quick to point to the lordship of Jesus who reigns over all things and can solve all problems – that is, no problem is greater than the power of his person and resources (Phil 4:19). Furthermore, this Lord Jesus is the savior of his people (Phil 3:20) and his attitude and disposition towards his people is one of grace, favor, and generosity (Phil 1:7, 29; 2 Cor 8:9). Like he does in his prescript (Phil 1:1–2), then, Paul could have added to his postscript a word of peace (*eirēnē*) as well; knowing the empowered and steadfast love, grace, favor, and generosity of the Lord Jesus Christ, his people can live with deep peace and joy.

Finally, we are left to address Paul's reference to "your spirit." We should note that some ancient manuscripts omit this and simply end with "be with you all" (see KJV). Text critics agree, though, that there is strong manuscript support for "your spirit."[445] Bruce Metzger proposes that a scribe may have left "spirit" (*pneuma*) out in conformity to Paul's pattern in other letters such as Rom 16:20. So, if Paul does bless them with God's grace toward their "spirit," what does that mean? We can quickly dismiss any notion that this is about a "spiritual" part of the human versus the "physical" part. We can simply say that Paul had several different ways he could talk about a person in general. Notice, for example, how in 1 Kgs 21:5 Jezebel says to Ahab, "How is it that your spirit[446] is so sullen that you are

---

[445] See Metzger, *Textual Commentary*, 550.
[446] The Hebrew text has *ruuḥ* here, the Septuagint Greek text *pneuma*.

not eating food?" This is such a general reference to Ahab that most translations do not even mention "spirit" ("Why are you so depressed that you will not eat?, NRSV).

We must be careful not to overinterpret what Paul writes in Phil 4:23, but at the very *least* we can say that he was reinforcing the sense that Christ – while "in heaven" in some sense (Phil 3:20–21) – is deeply attentive to the problems and needs of his people (Phil 4:6–7) and is eager to bless them with his grace and with the empowering presence and work of the Spirit (Phil 3:3).

# Author Index

# Ancient Sources

Aristotle
  *Nich. Et.* 8.3.6 66
Athanaeus
  *Deipn.* 97c 159
Cicero
  *Off.* 2.4 190
  *Rab. perd.* 4.13 27, 83
  *Tusc.* 2.40.58 1n2
Dio Cassius
  *Roman History* 51.4.6 3n7
Dio Chrysostom
  *Disc.* 69.1-3 179
*Diodorus Siculus*
  17.41.7-8 177
Diogenes Laertius
  *Lives* 7.116 96
Horace
  *Sat.* 1.6.23-24 70
Pliny
  *Ep.* 10.96-97 17
Plutarch
  *Adul. amic.* 96E 67
  *Alex.* 24.5-8 177
  *De Coriolanus* 11 164
  *Mor.* 778 96
Pseudo-Demetrius
  21 183
Quintilian
  *Decl.* 274 83n155
*Res Gestae*
  34 179

Seneca
  *Ad Marc.* 10.5-6 55
  *Ep.* 2.39 188
  *Ep.* 4.6 55
  *Prov.* 3.4 94
Tacitus
  *Ann.* 15.44.4 83
  *Histories* 5.5 11
Augustine
  *Conf.* 13.19-26 174
  *Ep.* 20.3 174
Chrysostom
  *Hom. Phil.* 1 36
  *Hom. Phil.* 11 139
*Epistle to Diognetus*
  5.5-9 164
Eusebius
  *Hist. Eccl.* 3.4 34
Ignatius of Antioch
  *Trall.* 2.3 38
Justin
  *1 Apol.* 65.5 38
Polycarp
  *Phil.* 1.3 42
  *Phil.* 4.2-3 37–38
  *Phil.* 6.1 37–38
  *Phil.* 9.2 58
  *Phil.* 11.1 37–38

Printed in the United States
by Baker & Taylor Publisher Services